Stage Management

A Guidebook of Practical Techniques

Second Edition

Lawrence Stern

Allyn and Bacon, Inc.
Boston   London   Sydney   Toronto

The author wishes to acknowledge his gratitude for permission to reprint excerpts from the following sources:

Hildegard Knef, The Gift Horse, translated by David Anthony Palastanga. New York: McGraw-Hill Book Company, 1971. English translation copyright © 1971 by Hildegard Knef.

The Son of Any Wednesday, Muriel Resnik. Reprinted by permission of the William Morris Agency, Inc. Copyright © 1965 by Muriel Resnik

Library of Congress Cataloging in Publication Data

Stern, Lawrence, 1935–
    Stage management.
    1. Stage management.   I. Title.
PN2085.S77   1982   792'.068   81-3590
ISBN 0-205-07384-0   AACR2

Managing Editor: Robert Roen

Printed in the United States of America.

10   9   8   7   6   86   85

In memory of Xenia Chekhov

A CHRONOLOGICAL APPROACH AND PRIORITIES

TASK	PAGE	PRIORITY	COORDINATE WITH
BEFORE REHEARSALS BEGIN			
Get things to run smoothly on stage and backstage	1	A	
Gather equipment	58	B,E,F	
Be aware of police, fire, and municipal regulations	232	A	Producer, Tech Dir
Inspect safety conditions	129	A	
Get to know the theater	61	B	
Make a diagram of the stage	61	C	Tech Dir
Check out the fuse boxes	63	C	Tech Dir
Make a diagram of lighting instruments	66	C	Tech Dir, Light Design
Keep a do list	134	B	
Make a prompt script	20	A,B,D	Director
Identify the problems of the script	25	A	Director
Write out plots	26	B,C,G	Dir, Technicians
Make master calendar	37	B,C	Everyone
Schedule staff meetings	41	C	Producer
Distribute rehearsal schedules	42	B,C	Producer, Director
Arrange the callboard	48	C	Producer
Distribute and explain company rules	46	C,G	Producer, Director
Keep a budget and record of your expenses	97	A	Producer
Obtain audition forms	84	B,C	Producer, Director
Prepare staff, crew, cast lists	90	C	Prod, Dir, Staff, Crew
Make gel patterns	167	D	Technicians
Make supply directory	228	E	
Post emergency numbers	50	A	
DURING READINGS AND REHEARSALS			
Prepare audition rooms	73	B,C,D	Producer, Director
Post notes for readings	75	B,C,D,F,G	Prod, Dir, Publicist
Accept resumes	79	E	Director
Control scripts	82	B	Director
Make preset diagrams	105	A	Dir, Tech Dir, Sc Des
Prepare for rehearsals	107	B,D	Director
Post running order	125	B,D	Director
Supervise department heads	149	C	Prod, Dept Heads
Control required forms	85	C	Producer, Director
Conduct deputy election	92	B	Union, Cast
Keep cast on time	141	A,B	Director, Cast
Distribute itineraries	219	C	Producer, Cast
Distribute touring agreement	221	C	Cast
Post duty roster	203	C	Everyone
Make check lists	189	B	
Supervise props	151	A	Property Master, Producer, Director
Distribute scene shift diagrams	182	B,C,D	Scene Designer
Contribute to advance letters	224	C	Producer
Maintain order	121	B,E	Director
Call rehearsal cues	108	A	Director
Take blocking notation	109	B,C,D	Director
Make French scene diagrams	115	E	
Spike set pieces	115	A,C,	Tech Dir
Prompt	117	C	Director, Cast
Give rehearsal, publicity, costume calls	121	A	Everyone

KEY: A. I've got to do this first. The quality of the production will be adversely affected if I don't.

B. I've got to do this because if I don't, time and energy of staff and cast will be wasted.

C. Someone else may do this well, but I've got to make sure it gets done.

D. I can assign this task to a subordinate if I make sure it gets done.

TASK	PAGE	PRIORITY	COORDINATE WITH
Warn cast	120	E	Director, Cast
Keep rehearsal log	129	E	
Submit rehearsal reports	129	B,G	Producer
Time rehearsals	126	B,D	Director, House Manager
Post photo calls	122	E	Publicist, Director, Costumer, Cast
Prepare lighting sheet	162	B,C	Light Techs
Work on take-in; brief crew	173	C,D,B	Scene Designer, Tech Dir, Crew
Make shift plot chart	169	C,D	Tech Dir
Supervise arrangement of scene dock	177	C,D	Tech Dir
Supervise technical rehearsal	185	A	Director, Tech Dir
Choreograph scene changes	178	B,D	Tech Dir
Prepare area lighting diagram	165	C	Light Designer
Prepare regeling plans	165	C	Light Designer
Post sign-in sheets	142	B,C	
Place curtain call light cues on lighting sheet	196	B	Director, Light Techs
DURING PRODUCTION			
Conduct lighting check	159	A	Light Designer, Light Techs
Post scene shift diagrams	169	B,C,D	Tech Dir
Give calls (prior to curtain)	145	A	Cast
Caution audience	182	C	Producer
Call late actors	141	A	Cast
Coordinate with house manager	199	A	House Manager
Give cues	191	A	Technicians
Check immediate effect of each cue	193	A	
Supervise shifts	169	C,D	Tech Dir
Inspect shifts	178	B,C,D	Tech Dir
Time performances	126	B	Director
Walk the curtain	196	D	Tech Dir
Time curtain calls	194	A	Director
Maintain sets	183	D,C,D	Tech Dir
Be aware of cast morale	211	A	Cast
Keep the show in hand	209	A,C	Director, Cast
Post V.I.P. list	207	F	Producer
Rehearse understudies, block replacements	213	C	Producer, Director, Cast
POST PRODUCTION			
Distribute strike plan	215	B,C,G	Tech Dir
Post changeover schedule	218	C,G	Producer, Tech Dir
Supervise moves	218	A,B,C	Producer
Write letter to next stage manager	239	F	
Write critique	240	D	
Write letters of recommendation, thank-you notes	241	F	
IN GENERAL			
Make contact file	229	E	
Make a theater information packet	68	C,F,G	Producer, Tech Dir
Get acquainted with unions	235	C,E	
Send out resumes	244	A	
Read theater news	226	E	
Keep in contact with theater acquaintances	250	F	
Start a theater library	229	F	

E. I'll do it if I have time, and it would help, but we'll survive without it.

F. A luxury; I'll leave it for last.

G. This might be helpful for another show, but wil¹ be υs less here.

Contents

Contents

Foreword

The best way to introduce this book is to speak well and perfectly about the Author. For you can't expect a stage manager like Lawrence Stern to stand up front and blow his own horn. Someone who knows him must do it for him, and I gladly assume the task.

Now there are all sorts of virtues a stage manager must have. You will find them listed and profusely described in the pages of this book. But the supreme virtue among many is: The stage manager must arrive before everyone and leave long after everyone else is gone.

Of course that is the essence of creativity in any field you may want to mention. Those who love writing stay up until dawn to finish a story. Those who love painting work around the clock until they drop dead in their tracks. Stage managers . . . ?

Lawrence Stern is one of those superb men who quietly go about their business, keep charts, arrive two hours early and, long after the play has closed or collapsed, or both, can be found carrying out the trash, cleaning up the lobby, filling in the final forms, or holding the flashlight while the author of the play crawls around on the floor of the ladies' room helping some poor blind thing find her lost contact lens.

All this Lawrence Stern has done, and more. His passions may be quiet, but they are there. Instead of your usual slob, found all too frequently in our unhappy society these days, Lawrence Stern is one of those who gives you 150 percent of himself. I know that sounds impossible, but I have seen him do it. And this book, with its incredible amount of detail and huge compilation of first-hand knowledge is proof of all that I say.

Frankly, I don't know how your average stage manager ever got along without this book, just as my own Pandemonium Theatre Company was never the same once Lawrence Stern moved on to other fields.

There you have it: some sort of idea of the man who wrote this book. But you needn't take my word for it. Just leaf through the book swiftly, checking chapters, pages, paragraphs. You'll soon find that a sub-title of the book could well be More Than You Ever Wanted To Know About Stage Managing. Except of course, that would be foolish: you can never know enough.

Let Lawrence Stern be the best teacher you ever had. He's here. Listen to him!

Ray Bradbury
Los Angeles

Preface

In the many levels of live theater—educational, children's, community, showcase, and professional—there are few provisions for training in stage management. It is often assumed that anyone can do the job reasonably well who has a mind to, without previous training or experience, and the result of this is a great deal of trial and an enormous amount of error. A new stage manager typically makes his or her own kind of improvised performance, trying to carry out the functions of stage management without ever being able to find out for sure what those functions are, except by trial and error. Unfortunately, there are few places where anyone can find any written summary of useful principles or primary needs of stage management, and what they do find by gleaning from texts on directing, stagecraft, or the like, is not usually appropriate to any one person's theater situation, much less to a reliable or professional standard for this kind of work. Most managers solve their problems with whatever organizational skill and inventiveness they possess— but at an unwarranted cost in time, effort and uncertainty.

At the amateur levels of live theater, particularly in educational and community theater, the problems resulting from such a lack of guidelines for stage management are compounded by the fact that often the duties of the producer, director, stage manager, and even business manager are assumed by one person. This individual is frequently a faculty member or volunteer who has had little or no experience in stage management. It is this person who stands to profit most from this book. However, this guide is written in the hope that it will prove to be a valuable tool for all producers, directors, stage managers, and supervisors of theatrical programs, regardless of theater level or staging environment.

L.S.
Los Angeles, 1973

Preface to the Second Edition

A very great reward of having written this book has been hearing from so many readers. Unfortunately, too much of what I heard was flattering and not enough was critical.

It's hard to resist flattery. So will you please help me. If, after reading this manual, you find that there is information missing that would be useful to stage managers, please let me know. Many readers will work in staging environments unfamiliar to me: theme parks, ballet, dinner theaters, ice shows, lounge acts, etc. If you look back on your experience and say, "I wish I'd read about that in *Stage Management*," please let me know.

On page 283 you'll find a reader's comment form.

Thanks for your help.

L.S.
Hollywood, 1981

· 1 ·

Making Things
Run Smoothly

A Point of Departure

The cast, staff, and crew of a live theater work together toward a common goal: a good performance Thus, theater is necessarily a group effort in professional, amateur, or educational theater. However, it is *never* a group effort of vague fellow committee-members, but of associated autocrats—a playwright, a producer, a director, a stage manager, designers, and above all, actors Each accommodates the others, and to some extent may overlap others in function when necessary, considering the wide variety of differing conditions for each show and every kind and level of theater. But each autocrat assumes distinct responsibilities and accepts them completely: The *producer* is the general manager who has responsibility for obtaining the personnel and resources to make theater happen. The *actors* must serve as the most essential dramatic media, without whom no theatrical ideas or emotions can be communicated to an audience. The *director* must interpret the playwright's script through the medium of actors and designers. The person who has responsibility for making the entire production run smoothly, on stage and backstage, in pre-rehearsal, rehearsal, performance, and post-performance phases, is the stage manager.

Stage management in general involves more responsibilities

1

and resources than any one manager ever needs to apply to any single production. So with this guidebook I shall describe and give examples of many more methods for stage management than should be applied to any one production, and you will need to use your judgment in determining which will be most effective for you. However, at this point you might also benefit from some overview of these functions to show how the responsibilities of stage management are needed and applied. I can provide this best through a personal anecdote about a situation in which I did not even act as stage manager.

The Care and Feeding of the Amateur
Stage Manager: A True Tale of the Theater

The North Covina Theater Guild was about to present *Take Me Along*, and I had been asked to direct. Their producer, a housewife, was Mrs. Betty Spelvin (all names changed to protect the very innocent). She had been with the group since its inception, or, to put it another way, she was the inception. She had statuettes on her desk from the Adult Drama Festival, and a gavel that proclaimed her "Best Producer" on her bookcase.

My first encounter with my producer concerned the absence of the stage manager. At the production conference prior to rehearsals I asked where he was. When she told me he could not be there for the meeting, I shrugged and assumed that he would appear for the following nights' meetings, since his name appeared on the staff list.

At the first reading I again asked for the stage manager. "Oh," said Betty, "he doesn't come in until production week." Production week was her term for the week of strenuous rehearsals prior to opening night.

"When he does come in, what does he do?"

"Why he gives the actors their calls and pulls the curtain," said Betty.

From my five years as an Equity stage manager I knew there was more to it than giving calls and pulling the curtain. I also knew that I could not function as stage manager if I waited until the week of technical and dress rehearsals to join the company. "Who gives the light and sound cues?" I asked.

"The light and sound men take their own cues. They can see from the booth in back. They're junior high school kids, but very dependable."

"Well, who is supposed to assist me during auditions?"

2

"You're doing just fine. You're really organized. If you need any help, just yell." And she dashed off before I could.

After the readings I cornered her in the box office to ask who would be taking blocking notation during rehearsals. "The director always does that," she answered.

"Who calls the cues, warns the actors, and sets the furniture and props during rehearsals?"

"We all pitch in," smiled Betty reassuringly, "and it all gets done, so don't you worry."

"Who mimeographs and distributes the rehearsal schedule?"

"The girl in the box office. She's very good. She'll join us in two weeks. Listen, I know this isn't the way you're used to doing things in Hollywood, but believe me, it all comes together like magic on the night."

(When I was six years old, my seven year old neighbor attempted to saw the lady in half using a rusty saw and me as the lady. I don't believe in magic!)

"I must have a stage manager to assist me starting tomorrow night," I said.

"Impossible," she replied. "We just haven't been able to find reliable people to work as stage manager. We have no budget for them. It's always worked out that the director is better off doing it himself."

"Let me put it this way, Betty. Find me a stage manager or find yourself a new director."

Betty Spelvin, I found out later, had been running little theater groups in Little Rock, Arkansas, Omaha, Nebraska, Boulder, Colorado, Manila, the Philippines, and a few other places her husband was stationed. She had been known to sew entire wardrobes overnight, paint complete sets after dress rehearsals, get up on lines in an afternoon to stand in for an ailing actress, and fire, replace, or take over for directors on the spot.

There must have been a short supply of directors in North Covina that week. Also, Betty was moving to a new home and her daughter was about to be married. And Betty was expedient. So the next night I had a stage manager.

Paul Crowell was young and inexperienced but alert, intelligent, and personable. He was anxious to learn and caught on quickly. I gathered examples of work I'd done as a professional stage manager—schedules, prompt book, sign-in sheets, cast lists, scene shift diagrams, etc.—and turned them over to him. I explained to him the only thing I thought essential.

"As stage manager you will have total responsibility for making

3

things run smoothly. As producer, Betty's function is to obtain the personnel and materials to make our production happen. As director, my function is to interpret the script. Both Betty and I are concerned that things run smoothly, but you are the only one on the staff who is totally in charge of smooth running. If there's a minute delay in rehearsal or production, it's your fault, and for every second within the schedule that you can deliver productive rehearsal time, you, personally, will be improving the quality of the group's performances."

Paul had been a class officer in high school. He'd lettered in baseball and football. He was efficient and had a way of getting people to move with him.

The North Covina Theater Guild was immediately responsive to what they assumed were innovations in making theater. The cast and staff had never had complete schedules and cast lists so early. Cast members were surprised when labeled prop boxes and backstage mapped prop tables appeared before they had even set aside their scripts. Most of all, they were shocked when they found rehearsals beginning at the moment called, and ending at the time specified. At rehearsals all of the light and sound cues were called by the stage manager. Sound effects were used at rehearsals a week prior to the tech. Costumes were paraded well before dress rehearsals. There were no last minute rushes. There were no late rehearsals. The tech rehearsals ended at 11 P.M. And was I amused when I overheard cast members talking about "the new method from Hollywood."

A few years have passed since Paul stage managed his first show in North Covina. A Christmas card from Viet Nam informed me that "tanks are less temperamental than actresses and easier to stage manage." He is now in law school.

And Betty Spelvin, bless her heart, is still running the North Covina Theater Guild. With her husband retired from the military she is probably dug in to stay—producing, directing, stage managing, serving coffee in the lobby at intermission, and selling theater parties.

I know I've mellowed. I certainly realize that stage management is not understood at many amateur theaters.

But I still think it's desirable. So for all of the Betty Spelvins of the world, here are five suggestions for the care and feeding of the amateur stage manager.

Get a Firm Understanding of the Function of the Stage Manager

There is no definitive list of duties of a stage manager that is applicable to all theaters and staging environments. A stage manager for

4

a comedy performed in a theater in the round might carry out specific duties that are totally different from those of a stage manager for a traveling pantomime troupe. But the function is the same. Regardless of specific duties, the stage manager is the individual who accepts responsibility for the smooth running of rehearsals and performances, on stage and backstage. If you understand this function, you can derive the specific duties for your theater. (This book is intended to help you do this.)

Give your stage manager her or his rightful function and the responsibility to carry out that function—not just a list of duties.

In Betty's case, understanding the function of the stage manager might mean sharing some of her responsibility with him or her. Not a bad idea. Betty felt that she had to do everything herself if she wanted it done right. As a result she did everything. If she could get over her I-am-the-savior-of-the-theater complex, perhaps she could devote more of her creative energy to the producer's function of obtaining personnel and materials. Obtaining a proper stage manager would have saved herself and her directors a lot of work.

Get Firmly into Your Mind the Qualities that Make a Good Stage Manager, and Don't Settle for Anything Less

Organizational ability is one of the primary qualities of a good stage manager. Leadership ability is another. The stage manager must be able to influence the staff, cast, and crew. He or she must be a take-charge type and a self-starter and must be the kind of person who has the capacity to accept responsibility. (This book describes and applies most of these qualities in detail.)

As a producer you are expected to control quality in selecting your staff. You should select the stage manager with the same care that you use to select your director, scene designer, and costumer.

Motivate Your Stage Manager

If your stage manager is new to the work you must make her or him see that everything she or he does contributes to the improvement of the production. It is not enough for the stage manager to understand his or her function and specific duties. Point out, for example, that in setting rehearsal furniture fifteen minutes prior to rehearsal three hours of cast time may be saved, time that can be devoted to rehearsing that will result in a more polished performance.

In short, make sure that your stage manager knows that every bit of work he or she does is desirable, necessary, and appreciated.

Collect the Work of Past Stage Managers as a Reference

It is easier to set up a rehearsal schedule if you have a well ordered one in your hand. It is easier to improve a rotating duty roster if you have a past example to imitate. It would save a new stage manager considerable time and energy in making a shift plot chart if she or he had an old form to work from.

Collect such materials in a loose-leaf notebook arranged in the general order of their use: pre-rehearsal materials, rehearsal materials, production materials, post-production materials. (The material in this book provides a start in this direction.)

Reward Your Stage Manager

Cast members are generally rewarded by the response and applause of the audience. Directors clip their reviews. Producers count the money at the box office. But in most amateur theaters, the stage manager is forgotten.

Kind words and letters of praise would be a good start. But why not let your stage manager in on the rewards available to other cast and staff members? Give her or his name prominence in the program. Publish her or his biographical sketch along with those of the cast. At the annual banquet when your theater group gives out its awards for best actress, best director, etc., why not select a best stage manager, too? Could you put a plaque that records the name of the outstanding stage manager of each year in the lobby? Find other ways to honor your stage manager—and he or she might come back for another production.

A new director who finds a stage manager who has been through several productions with a group on hand inherits an experience level that can get the director off to a flying start.

Well, Betty, that's the way it should be. But, if as in so many amateur theater groups, you want to continue to distribute the stage manager's duties while holding on to the function—if you want to continue to bring in people at the last minute to pull the curtain and give the actors their calls, and call them stage managers—if you want to continue to paint scenery and sew costumes at the last minute because you haven't done your work of obtaining a stage manager who could schedule work calls—if you want to continue to make amateur theater amateurish—then that's your problem.

· 2 ·

Characteristics of a Good
Stage Manager

I have since learned what a stage manager does. Everything. In production he is master of all details, liaison with Actors Equity and the hairdresser, maker of appointments and planner of time for the cast, assistant to the director, rehearser of understudies and replacements, supervisor of all moves in and out of theaters, confidant and hand holder of cast, director, and author. Once the play opens he's the man who runs the show, attends every performance and is responsible for the condition and upkeep of the set and costumes, the temperature of the theater, as well as the cast, and is responsible for the level of performances. He's Big Daddy. And Porter (stage manager for *Any Wednesday*), unobtrusively but meticulously organized, highly efficient, funny, warm and caring, was perfect casting.

from the book by Muriel Resnik, *The Son of Any Wednesday*. Reprinted by permission of Muriel Resnik. Copyright © 1965 by Muriel Resnik.

In the quotation above, playwright Muriel Resnik praises her stage manager as, "Unobtrusively but meticulously organized, highly efficient, funny, warm, caring." Are these the highest attributes? Let's examine some of the qualities of a good stage manager.

Proposition 1

Good stage managers assume responsibility.

They say to themselves, "I am *the one* who must make things run smoothly on stage and backstage. Beyond me the buck does not pass." This is an active role, not passive. It is not merely coordination. It is not merely doing what one is told. It is not merely the sum total of the myriad little duties. It is taking charge. It is accepting responsibility.

Professional Attitude

The significant difference between professional and nonprofessional stage managers is not whether or not they are paid or are members of a union. The significant difference is whether or not they are willing and able to accept responsibility for making the production run smoothly on stage and backstage in pre-rehearsal, rehearsal, performance, and post-performance phases.

Your professionalism will make a significant difference in your relationship to the theater staff. The producer, director, technical director, and other staff members are also concerned that things run smoothly. But they have higher priority responsibilities. You are the only one on the staff for whom this is the primary responsibility.

If you can and will accept this responsibility, you are an equal of the producer and director on the team that makes theater. If you do not accept this responsibility, and simply carry out a number of assigned tasks (pulling the curtain, giving the actors their calls, etc.), then you are a subordinate of the producer and director. Which are you?

Proposition 2

Good stage managers keep their cool.

Can you exercise emotional self-control during all phases of production?

You will be working with excitable, conceited, self-centered, temperamental, volatile, sensitive, nervous, explosive people. But you will serve them best by not becoming emotionally involved in their arguments, controversies, or displays of temper.

If the leading lady stalks out screaming and crying, hand her a tissue to show her you care, but don't tell her or the director who was right or wrong in their dispute. It's none of your business. They will resolve their problems without your help.

If the producer asks for the cooperation of the cast in nonacting chores (cleaning the dressing rooms, selling tickets, publicity, etc.), don't give a non-cooperative cast member a five minute harangue or diatribe on his or her responsibilities. It is your job to insure that cast members know what the director and producer expect of them—the time, the place. You may post a duty roster. You may hand out written memos. You may phone them to remind them. You may explain. But you may not lose your temper with a cast member for any reason at all.

If a cast member is late for half hour call, even habitually late, and fails to call the theater, you may remind, you may explain, you may plead, you may cajole, but thou shalt not lose thy cool.

In general, don't raise your voice to cast members. Reply to raised voices in calm, steady, controlled tones.

If a director or producer should reprimand you, privately or before the company, for your prompting technique (as an example) or anything else, don't sulk. Get on with the job the way she or he wants it done.

If you blow a cue, don't get upset. Concentrate on getting the next one right.

Know your own panic response. Then control it. You have reacted to crises in the past. You know you can survive the next one. In time of panic there must be only one question in your mind: "Is there any action I can take to alleviate this situation?" If so, do it. If not, keep your cool. Don't get swept up in the panic. Errors tend to compound.

Example:

During a performance a telephone bell failed to sound. The actors started to ad lib thinking that the cue was simply late. The stage manager in the booth realized that it was not late, but a mechanical failure. There was absolutely no way for the stage manager to get the bell to ring. There was no way to inform the cast on stage that the bell was not about to ring. The cast continued to ad lib until one actor picked up the phone saying, "Thought I heard it ring."

What should the stage manager have done?
Answer: nothing
The stage manager in this case panicked, left the control booth and ran backstage to repair the bell—even though it was not to be used again during the performance. As a result, the next two sound cues were omitted. The error was compounded.

It is terribly uncomfortable to watch a cast ad lib around a mechanical failure. But that's the price of insufficient preparation.

1. Did the stage manager test the bell during the precurtain routine?

2. Did he make sure that the bell wire was out from under the feet of backstage actors and crew?
3. Did he check to see that all connections were soldered?
4. Did he have a separate emergency bell wired in? (Do you think this is going too far?)

A week later during a performance of the same play, the bell failed again. It was unquestionable negligence on the part of the stage manager. But a bell was heard. A cast member had brought an emergency bell to ring off stage because she didn't want a repeat of that incident. (Apparently the cast member didn't think an emergency bell was going too far!)

Stage Manager, if a cast member has to ring your bell for you, it's time to hang up your clipboard.

Keeping one's cool means never appearing harrassed, belligerent, insecure, apologetic, or imposed upon. It's not enough to be doing your job well. You've got to let the cast know by your deportment and the relaxed smile on your face that everything is under control. This gives the cast confidence. In this way, your cool may often be a positive contributing factor to the overall quality of the production.

Proposition 3

Good stage managers keep their mouths shut and their eyes and ears open.

Do you tend to be quiet and observant? If what you say always has to do with the immediate improvement of the rehearsal or production, cast members, crew, and staff will listen to you. If you run off at the mouth endlessly, you will have to struggle to gain attention when you have something significant to contribute. Where between these two extremes are you?

If you have a choice between shouting across the stage to a subordinate to change some gel frames, and crossing the stage yourself to deliver quiet instructions, choose the latter. The cast, staff, and crew will come to appreciate the fact that you are the great mover without the vocal display.

Don't waste your own time promoting yourself. Efficient work is hard to hide so you need not explain how efficient you are to staff members.

Be alert to what is going on around you. During breaks, stick with the director. In casual conversations with actors and staff she or he will agree to changes in lines, props, cues, or design. You should make these changes, or cause them to be made, without further instruction.

Example:

During a break, an actor approaches the director and asks if he may omit a line that's been troubling him. She agrees to the omission. You were getting a cup of coffee instead of staying at the director's side. At the next rehearsal of the scene the actor omits the line. You prompt. The actor breaks character to advise you that the line was cut. You turn to the director for confirmation. The director doesn't remember since it has been three days since this scene was last run. The actor and director discuss it. They agree to omit the line, or the director decides at this time she wants the line delivered. The rehearsal resumes. But there has been a delay that you might have avoided if you had stuck with the director and kept your ears open.

There are no breaks for stage managers. If you must have refreshments, bring a thermos and pack a sandwich or snack in your kit.

Don't gossip with the cast. You will often be privileged to know things that are going on at the administrative level, or between the producer and the director, or between the conductor and the harp player, or about closing date, casting history, salaries, etc. Keep it to yourself.

If a cast member should ask you what you think of the director, staff, crew, or another cast member, try the following delivered by rote in a loud if not sincere voice: " 'X' is the best director (producer, scene designer, publicist, actor, actress, etc.) I've ever had the pleasure of working with." When you are no longer associated with that production you can say what you really think, but until then, a complete, beguiling display of "I-know-how-to-play-this-game" is the most effective way to fly.

Don't align yourself with any clique of actors, within a cast. The stage manager is a friend to the whole cast. If you choose to go out after the show with one group habitually, make it clear to the others in the cast that you would also like to be with them. Invite them to come along some time.

Proposition 4

Good stage managers think ahead.
Don't just sit there, anticipate!

11

What is the company going to be doing later today? Tomorrow? Next week? Does everyone know about it? Is everything ready? You have made a master calendar, schedules, do-lists, duty rosters, a prompt script, and check lists. All of these are instruments to help you think ahead. But there is no substitute for constant vigilance.

If something is changed suddenly, what future effects will the changes have? What other changes must be made as a result of that change? Who must be notified?

One of your greatest contributions to the performance quality is making the most of every minute between first reading and final curtain. If there is any delay in rehearsal or production, it's your fault.

Stage managing may be compared to flying a high-performance aircraft. Once you're in the air, you can't make repairs. Once the curtain goes up you can't stop the performance to make changes in the location of set pieces and discovered props. Pilots and stage managers both have extensive preflight check lists for these reasons.

To land a high-performance aircraft you must take several steps prior to entering the landing pattern, because the aircraft moves so fast there is no time to accomplish everything once in the pattern. To carry out a tight sequence of light changes and sound effects, the stage manager must also take several steps in advance, like insuring that tapes are cued, that dimmer board presets are cranked in and patches made, and that all hands are rehearsed in the execution of that sequence and understand their cues, because once the sequence starts, there is no time to do all of the things that must be done in advance if the sequence is to be brought off successfully.

Although the comparison might be extended, the point is clear: pilots and stage managers must have the same think-ahead discipline in order to be effective.

Serious emergencies call for both keeping cool and thinking ahead.

A fire should be expected momentarily (see Figure 15-1). Do you have a fire extinguisher in the control booth? Do you have another one backstage? Do you have a phone in the booth? If it's a pay phone, do you have an emergency dime taped nearby? Do you know the number to call? Is there a clear unblocked space for you to get out from behind your equipment? Can you give calm instructions to your audience in a tone of voice that will convince them to leave the theater in an orderly fashion? In a huge theater, do you have a working microphone in the booth that will allow you to reach the entire audience via the public address system? Do you know how to drop the fire curtain (the asbestos curtain that hangs immediately in front of the main curtain and seals off the stage from the audience in the event of fire)? Are all of the exit aisles, doors, and alleys unblocked? Will the emergency exits open? Is your scenery flame-proofed in accordance with city ordinances? Is all electrical equipment wired safely?

If the answer to any question above is no, the stage manager and the producer are derelict in their responsibility for the safety of the audience and the cast.

Stage managers must force themselves out of the rut of thinking that it can't happen here. It can happen here, and everyone in your theater will be safer if you will just assume that it is going to happen here within the next thirty seconds.

Plan ahead for the worst possible type of medical emergency. Assume that a member of the cast or crew will suffer a severe injury or heart attack in the course of mounting, rehearsing, or presenting.

Do you have a company doctor? Is her or his office or home near the theater? Do you have the doctor's office, home, and service numbers posted? Do you know the location of an all-night clinic? Have you driven there on a test run from the theater? (It is maddening to find that the clinic entrance is located on a one way street and you will have to drive three extra blocks because you didn't make the right approach—while your passenger is losing blood!)

During such emergencies keeping your cool and thinking ahead become traits of paramount importance.

Proposition 5

Good stage managers are considerate.

Do you have that quality of selfless caring which prompts a man to give a woman his jacket when he knows he'll be cold? Can you put the comfort of every cast member before your own comfort?

Is the theater warm enough? Can you get there a little earlier to turn on the heat so that cast members don't walk into a cold theater? Can you turn on the lights so cast members won't have to enter dark dressing rooms?

Is the backstage area too drafty? Can you close some doors or make some baffles out of extra flats?

Do the actresses have to walk to their cars from the theater along a dimly lit street? Can you walk them to their cars or ask other cast members to do so? If it's raining, can you provide an umbrella?

Is there drinking water backstage and in the dressing rooms? Can you arrange for water service or provide pitchers and cups?

Did you dust the rehearsal furniture before the cast sat down?

Do you really listen when cast members speak to you?

Can you offer your cast a natural affection?

Backstage in Hollywood theaters I found the lavish affection and terms of endearment that pass between casual acquaintances to be quite surprising. It did not seem very natural to me. But insecurity seems to be a very common trait among theater people, and they find warmth and affection reassuring. This display of warmth does not come naturally to all people. It is certainly not recommended if it must be forced. But if you can display a natural affection for your cast, as if they were all dear old warm friends or members of your family, why not?

Are you considerate with respect to the creativity of others? Can you offer constructive criticism effectively without stamping out creative instinct? It's very difficult to do.

Many of the creative people—the scene designers, costume designers, choral directors, choreographers, and directors—carry their gifts wrapped preciously within thin skin. Yet, in the theater situation, no creator can work alone. He or she must communicate with, and gain the cooperation of all the others on the staff to see his or her own creativity come to fruition. The stage manager, unfortunately, is frequently placed in the position of coordinating the creative efforts of the super-sensitive. It requires a great deal of patience and tact.

Example:

Set construction is running behind schedule. The technical director complains to you that the scene designer has no concept of economy in design, that he tries to present in total rather than sug gesting. She complains that the designer is overburdening the shop with an unconscionable amount of work.

The scene designer complains to you that the technical director has ruined more scenery than a termite on a showboat, that inefficient methods are being used in the shop, and that for two nights running, one of his ornamental set pieces has not been placed on stage because it is waiting to be repaired and that this ruins the entire aesthetic balance of the set.

Your chief concern as stage manager is to have the set for the next production ready for the take-in one night hence.

This is the type of situation that requires tactful soothing, and massive doses of consideration. If you try to fix the blame at this point, you are likely to find your next production hung up. Cool them off separately. Commiserate with each, separately. Tell them what an incredibly good job they've been doing up to this point. Praise their strong points. Overlook their weaknesses. Sympathize with their problems. Pep them up and send them back to work. They'll get the scenery finished.

Proposition 6

Good stage managers keep their sense of humor.

Making theater should be a happy experience for all concerned. Unfortunately, delays, deadlines, economic pressures, personality conflicts, and other factors sometimes make the process grim.

Don't contribute to the grimness. Leave your personal problems at home. Come to work with a resolve to stay happy.

"I find that most people are just as happy as they make up their minds to be," said Abraham Lincoln. Lincoln considered humor a "labor-saving device" and a "multiple-purpose tool."

"A sense of humor is part of the art of leadership, of getting along with people, of getting things done," said Dwight D. Eisenhower.

Try to keep a smile on your face, and have a good reason for its being there.

A cheerful stage manager can be a great asset to any theater group. Sometimes a cheerful word can get the whole company over a rough spot.

Knowing jokes is not a substitute for having a sense of humor. There are occasions, however, when a good theater story will put the company at ease. A successful director with whom I worked greeted each new cast with a story; it seemed to break the ice and to be very effective for him. The appendix contains a few of my favorite stories.

A corollary of Proposition 6 is that *good stage managers do not have personality conflicts with anyone.* Holding grudges or showing hostility toward any member of the company cannot be a part of your behavior. Go home and kick your cat, but don't let any member of the cast, staff, or crew feel that you dislike her or him. It simply does not expedite production.

Proposition 7

Good stage managers are organized and efficient.

Throughout the chapters that follow the emphasis will be on organization and efficiency, so no further comment should be needed here.

Proposition 8

Good stage managers are punctual and dependable.

If you are not there on time or early, or cannot be depended on, you simply cannot be a stage manager.

In summary, good stage managers

accept responsibility,
keep their cool,
keep their mouths shut, eyes, ears open
think ahead,
are considerate,
keep their sense of humor,
are organized and efficient,
are punctual and dependable.

How do you compare?

· 3 ·

Getting the Play and Understanding It

During readings, rehearsals, and production, you must have a copy of the script and a thorough understanding of it. In order to expedite readings and rehearsals, you should check to make sure that there are enough scripts on hand for actors and staff.

Usually copies of the script are ordered when the rights of production are obtained from the play service (Samuel French, Tams-Witmark, etc., see below).

If, however, you are going into production with one copy of the script, or a vague memory of it, one of the first things you must do is make sure you have on hand an adequate number of scripts. This may possibly be limited to determining how many are necessary, or it may mean actually going to pick them up.

It is desirable to have for reference the catalog of at least the major play services. A postcard will get them from:

Anchorage Press
Cloverlot
Anchorage, Kentucky 40223

Baker's Plays
100 Summer Street
Boston, Mass. 02110

McKay's Contest Plays
David McKay Company, Inc.
750 Third Ave.
New York, New York 10017

Music Theatre International
119 West 57th Street
New York, New York 10019

17

I. E. Clark
Box 246
Schulenburg, Texas 78956

Drama Book Specialists
150 West 52nd Street
New York, New York 10019

Dramatic Publishing Co.
86 East Randolph Street
Chicago, Ill. 60601

Dramatists Play Service, Inc.
440 Park Avenue South
New York, New York 10016

Edridge Publishing Company
Franklin, Ohio 45005

EMA Plays
280 Riviera Drive
Harvey Cedars, New Jersey 08008

The Hever Publishing Co.
P.O. Box 248
Cedar Rapids, Iowa 52406

Performance Publishing Co.
978 N. McLean Blvd.
Elgin, Illinois 60120

Pioneer Drama Service
2172 S. Colorado Blvd.
Denver, Colorado 80222

The Rogers and Hammerstein
Library
598 Madison Avenue
New York, New York 10022

Samuel French, Inc.
25 West 45th Street
New York, New York 10036 (or)
7623 Sunset Blvd.
Hollywood, Cal. 90046

Tams-Witmark
757 Third Avenue
New York, New York 10017

Check with your post office to determine the type of mail service that you must have to insure that the scripts get to you on time. It is usually worth the cost of specifying airmail, special delivery, or at least first class, rather than the less expensive book rate, to make sure that your scripts won't be delayed in the mail.

In determining the number of scripts you will need, consider:

1. Will all speaking parts need scripts? Check your visual display of characters on stage (discussed later in this chapter) to see whether a few pages of one script can be removed for one or two other speaking parts.
2. Will the costume designer, scene designer, property master, or any other staff member need a script? The publicity person can often make good use of a script.
3. Will a lonesome follow-spot operator or any other crew member need one?
4. Will understudies or replacements need them?
5. Can the budget allow for a few extra copies?
6. Do you have copying equipment?

It is not legal to reproduce any part of a published script unless the copyrights have expired. But in the event that you are working on an original, unpublished play, you would want to have the address and phone number of a copying service in your contact file. Perhaps you will want to use a mimeograph or spirit duplicator to make additional scripts or sides yourself. Hectofax masters for a spirit duplicator, which can be made on a Thermofax machine, can save a lot of typing, assuming that you do not have access to even more sophisticated copying equipment.

Sides, a part of a script giving only one character's lines, each preceded by the cue for the line, may be typed or hand copied by apprentices or the actors, if necessary.

When script shipments arrive, you should immediately check the content against the invoice or manifest. It is quite possible to find the score of *South Pacific*, scripts for *Oklahoma*, and sides for *Flower Drum Song* in a shipment sent out for a production of *The King and I.*

Such errors must be called to the attention of the play service as soon as possible in the hope of obtaining the correct materials in time. You may have to resort to long distance phone calls.

Lock up your scripts and let them out only on a sign-out basis. Otherwise, they will disappear. It's not usually criminal intent. It may be the chorus girl who wants to read for a principal part in next week's production who loses her script on a cast picnic. This does not mean to imply that she should not be permitted to see a script in advance of readings, but she should have to sign it out.

All scripts and sides should be signed out when issued to cast members and staff. Lock up the sign-out sheet in the same cupboard as the scripts. Scripts, sides, and scores are usually due back from cast, staff, and musicians on the day preceding or coinciding with the close of the show. (This is payday in professional companies; the cost of lost materials can then be deducted on the spot.) Post a notice to this effect and a price list on the call board. Note your intent in the company rules.

Frequently a cast member with just a few lines will elect to copy them rather than sign out a skimpy side, thus avoiding the possibility of losing it. You would be wise to encourage this.

Normally in musical stock and musical comedy, the scores, scripts, and sides are packaged and returned within a week after the close of the production in order to decrease rental costs. This task is usually assigned to an apprentice or the company "gopher" (a production assistant sent to "go fer" things). If a closing night review of the past year or season is to be presented, you may want to retain one score and one script from each of the shows.

On straight play-book shows you may allow the actors to keep the scripts, or you may ask that they return or pay for them. Determine your policy and relay it to the cast.

All too frequently you may be held responsible for missing scripts and asked to pay for them. So it is a good idea to mark each script with a number so that each may be accounted for.

Scripts sometimes get tied up for unusual reasons.

Example:

In casting a big name show, an actor may be sent a script even though there is no intent to cast that actor. You may even be called upon to deliver the script to the actor's home. The script is never seen again until a few weeks after opening, when it comes back through the mail with a hard to read note, "Not my cup of tea," and the big name actor's initials.

Agents for professional actors often beg directors or managers for scripts, and receive them, even though there is no intent to cast the agents' clients. The agents feel that showing the scripts to their clients is tangible proof that they are working and that their clients are being considered.

When a script is issued for any unusual reason, don't count on its being returned in time to meet your needs. It is best to replace that script immediately if you have on hand only the necessary minimum with which to begin rehearsals.

Although your responsibility for scripts may be very limited, you should know how to get, replace, reproduce, lock up, control, and retrieve scripts as part of your work in expediting auditions and rehearsals.

Of even greater concern is the processing of your own script—making it into a working tool.

The Prompt Script

Turning a script into a prompt script increases the size of the margins (see Figure 3-1). This allows you to make all of your cues and warns (warning alerts) large and clear. It gives you adequate room to make clear blocking notations and diagrams. It also gives you sufficient room to make production notes.

To make a prompt book, cut or "unbind" the pages of a script and mount each page on a standard size (8½ × 11) loose-leaf sheet (unruled) so that both sides of the script can be seen (see Figure 3-2).

ACT I]   OF BEING EARNEST   47

the servants invariably drink the champagne? I ask merely for information.

Lane. I attribute it to the superior quality of the wine, sir. I have often observed that in married households the champagne is rarely of a first-rate brand.

Algernon. Good Heavens! Is marriage so demoralizing as that?

Lane. I believe it *is* a very pleasant state, sir. I have had very little experience of it myself up to the present. I have only been married once. That was in consequence of a misunderstanding between myself and a young woman.

Algernon (languidly). I don't know that I am much interested in your family life, Lane.

Lane. No, sir; it is not a very interesting subject. I never think of it myself.

Algernon. Very natural, I am sure. That will do, Lane, thank you.

Lane. Thank you sir. *(LANE goes out.)*

Algernon. Lane's views on marriage seem somewhat lax. Really, if the lower orders don't set us a good example, what on earth is the use of them? They seem, as a class, to have absolutely no sense of moral responsibility.
                ENTER LANE.
Lane. Mr. Ernest Worthing.
                ENTER JACK. LANE goes out.
Algernon. How are you, my dear Ernest? What brings you up to town?

Jack. Oh, pleasure, pleasure! What else should bring one anywhere? Eating as usual, I see, Algy!

· **Figure 3-1** ·
A Prompt Book Page with Script Page Numbers Visible

If you are willing to use two printed scripts to produce one prompt script, this is by far the fastest method: you simply paste alternate printed pages to opposite sides of each loose-leaf 8½ × 11 page.

Whether your prompt script is made from two scripts, or by the "economy" one-script method, you need to consider the best placement of loose-leaf page space around the printed script, and Figure 3-2 shows the alternatives. Note that for the one-script cutout method with loose-leaf page pasted around printed script edges, pattern 1 calls for cementing, taping, or gluing four sides of every page while

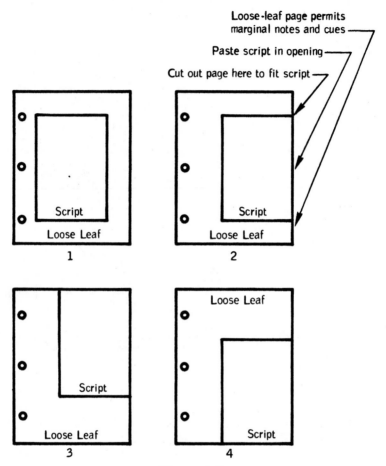

· **Figure 3-2** ·
Four Patterns for Mounting Script Pages

patterns 3 and 4 require that only two sides of each page be attached. I feel that pattern 2, which requires that three sides be attached, gives me the most desirable distribution of additional space.

   If you cannot spare an extra printed script and must paste loose-leaf around printed pages to show both sides of each printed sheet, then start by making a heavy cardboard template cut to show all the printed area of each script page (see Figure 3-2). With a single-edged or mounted razor, you can then cut about five loose-leaf sheets at a time to the correct size, making one loose-leaf cutout page for each two page leaf of printed script.

   Use Scotch Magic Transparent Tape, a crayon-shaped glue stick, or rubber cement to attach script pages to the cut out loose-

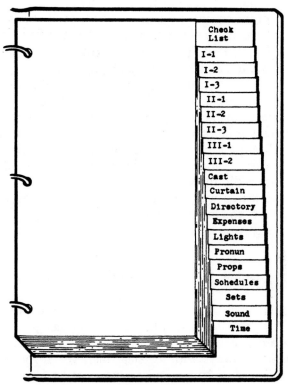

· **Figure 3-3** ·

Page Tabs for Rapid Reference in a Prompt Script. Note that the tabs are in alphabetical order so that the stage manager has extremely easy access to any information that he needs during rehearsal or production.

leaf sheets. Rubber cement is the most forgiving. Errors can be corrected without cutting as rubber cemented pages can be pulled apart and restuck without damage to the pages. Glue sticks are faster and more convenient. I have found the Pritt Glue Stick to be excellent. Some liquid glue sticks wrinkle the paper when dry. It is best to experiment and find the right glue stick before pasting up your entire script.

With the help of a few apprentices, using assembly line methods, you can assemble an "economy model" prompt script in less than one hour. Allow several hours if you are making your first script by yourself, and five hours with a hangover following a cast party.

Next you should make tabs for each scene so that you can quickly turn to any scene without thumbing through the script. You may purchase tabs at a stationery store or you can make your own, using tape. Each tab should be labeled (see Figure 3-3). Place the scene tabs on the last page of the previous scene, not the first or second page of the scene, so that the tab will open your script properly, with the desired scene immediately displayed.

Rehearsal schedule, pronunciation guide, plots, set sketches, and cast lists should also be tabbed so that you can turn immediately to whatever information you need during a rehearsal without wasting time by shuffling through a lot of paper.

A neat, well-made prompt book is an asset, but no critic will ever review your prompt book. Great paperwork does not necessarily make great theater. It might be possible for some people to keep all of their blocking notation in their head and make sound and light cue notations in the margins of uncut scripts, but most managers could not work this way, and most wouldn't feel secure or comfortable. I advise you to do whatever works best for you, but I would suggest that super-organization of your prompt book is a great system.

Keeping the Prompt Script in a Safe Place

Once a skilled stage manager has worked on a prompt script it becomes a valuable tool and should therefore be safeguarded.

There are two possible ways to do this. The first is that the prompt script is *always* with the stage manager. It goes home with the stage manager. If anyone needs information from the prompt script in the middle of the night, he or she calls the stage manager. The stage manager is so prompt and so reliable that there is never any question in anyone's mind that the prompt script would be missing when needed.

The other possibility is that the prompt script is kept in a secure place in the theater—locked up when the stage manager is not using it during rehearsals. The idea here is that if something should happen to the stage manager, someone else could pick up the prompt script and run the rehearsal or show.

You will have to decide which of these two possibilities is best for your theater.

Access

Anyone who needs information from the prompt script should ask the stage manager for that information. The prompt script is the stage manager's tool, and as a courtesy to the stage manager, no one should go into the prompt script without the stage manager's permission.

Key or Code

In educational theater the stage manager is often advised to set up the prompt script so that anyone can read and understand all the cues and notes, as well as the blocking notation. The stage manager is instructed to make a key for abbreviations and symbols on the front page of the prompt script. Couldn't hurt.

Understanding the Script

You must understand the script. You must understand it well before casting and before rehearsals begin if you are to be effective. To understand it you must analyze it and identify its problems. The word "problem" is used to mean anything that must be done to run the show.

Try to allow a quiet time of intense concentration for your first reading. It can pay off in the accomplishment of a lot of work. And all of this pre-rehearsal work can pay great dividends in time-saving during rehearsals.

As you read, use light pencil in the margins of your script to identify all possible light cues, sound cues, special effects, costume changes, or peculiarities, properties, entrances, exits, and pronunciation questions.

You might want to use the following code:

L — Light cue
S — Sound cue
Ef — Special effect
P — Property
E — Entrance or exit
? — Pronunciation question

Of course, any code that works for you is fine.

For every light, sound, and special effect, using a ruler and working in light pencil, you should draw a horizontal line closest to the line of dialogue preceding an oral cue, or under the description of a visual cue. This line should cross the entire prompt book page so that you can see it quite easily during rehearsals.

About a half page preceding the line, draw another horizontal line marked "warn lights" or "warn sound." In the case of two light cues and a sound cue in a tight sequence, you need put in only one warn line before the sequence, but it should be marked "warn light/sound series" (see Figure 3-4).

accepts me, I am going to kill my brother, indeed I think I'll kill him in any case. Cecily is a little too much interested in him. It is rather a bore. So I am going to get rid of Ernest. And I strongly advise you to do the same with Mr. . . . with your invalid friend who has the absurd name.

Warn
Bell

Algernon. Nothing will induce me to part with Bunbury, and if you ever get married, which seems to me extremely problematic, you will be very glad to know Bunbury.   A man who marries without knowing Bunbury has a very tedious time of it.

Jack. That is nonsense. If I marry a charming girl like Gwendolen, and she is the only girl I ever saw in my life that I would marry, I certainly won't want to know Bunbury.

Algernon. Then your wife will.   You don't seem to realize, that in married life three is company and two is none.

Jack (sententiously). That, my dear young friend, is the theory that the corrupt French Drama has been propounding for the last fifty years.

Algernon. Yes; and that the happy English home has proved in half the time.

Jack. For heaven's sake, don't try to be cynical. It's perfectly easy to be cynical.

Algernon. My dear fellow, it isn't easy to be anything now-a-days. There's such a lot of beastly competition about. *(The sound of an electric bell is heard.)* Ah! that must be Aunt Augusta. Only relatives, or creditors, ever ring in that Wagnerian manner. Now, if I get her out of the way for ten minutes, so that you can have

Bell

· **Figure 3-4** ·
Lightly Penciled Cues and Warns
for Use during Rehearsals

It is too early to number these cues or to write them in ink, since there may well be changes during rehearsals. You will use the penciled lines to call the light and sound cues during rehearsals.

Plots

As you identify the problems and put in your light pencil lines, you might also wish to list the problems. A list of problems is a *plot*. A functional plot is one that allows your associates to obtain a complete

COSTUME PLOT	Actor Provides	Borrow	Rent	Purchase	Responsible; Date
MRS. JONES:					
Green and white silk polka dot dress					
White shoes					
Long white gloves					
White bracelets and earrings					
Pink silk fringe dress and stole					
Pink shoes and white beaded evening bag					
FRED:					
Light blue shirt					
Grey flannel pants					
Dark red tie					
Black shoes					
Red wool school jacket (Monroe High School)					
FATHER:					
Pajamas, orange and white stripe cotton					
Black shoes					
Grey suit					
Print shirt					
White shirt					
Soft grey hat					
JANE:					
Green jumper and white blouse					
White low heel shoes					
White bag					
White dress					
Light blue suit					
White gloves					
White high heel shoes					
HENRY:					
Dark blue and white stripe shirt					
Print shirt					
White shirt					
Blue dungarees					
Grey sneakers					
Grey socks					
Brown socks					
Tan shoes					
Light brown double breasted suit					
Blue apron					
JEEVES:					
Black double-breasted tuxedo					

· **Figure 3-5** ·

Costume Plot as Modified from the Script

grasp of the problems in their areas without having to refer to the script. In other words, *plots allow you to digest the script for others.*

In deciding whether making plots will be of practical value, ask yourself this question: "If I were the sound technician on this production, would it help if I were handed a sound plot?" In productions where the technical people come in just a few days before opening, having plots ready is particularly valuable.

Copies of your plots should be given to all staff members concerned. Your copy should be kept in your prompt book, properly tabbed, to be changed in rehearsals as necessary.

page	lt. effect	cue	cue #	instr dmmrs	int	tmg
114/64	Shop up	after Fore-man's entrance				
114/70	Shop out	David: "Whee" and Marvin's exit				
115/71	Dressing room in	following David's exit				
115/78	Dressing room out	David: "No, he's a hard-ware salesman!"				
116/78	Stage and Stage Mana-ger's area (Now the foots!) (But no worklight!)	after entrance of cast				
116/82	Stage and Stage Mana-ger's area out	David: "I am your older brother! By a former mar-riage!"				
117/82	Stage to general with worklight, no foots	when cast in place				
117/83	Stage down to effect of single work-light	Mother: "A very nice young man." & her exit				
117/84	Worklight out	David: "I trust I haven't kept you waiting to long."				
	Curtain calls lighting					
	Curtain lights out					
	House in					

· **Figure 3-6** ·

Light Plot, Listing Cues. Note that cue numbers will not be established until the technical rehearsal. The columns left blank for "instruments/dimmers," "intensity," and "timing" will normally be filled out by the light technician working with the SM.

If, as you read, you listed problems on separate sheets of paper headed "Light plot," "Sound plot," "Special effects," "Properties," and "Pronunciation," then you now have rough plots ready.

Some acting editions of plays contain costume and property plots. They do not always contain all of the information you will need, but you will be able to modify them easily (see Figure 3-5).

	ACT SCENE PAGE	SOUND CUE SHEET	VOLUME	TONE	SPKR SLCTN	TIME	OTHER
1. Intro music		30 min prior to curtain in time	4	balance	1,2,3	30 min	fade out Gently
2. Fade out intro		to cue up 3rd cue (on "places")	—				
3. Roar of airplane	I-1	just prior to curtain	8		1	20 sec	
4. Thunder, lightning, heavy rain	I-1	"You won't be needing your raincoat."	7		2	90 sec	
5. Bells and light rain	I-2	"Hold on to my hand."	5	Treble	2	20 sec	
6. Car approach motor sick	I-6	"I don't hear anything."	6	balance	3	20 sec	
7. Motor strangles, car door slams	I-6	"...His usual cheerful self."	8		2	10 sec	
8. Bicycles (like loud crickets)	I-10	"We'll meet you there." & ad libs (as they exit)	4-9 (fadeup Gently)		2	90 sec	

· **Figure 3-7** ·

Sound Plot, Listing Cues. Space should be left between cues so that additional cues may be entered. The last five columns are set through coordination of director, stage manager and sound technician during rehearsals.

In general you will want to cite on each plot for each entry the following information: the page, the act and scene, and a complete description of what happens.

Light Plot

Leave plenty of room between entries (see Figure 3-6). The director may add lighting effects not called for in the script and may add many dimmings and brightenings of areas during rehearsals.

Sound Plot

Frequently at sound recording sessions, the sound technician and staff members, each holding a copy of the sound plot (see Figure 3-7), work at selecting and rerecording, or creating and recording sound effects. At such sessions you will insure that all the needed sounds are recorded, in proper order, and of appropriate length.

Costume Plot

Besides giving some indication of the clothes to be worn (see Figure 3-5), you should also identify quick changes that will require change booths in the wings or at the tops of aisles and/or series of changes that will require that an actor be assisted.

The costume plot published in the actor's edition of a contemporary non-costume play in which each cast member wears one costume throughout might require only the director's approval. But in a musical like *Little Me*, in which the lead plays several roles and is forever making quick changes, you will need to write a meticulous plot with cues for costume assistants and presets for costumes.

Properties

Note whether the prop is discovered or carried on—if discovered, where, and if carried on, by whom (see Figure 3-8). During rehearsals, note whether the prop enters stage left or stage right, so that if there are two or more prop tables backstage, you will know where to preset that prop.

Property control is discussed at greater length in Chapter Ten.

Entrances and Exits

List each character, the scenes he or she is in, and the pages on which he or she enters and exits, in the following way:
Irene:

I-1, 16-24; I-2, 26-30, 50-53;

II-1, 57-73, 78-83; II-2, 84-112

Constance:

I-1, 5-19; I-2, 26-45; etc.

(In Act I, Scene 1, Irene enters on page 16 and exits on page 24. In Scene 2 of Act I, she enters on page 26 and exits on page 30, then reenters on page 50 and exits again on page 53.)

You may wish to post your list of entrances and exists prior to a casting call so that actors may easily find lines to read for their parts.

You may also want to put in light pencil line warns for entrances of actors, about a page preceding each entrance. It is not a stage

THE BEAUTY PART

Act I Scene 4

Stage Right Prop Table

PROP/SET PIECE	person1	preset	WHO/WHERE	work	SOURCE	final
coffee cup, white take-out	X		Quagmeyer	X		X
attache case	X		Hubris	X	Bill	X
script	X		Hubris/in attache	X	Lawrence	X
artist's smock	X		Hubris/in attache	X	Maria	
April Monkhood's picture	X		Hubris	X	Lawrence	X
phone, old beat up		X	on table	X		
radio, old beat up		X	on table	X		X
vase to hold brushes		X	on table	X		X
brushes		X	in vase	X	Dinah	X
small white paper bag		X	on table	x		X
push broom		X	behind easel	X		X
oil paintings		X	on chair	X		
abstract of woman		X	on easel			
bottle of whiskey in white bag		X	Quagmeyer	X		
easel, paint smeared						
table, beat up, paint smeared						
2 beat up, non matching chairs						

· **Figure 3-8** ·
Property Plot (May Double as Control Form)

manager's function to warn actors for their entrances during performances. But you will find that warning them during rehearsals is helpful. This aspect of rehearsal procedure is discussed in Chapter Eight.

Long strips of paper rather than penciled lines may be used for entrance warns. The marker warns are harder to miss than the light lines and may be completely removed from the prompt script prior to opening night. The marker may also be handed silently to an assistant to summon the actor. (See Figure 3-9).

From your notations of entrances and exits you may now make up a visual display of characters on stage, a graph that shows at a glance which actors work together on what script pages (see Figure

· **Figure 3-9** ·
Actor Warn in Prompt Script for Quick Access during Rehearsal

3-10). This device will be invaluable to you in planning rehearsal schedules, finding appropriate pages for readings, double casting, and removing script pages to serve as sides for a minor role. The visual display should be placed in your prompt script as a reference tool.

Actors and Their Entrance Cues

During performances actors are responsible for making all of their entrances on cue. They alone have this responsibility. This arises out of very understandable circumstances: during the performance the stage manager can only be in one place—the work area—where she or he is busy following the book and cuing sound, lights, and curtain. Cues sometimes coincide with an actor's entrance, i.e., door-bell rings prior to the entrance or the director calls for a subtle increase of light intensity on the door area as he or she enters. So the stage manager cannot be in two places at once, cuing and pushing

	5 10 15 20 25 30 35 40 45 50 55 60 65 70 75 80 85 90 95 100 105 110 115				
	I 1	I 2	II 1	II 2	III
Maureen					
ESTELLE					
Karen					
Philip					
JOSEPH					
Dick					
Blocked					

· **Figure 3-10** ·

A Visual Display of Characters on Stage. Numbers denote script page numbers. Note that the "blocked" line allows you to see what scenes have yet to be blocked, and who's in them. The "v" denotes voice only.

the actor on stage. There might be several actors entering from more than one entrance. So out of very practical considerations it is necessary that each actor be responsible for her or his own entrance. In professional theater, the union insists on this.

There are some exceptions: The stage manager is responsible for actors being in place when they are discovered at the rise of the curtain, and when they are offstage about to enter within the first few seconds after the curtain. After calling "Places, please," the stage manager checks that all discovered cast members are in their appropriate blocked positions. The procedure for checking this, in a theater-in-the-round example, is discussed in Chapter Twelve under "Shift Inspection."

And there are even some exceptional exceptions: Occasionally a producer or director overrides normal procedure and asks that the stage manager "supervise" the entrance and exits of an actor who has particular difficulties. Such an exception is discussed as an example under "Calls" in Chapter Nine.

During rehearsals the situation is different. In the role of expeditor of rehearsals, the stage manager should closely supervise the entrances of cast members. In many theaters there is no monitor system that broadcasts the rehearsals to offstage areas where the actors may wander for fittings or to run lines. So the stage manager

33

warns them of their entrances, following the procedures described under "Warning" in Chapter Eight.

Pronunciation Questions

You may wish to make a list of all words in the script about which there is a question of pronunciation. Give the pronunciation of all proper names in the script which might be pronounced in two ways.

Example:

Middle of the Night by Paddy Chayefsky—"Mrs. Nieman." Obviously, all members of the cast should pronounce this name the same way. Should it be pronounced Nē–man or Nī–man?

List foreign words and phrases and give both the pronunciation and meaning.

Example:

A Majority of One by Leonard Spigelgass—"mashugina"; *ma–shoog'–i–na*, Yiddish meaning crazy.

List unusual and uncommon words and give pronunciation and meaning.

Example:

The Emperor by Hermann Gressieker—"trīreme"; trī–rēm, an ancient Roman galley with three banks of oars on each side.

Example:

The Cherry Orchard by Anton Chekhov—"Epihodov"; "Ep–(i)–hóe–doff, a clerk who proposes to Dunyasha.

Cast members aren't expected to be Russian scholars but should be provided with correct pronunciations of characters' names.

This list may be posted as early as the readings for the benefit of those trying out for parts. But it is especially beneficial to you, since you must pronounce the words correctly while prompting. You should keep a copy in your prompt script.

Special Effects

If there is only one special effect in a play, there is obviously no need for writing a plot. But if you are doing a play that calls for many, you will want to list them for consideration by the scene designer and technical director. Such a list might include a heavy fog, walls shaking and dishes falling off shelves, a trap door disappearance accompanied by a flash of smoke, a sliding panel, firing of weapons, etc.

Making plots and lists seems far removed from making theater happen. It is not recommended unless you can clearly see that it will expedite your production.

However, hard work in analyzing the script and identifying its problems before rehearsals begin pays off—your work becomes easier with every day that passes. Lack of preparation before rehearsals begin results in a terribly overworked and panicked feeling as opening night approaches. I've always preferred the former.

· 4 ·

Scheduling
and Company Rules

The Master Calendar

Time, management of time, and the coordination of the cast, crew, and staff are very important to every theater. In order to keep everyone on time and their efforts meshing smoothly, it is desirable to post a master calendar—and only one master calendar—in a convenient place so that it is available to everyone on the staff. The master calendar can be your most effective tool for coordinating the staff.

The master calendar (see Figure 4-1) should be large enough so that several lines may be written legibly in the space allotted for each day. It should, of course, be developed after consultation regarding the needs of producer or management, department heads in various phases of production, and above all, after conferring with the director, with whom you work in a direct supporting role. The calendar should list many of the following kinds of events, but not necessarily all of them, and not necessarily in the following order:

Deadline for set drawings/line drawings (see Chapter Eight)
Deadline for lighting plans (see Chapter Eleven)
Deadline for cleaning/repairing lighting instruments (see Chapter Eleven)

37

Sunday	Monday	Tuesday	Wednesday
		1 10 STAFF CONF.	**2** 7:30 Readings 9:30
6	**7** 1ST DAY THTr. AVAILAble 10 AM 1ST Rehrsal (contracts) 2:00 Pub. Photos	**8** 10 AM Rehearsal 11:30 STaff Conf.	**9** 10:00 STAff conf. 10:30 REHEARSAL
13 10:00 WORK CALL	**14** 10:00 rehearsal	**15** 10:00 REhearsal	**16** 10:00 Staff Confer. 10:30 REHEARSAL
20 10:00 WORK CALL	**21** CAST DAY OFF 8:00 TAPE ALL SOUND CUES MUSIC	**22** 10:00 AM REhearsaL 10:30 STaff Meet.	**23** REHRSL 10 AM Staff Conf. deadline: Reserve opening night & invitations
27 9:00 Work Call SET COMPLETE 8:00 Rehearsal Run Through	**28** Cast day off 10:00 Focus lghts 2:00 Flameproof sets	**29** 10:00 STAFF CONf. 8:00 Tech Rehearsal	**30** DEADLiNE: All COSTUME COMPLETE 8:00 Tech Rehearsal

· **Figure 4-1** ·
A Master Calendar

Deadline for obtaining sufficient copies of the script (Chapter
    Three)
Readings/auditions (Chapter Six)
Deadline for complete casting (Chapter Six)
Understudy casting (Chapters Six and Sixteen)
First rehearsal (Chapter Eight)
All subsequent rehearsals (Chapter Eight)
Work calls (Chapters Four and Twelve)
Staff conferences (Chapters Four and Eight)
Deadline for memorization of lines (by act) (Chapter Eight)
Deadline for obtaining all rehearsal props (Chapters Eight and
    Ten)
Take-in day (see Chapter Twelve)

Thursday	Friday	Saturday	**NOTES**
3 2:00 – Readings 4:00 *reading* 6:00 *reading* 7:30	4 2:00 Readings 5:30	5 DEADLINE: SET DESIGN LINE DWGS.	
10 10 AM REHEARSAL 2:00 COSTUME FITTINGS	11 10:00 Rehearsal	12 CAST DAY OFF 10:00 WORK CALL	
17 *Deadline: Live sound effects obtained* 10 AM Rehearsal	18 DEADLINE ALL REHEARSAL PROPS 10:00 rehrsal.	19 *Cast day off* 10:00 WORK CALL	
24 11:30 Rehearsal DEADLINE: *All props final*	25 DeadLine: All lines memorized 10 Rehearsal INTEGRATE SOUND	26 *Take-in Day:* 10 *work call* 8:00 REHEARSAL RUN THROUGH	

· **Figure 4-1** ·
(Continued)

Deadline for completion of sets (Chapter Thirteen)
Deadline for completion of sound effects (Chapter Thirteen)
Focus lights (Chapter Thirteen)
Fittings of costumes (Chapters Eight and Thirteen)
Publicity picture calls (Chapter Eight)
Publicity interviews (Chapter Eight)
Deadline for reservation of opening night tickets
Deadline for obtaining all final props (Chapter Ten)
Integration of sound effects into rehearsals (Chapter Thirteen)
Integration of film effects into rehearsals (Chapter Thirteen)
Costume parade (Chapters Eight and Thirteen)
Special costume rehearsal
First rehearsal with musicians

No-actor tech/all set changes (Chapter Thirteen)
First technical rehearsal (Chapter Thirteen)
Second tech (Chapter Thirteen)
First dress rehearsal (Chapter Eight)
Second dress
Invitational dress/previews
Flameproofing of set (Chapters Eight, Fifteen, and Eighteen)
Fire inspection
Opening night
All performances (Chapters Fourteen and Sixteen)
Understudy rehearsals (Chapter Sixteen)
Closing night (Chapter Seventeen)
Strike (Chapter Seventeen)
Take-out day/sets and props returned (Chapter Seventeen)
All other use of the stage

If you plan to have every aspect of the production in final shape all at the same time, you are likely to have problems. But by spacing deadlines for various aspects of the production, you may check on, and overcome, small crises rather than have to face (and hopefully surmount) total panic.

Example:

If you wait until the technical rehearsal ("tech," Chapter Thirteen) to check on the progress of your sound effects, you may find that the tape is not ready and the source records that the sound technician expected to tape at the last minute are missing. At the second tech the sound technician finds that wires to a backstage speaker are missing and there is no spare wire in the theater. So you may get your sound effects working by dress rehearsal, if then.

But if you put your sound tape completion deadline two days before your target date for sound integration at a rehearsal, and put the date of integration two days before your technical rehearsal is scheduled to run, you can afford to slip one day, even two or three, and still be ready for tech with all sound ready for plug-in. Similarly, you must try to plan checkpoints in other areas and get your co-workers to try to meet these checkpoints so that everything shapes up neatly for the first technical rehearsal.

Some deadline dates must naturally fall before others. "Take-in" day, for instance, must come before "focus lights" day, since focusing of instruments is dependent on placement and shape of set pieces. Rehearsal props deadline (Chapter Ten) should precede line memorization deadline so that actors may pick up their props (or substitutes for them) as they set down their scripts.

If all staff members are required to post their requirements for use of cast members and stage and rehearsal space on the master calendar, conflicts will be avoided.

Example:

The crew arrives for a work call and finds the cast on stage for an extra rehearsal. After it is determined whose needs are greater, cast or crew depart, losing time. If all of the stage requirements had been posted on the master calendar, this situation would have been avoided.

The master calendar should not be placed on the callboard or made available to the cast under normal circumstances. It is kept away from cast members so that actors do not become confused about their rehearsal schedule or concerned about technical deadlines. All information that cast members need from the master calendar should be made available to them by other means, particularly the rehearsal schedule (see below).

Staff Meetings

Some theaters have regularly scheduled staff conferences. Most do not. If conferences have not been held in the past, you should initiate them. Getting everyone on the staff to sit down at once to discuss problems and progress can save a lot of time and grief.

At staff meetings you should ask intelligent questions that will urge your co-workers to reveal specifics about what they are doing. "Everything is going just fine and on schedule," is not a satisfactory contribution to a staff meeting from any department head. It should be show-and-tell time, with every member showing diagrams and drawings and discussing the specifics. (For examples of typical situations, see Chapter Ten on Properties.)

Example:

At dress rehearsal it is found that the leading lady's costume blends perfectly into the set designer's flats to the point where all but her face and hands disappear when she stands against them. Something has to be changed at the last minute. This problem would have been avoided if the set designer and costume designer had talked it out at a staff meeting.

A full review of the master calendar is a good way to start the first staff meeting.

Rehearsal Schedules

Carefully oversee the preparation, posting, and distribution of the rehearsal schedule. If possible, the schedule should be posted at the very first reading and distributed before the first rehearsal.

This takes a lot of coordination with everyone in a supervisory position. If you are working with amateurs who are not expected to be at the total disposition of the rehearsal schedule, you will have to coordinate the schedule with the cast as well. If you are working with professionals who are at the total disposal of union restrictions, you will have to crank into the schedule the exact union requirements, specifying days off as well as required coffee breaks on more complicated schedules.

Once content is determined, clarity should be your chief concern in writing the schedule (see Figure 4-2). Make sure that for each entry you give the time, date, place, and scenes to be rehearsed. It is not enough to identify the act (Roman numeral) and scene (Arabic numeral) i.e., II-1, III-2. You must list the names of the cast members involved. Do not assume that cast members will know which scenes they are in. Assume the worst, that cast members will find ways to misinterpret the schedule. Take the time to make reading and understanding the schedule easy for cast members. This is not done out of contempt for actors, but out of respect: if you can free them from the mechanics of production you may allow them greater concentration on their primary function.

Your schedule might also include a wallet-sized area with important numbers that can be clipped for the cast member's wallet or purse. Numbers to be listed are (1) a coordination number or numbers that cast members can call to leave messages when supervisory personnel cannot be reached directly, (2) your home phone number, (3) the home phone numbers of any other staff or supervisory personnel whose assistance may be required by members of the theater group, (4) the theater number, (5) rehearsal hall number (if different from theater number), (6) police emergency, (7) fire emergency, (8) ambulance emergency, (9) food service, (10) ticket reservations (if

```
THEATER TWENTY
                              Numbers You Need
5060 Fountain Avenue          (clip for wallet or purse)
phone 666 9059               ┌─────────────────────────────────────┐
                             │ Coordination (Jackie)    383 2171   │
                             │                    or    461 2028   │
                             │ Stage Manager (Frank)    272 9887   │
                             │ Theater                  666 9059   │
                             │ Reservations             938 1142   │
                   REHEARSAL │ Rehearsal hall           274 4301   │
                             │ Fire emergency           274 5421   │
                   SCHEDULE  │ Police emergency         274 7171   │
                             │ Ambulance                274 0126   │
                             │ Chicken Delight          274 0253   │
                             └─────────────────────────────────────┘
```

Act I Sc 1: Rita, Arlene, Sandy
       Sc 2: Jonas, Terry, Sylvia, JoAnne
       Sc 3: Arlene, Jonas
Act IISc 1: Sandy, Dee, Norma, Rita, Arlene, Jonas
       Sc 2: Jonas, Arlene
       Sc 3: JoAnne, Terry, Dave, Jonas
ActIIISc 1: Arlene, Larry, Rita, Sandy
       Sc 2: Terry, Jonas, Arlene

DATE	TIME	PLACE	SCENES
Sunday, Dec. 8	1-5 PM	Nursery 5	III-1
Tuesday, Dec. 10	7:30-10 PM	Nursery 5	I-3, II-2
	(all lines must be memorized by this date)		
Thursday, Dec. 12	7:30-10 PM	Room 203	I-2, III-2
*Saturday, Dec. 14	1-5 PM	Nursery 5	II-3
Sunday, Dec. 15	1-5 PM	Nursery 5	I-1, II-1
*Monday, Dec. 16	7:30-10 PM	Auditorium	runthrough
	(all costumes must be worn; make all changes)		
Tuesday, Dec. 17	7:30-10 PM	Auditorium	runthrough
Thursday, Dec. 19	7:30-10 PM	Auditorium	First Tech
Friday, Dec. 20	7:30-10 PM	Auditorium	Second Tech
*Saturday, Dec. 21	1-5 PM	Auditorium	First Dress
Sunday, Dec. 22	1-5 PM	Auditorium	Second Dress
Monday, Dec. 23	8 PM Call		Opening Night
Tuesday, Dec. 24	2 PM Call		Second performance
Thursday, Dec. 26	2 PM Call		Third performance
Friday, Dec. 27	2 PM Call		Fourth performance
Monday, Dec. 30	2 PM Call		Fifth performance

*On Saturdays, entrance to the building is by way of parking
lot only.

Open dates are not necessarily off. Stay flexible for extra
calls.

*Director wishes to see all costumes work on stage long
before dress rehearsal. If your costume is approved, you
need not wear it again until dress rehearsal.

· **Figure 4-2** ·
A Rehearsal Schedule

different from theater number), and (11) any other numbers that might be helpful as quick reference to the cast.

The rehearsal schedule need not (and probably should not) include any of the technical deadlines for staff members posted on the master calendar. This might be confusing to cast members. But line memorization deadlines should be included and dress rehearsals noted. Notes on parking, access to the theater and rehearsal areas, and other helpful information would also be appreciated by cast members.

If you are unable to fill in the entire rehearsal schedule with specifics, it is best to get out a tentative schedule, so labeled, with

```
TENTATIVE REHEARSAL SCHEDULE          The Chapel Theatre
                                      2222 Lomita Blvd.
                                      373 3636

Tuesday    Aug   4    Readings
Wednesday  Aug   5    Call backs
Friday     Aug   7    1st rehearsal   All rehearsals are at
Monday     Aug   10                   7:30 pm sharp!
Wednesday  Aug   12
Friday     Aug   14
Monday     Aug   17
Wednesday  Aug   19
Friday     Aug   21
Sunday     Aug   23
Monday     Aug   24
Wednesday  Aug   26
Friday     Aug   28
Sunday     Aug   30
Monday     Aug   31
Wednesday  Sept  2
Friday     Sept  4
Sunday     Sept  6    Deadline:  All Act I lines
Monday     Sept  7
Wednesday  Sept. 9
Friday     Sept.11
Sunday     Sept  13   Deadline:  All Act II lines.
Monday     Sept  14
Wednesday  Sept.16
Friday     Sept  18
Saturday   Sept  19
Sunday     Sept  20   Hold this day open for rehearsal.
Monday     Sept  21   1st Tech
Tuesday    Sept  22   2nd Tech
Wednesday  Sept.23    1st Dress
Thursday   Sept  24   2nd Dress
Friday     Sept  25   Opening Night
```

1. Everyone in the cast must be available for all rehearsals Please note in accepting roles that you are accepting a four night per week schedule and that starting Sept. 18, you are committed for 10 nights in a row without one night off!!!!!!!! Please do not accept roles unless you are willing to give this amount of time.

2. Dancers: Additional rehearsals, not on the schedule, may be called.

3. Performances: Six consecutive weekends, Sept. 25 - Oct. 31, Friday and Saturday nights with some additional performances on Thursday and Sunday nights, depending on group sales. (Pickup rehearsals: Wednesday or Thursday nights preceding first performance of the week.)

DAMN YANKEES DAMN YANKEES DAMN YANKEES

· Figure 4-3 ·
A Tentative Rehearsal Schedule

dates and blank spaces for the unknown variables, so that cast members may fill in the blanks (see Figure 4-3).

Sometimes it is effective to staple a second copy of the rehearsal schedule into each cast member's script on the premise that the script is less likely to be lost than a single sheet of paper.

It may be desirable for you to print the following lines at the bottom of your schedule: "Open dates are not off! They haven't been set yet. Please keep your personal schedule open for additional rehearsals as called." Keep in mind, when first making up the rehearsal schedule, that to include extra "safety" rehearsals initially, and then cancel them when they are determined to be unnecessary, is easier

REHEARSAL SCHEDULE

TUESDAY - JULY 14

TIME	AUDITORIUM	TENT	CHORUS ROOM	MUSIC ROOM	COSTUME SHOP
10:00		Frank			
10:30		II-5		Julie	Ravenal
11:00		II-5	Girl Sing. Dancers	Ravenal	Male Danc.
11:30	Frank, Karen	Ravenal Magnolia	Girl Sing. Dancers Male Danc.	Julie	Andy
12:00	I-1	(Lunch)	Girl Sing (All Danc. to lunch)	(Lunch)	(Lunch)
12:30	I-2	(Lunch)	" "	(Lunch)	Parthy
1:00	(Lunch)	All Danc.	(Lunch)	Joe	Magnolia
1:30	(Lunch)	" "	(Lunch)	Andy, Parthy	Steve
2:00	I-3	" "	Girl Sing	Ravenal	Joe, Frank
2:30	I-3	Male Danc.	" "	Queenie	Girl Danc.
3:00	I-4	All Danc., Girl Sing.		Ellie, Frank	Julie
3:30	Andy	" "		Magnolia	Queenie, Ellie
4:00	Piot. Call				
4:30					
5:00		I-2			
5:30					Local Chorus
6:00	Joe, Queenie		Local Chorus		
6:30	Ellie, Frank		" "		

Notes: Today is day off for Male Singing Ensemble.
Picture Call: 4 p.m. Aud. - Check sep. picture call sheet to see if you are needed. Report to costume shop, then aud.

· **Figure 4-4** ·

A Single Day Rehearsal Schedule

than to call extra non-scheduled rehearsals as opening night looms larger.

In some amateur theaters the cast may be told halfway into rehearsals that they will have to come to previously unscheduled work calls if they want to have scenery. There is much unhappiness. To avoid this, stage managers in amateur situations should plan work calls before rehearsals begin and put them on the schedule with a note that cast members will be expected to attend in work clothes.

When rehearsing a musical in one week, it becomes necessary to juggle principals, chorus, dancers, and extras between five or more different areas and still retain one's sanity. This calls for extremely careful planning of a more sophisticated schedule (see Figure 4-4), and the determination of all concerned to meet the schedule.

The worst problem in keeping to such a complicated schedule, where work periods are broken down to the hour and even half-hour, is that the staff members—musical director, chorus director, choreographer, and costume designer—are unwilling to release the cast members they are working with at the end of the specified time period. They are always in the middle of something very important and need five minutes more. It becomes difficult to cajole these creative people into keeping to the schedule.

A second problem is that a lot of cast time is lost in shepherding members between rehearsal areas.

With many work areas and short work periods a certain amount of confusion and delay cannot be avoided, but clear and careful scheduling can help to minimize it.

Is it desirable to mimeograph or duplicate schedules? Yes, it is. It is one of the ways in which you can assist the cast beyond the minimum requirements of announcing the next call. It saves the cast the trouble of individually copying the schedule.

Sometimes it is not enough to distribute the schedule, staple a duplicate in each script, post a copy on the callboard, and announce the next call at each rehearsal. You must "mother-hen" the schedule even beyond this. If a cast member is late, you must check to find out why, in the hope of eliminating future tardiness. If a cast member is absent, you must call to make sure that the actor knows the next call.

If there is any change in the schedule, it is your responsibility to see that every person concerned is informed of the change.

Keep several extra copies of the rehearsal schedule in your prompt script, always ready to hand one to a cast member who has misplaced his or hers, one to the upholsterer who wants to know when the stage will be free so that she or he can recover the sofa, one to the lady who lives above the theater and wants to know when not to play her TV, and more to all others concerned, *ad infinitum*. Of course, every staff member should be on your initial distribution.

Company Rules

A handout of company rules is a helpful device to let cast, staff, and crew know what is expected of them (see Figure 4-5).

Scheduling and Company Rules

Player's Ring Gallery
8325 Santa Monica Blvd.
December 13, 1964

The Company of
ONE FLEW OVER THE CUCKOO'S NEST

1. You must sign in each night. Never sign in for another actor.

2. Please call 555-2424 if you expect to be late for half hour call.

3. Please use the stage door, not the front door.

4. Please open and close the stage door quietly.

5. Please stay backstage after 8 pm (7:30 pm Sat.).

6. Cast members are not allowed in the box office.

7. Extremely important and emergency messages can get to you by calling 650 6920 during performance, and only that number.

8. Please leave costume laundry with st. manager on Sunday night after performance. You must fill out laundry slip.

9. Please stay out of the light booth.

10. Please do not speak to st. manager during light cues, sound cues, and set changes.

11. All cast members must take curtain call in complete cost.

12. Please smoke behind theater, & not in the backstage hlwys.

13. No visitors are allowed in dressing rooms during perf.

14. Please be alert to the monitors for your cues. The st. manager is responsible for warns only before acts, not before individual cues once the act has begun. (See your Equity rules.)

15. Please do not talk during perf. while backstage. If you must communicate, please whisper. The wall between aud. and dressing rooms is not sound proof.

16. Keep theater doors closed because of air conditioning.

17. Please do not congregate with aud. during intermission.

18. Please wear appropriate clothing backstage.

19. Please do not use the pay ph. during perf. because of noise.

20. Please help in Saturday night buffet cleanup.

21. Please stay out of the entrance areas during entrances & exits of other actors & during crew shifts. You can be seen by the audience.

22. Please do not use the men's room during perf. It is noisy and near an entrance. Both men and women may use the women's room during perf., but please wait until the water has stopped running before opening door, and hold door closed to prevent slamming.

23. Use good judgment about not using the water fountain during silent moments of performance.

THANK YOU IN ADVANCE FOR YOUR HELP AND COOPERATION!

Lawrence S.
stage manager

· Figure 4-5 ·
An Example of Company Rules

Categories of rules that you will want to include are:

A. Backstage behavior, noise, and cleanliness,
B. Tardiness,
C. Guests backstage and complimentary tickets,
D. Costume upkeep.

When the rules are approved, distribute them to all concerned, preferably at the initial meeting of the company. Post a copy on the callboard.

Just as you want to know what is expected of you, actors want to know what is expected of them. Take time at the first company meeting to review the rules and explain the reasons for them.

Example:

Tent theater rule: "Cast members must sit in the last two rows of the theater when not on stage during rehearsals." This brief rule alone seemed unjustifiable; after all, the empty seats in front were a much more convenient waiting place. The rule could have been explained in just a few lines: The asphalt surface of the center of the tent became so hot during rehearsal hours that the chair legs sank into and destroyed the surface. The back rows were not surfaced and were thus practically indestructible.

If there are good reasons for rules, try to make the reasons clear to cast members. This will result in greater cooperation on their part. Reasons for rules which seem obvious to you are not always so obvious to cast members—like the fire hazard of smoking backstage. Be patient in explaining.

The Callboard

The callboard has already been mentioned as the place to post the rehearsal schedule and company rules. Let us take a closer look at it.

The callboard is a backstage bulletin board for cast, crew, and staff (see Figure 4-6). It is usually located near the stage door where cast members can't miss it when they arrive and depart.

· Figure 4-6 ·

A View of a Well Organized Callboard. Frank Marino, stage manager for the touring company of *Grease*, posts a letter on the callboard at the Shubert Theater in Los Angeles. Note that the callboard is spacious, well-lit, and ideally located—at the stage door. Ushers' callboard is seen in background.

The basic items that every member of the company must be able to find are:

A. Emergency phone numbers (see Figure 4-7),
B. The next call (see Chapter Eight),
C. The rehearsal schedule (described above),
D. The sign-in sheet (see Chapter Sixteen),
E. Closing notice (see Chapters Thirteen and Seventeen),
F. Company rules (described above).

Some other items that you might wish to post are:

A. Helpful phone numbers (cab service, food service, and nearby restaurants and hotels if cast members are from out of town),
B. Cast list (see Chapter Seven),
C. Favorable reviews (if favorable to *all* cast members),

EMERGENCY

 FIRE 555-2419

 POLICE 555-4711

 AMBULANCE 555-3210

 ALL NIGHT CLINIC and how to get there 555 3699

White Memorial Medical Center
414 North Boyle
(West on Brooklyn past Soto to Boyle
turn left on Boyle)

 DIAL-A-PRAYER for producer's use only 555 2783

courtesy Lawrence Stern, stage manager 555 3179

· **Figure 4-7** ·
Emergency Phone Numbers for Callboard Display

D. Invitations to other theaters,
E. Advertisements of lessons and services of special interest to cast members,
F. Telegrams and letters to the cast,
G. Duty roster (see Chapter Fifteen),
H. Curtain call order (see Chapter Fourteen),
I. V.I.P. list (see Chapter Fifteen).

Take down the notes for readings (see Chapter Six) when casting is complete. Remove all items that are no longer timely from the callboard.

Bring your organizational skill and artistic ability to the arrangement of items on the callboard so that cast members can find what they want quickly. It might be advisable to divide the callboard into three areas: permanent, temporary, and urgent.

The callboard should be large enough to accommodate all of the bulletins that must be posted without having them overlap. Make sure that extra pins are available to put up additional material, and attach a pencil to your callboard so that cast members may initial bulletins and the sign-in sheet, as well as make notes for themselves, without having to search for a pencil.

With your master calendar discussed and posted, staff meetings arranged, rehearsal schedules coordinated and distributed, company rules determined and explained, and the callboard made orderly, you have made a good start at making things run smoothly.

• 5 •

Getting into Your Theater

Who Reports to Whom?

The stage manager should know who reports to whom in her or his theater. She or he should know not only to whom she or he is responsible, but also to whom everyone else on the staff is responsible. In the role of personnel coordinator this information is important.

The easiest way to find this out is to talk to people on the staff. If still uncertain, you should bring up the question at the earliest staff meeting. Even in theaters in which the distribution of tasks has become codified over the years, time may be taken at the first production meeting of a season to review and adjust for current staffing, personal preferences and capabilities of staff, and staff members' available time.

Figure 5-1 shows an idealized organizational chart for a hypothetical theater. I can readily guess that it does not apply to your theater. There are so many variations in staff organization that it would be impossible to provide charts for every theater here. Several factors causing variation are discussed below.

Designing an organizational chart for your theater might be desirable if you have a high turnover in personnel and you need to brief incoming personnel quickly. The more that your organizational chart differs from what might normally be expected, the more your theater needs an organizational chart.

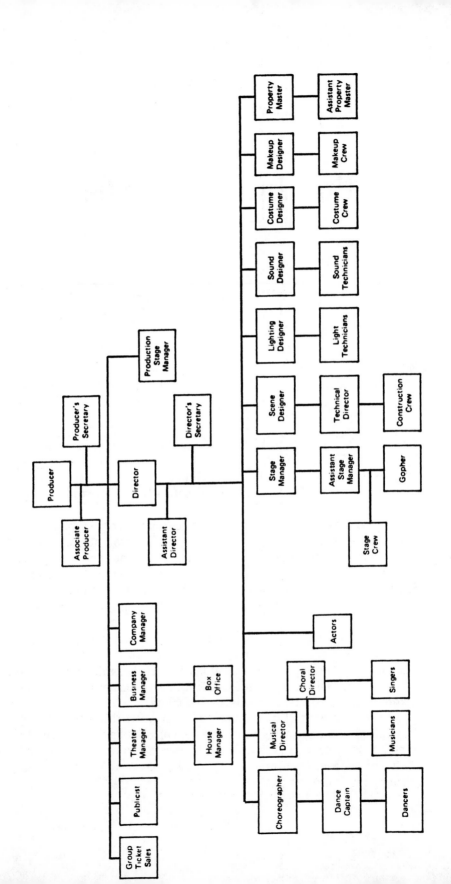

The chart is not as important as is knowing who does what. Authority in the theater generally stems from function. The authority of the lighting designer over the lighting technician stems from their relative functions. The function of the designer is to design the lighting effects. The function of the lighting technician is to repair, gel, hang, wire, and focus lighting instruments. Obviously, the lighting technician takes orders from, and is responsible to, the lighting designer.

As succinctly as possible, here are the functions of the theater staff:

The *producer* is to obtain the personnel and materials to make theater.

The *director* is to interpret the script through the use of actors and designers.

The *stage manager* is to insure that everything runs smoothly backstage and onstage.

The *actor* is to deliver the playwright's words, actions, and characterization, as interpreted by the director, to the audience.

The *technical director* is to execute scene designs and staging devices. (Confusion about the role of the technical director is discussed below. If you as stage manager have any doubts about your working relationship with the technical director, talk it out with him or her. If unable to resolve the conflict, talk with the producer.)

The *theater manager* is to insure the safe, efficient, and clean operation of the theater. (This includes care of the physical plant, box office operations, rest rooms, garbage disposal, gas, electricity, water services, and compliance with city regulations concerning the health and safety of the audience. It may include parking lot operations.)

· **Figure 5-1** ·

Organizational Chart. This chart represents an idealized hypothetical theater and most probably does not represent the organization at your theater. There are an infinite number of variations in the organization of a theater's staff. Some of the causes of variation are discussed in the text. This chart shows primary lines of responsibility only. The stage manager, for example, reports to the production stage manager and to the producer, as well as to the director. Also, the organization shifts *when the curtain goes up*. Actors who reported to the director now report to the stage manager and light and sound technicians who reported to designers now report to the stage manager.

The *house manager* is to greet and to seat the audience and to
attend to the audience's comfort.

The *designer* (costumes, lighting, scene, sound, or makeup) is
to plan turning the director's and playwright's concepts into
the realities that make stage illusion.

The *technicians* (master carpenter, master electrician, stage
hand, etc.) are to turn designs into reality and to run the
show.

The *company manager* is to supervise the transportation and
housing of the company.

There may be several other titles, real or honorary, on your staff.
If you are uncertain about what they do, ask them.

The title of production stage manager may take on different
meanings. In some theaters it is simply an honorary title for the stage
manager. Sometimes this title is assigned only when there is more
than one show being rehearsed and presented in the same theater
or theater complex. In this case the function of the production stage
manager is to coordinate and supervise the use of the theater's facilities, crews, and subordinate stage managers.

Sometimes the title of production stage manager is assigned to
the producer's assistant. In this case, the production stage manager
has no specific duties relevant to any one show but troubleshoots
and supervises, reporting only to the producer.

Sometimes the production stage manager and stage manager
divide duties. The stage manager works rehearsals and turns the
prompt script over to the production stage manager at tech rehearsal;
then, the production stage manager calls the show, while the stage
manager runs the stage crew. Or, in some theaters, the production
stage manager runs rehearsals and then turns the prompt script over
to the stage manager who runs the show; the assistant stage manager
supervises the crew and the production stage manager sits in the
audience and gives notes to the cast after each performance. This
sharing of duties is common in musical theater and opera.

There is no single correct distribution of duties between the
production stage manager and stage manager, or between the stage
manager and assistant stage manager.

Some of the factors that determine the distribution are the same
factors that might influence the distribution of duties between the
technical director and the stage manager:

1. Will of the producer or director,
2. Tradition of the particular theater,

3. Number of people available,
4. Layout of the theater,
5. Personality of individuals filling the slots.

Again, the stage manager gets an understanding of who reports to whom by talking with coworkers. She or he tries to avoid problems by anticipating work that will have to be done and insuring that everyone involved knows his or her specific duties in getting that work done.

Some general principles to keep in mind:

1. Treat everyone on the staff with respect for his or her function.
2. Many hands make light work.
3. If you have subordinates, one of your responsibilities is to insure that they are not overworked. (Sometimes a stage manager feels that since she or he served as assistant stage manager and got the work done, she or he can now lean on the assistant stage manager. If you are the assistant stage manager, you have to appeal to the stage manager's ego: explain that you are not the same terrific, outstanding, well-organized, industrious assistant stage manager that he or she was, and that you need help.)

Example Problems:

(1) The technical director (TD) tells you that he is in charge of the lighting designer, the sound designer, the shop foreman, the makeup crew, as well as the stage manager. He states that he runs the crew during performances and that you (SM) call the cues. He says that you will report to him for work in the shop on scenery construction prior to rehearsals.

Could be. In some educational and community theaters the TD has extensive responsibility. If you feel that a different system would improve the operation of your theater, speak to the producer. If you feel that you are being overworked and/or need help (an ASM or gopher), speak to the TD and/or the producer.

(2) The production stage manager (PSM) tells you that your first duty as the new ASM is to help build a fence around the theater.

Probably. Your duties are what the PSM says they are, even if those duties don't fit your mental picture of the job. If you are a member of a union, you might complain to your union rep. Will

57

building the fence interfere with your other duties? If so, you had best make that clear to the PSM.

(3) The director's secretary tells you, the new SM, that he will be holding book during rehearsals and will also supervise understudy rehearsals.

How do you feel about it? Do you feel that you have lost some of the authority that goes with your title, or do you welcome the help? Or do you have mixed feelings? Perhaps you welcome the help at rehearsals yet feel that the director's secretary is not as capable of supervising understudy rehearsals as you are. Perhaps you feel that you really need to hold book during rehearsals in order to prepare yourself for running the show successfully.

This is a typical problem of the distribution of tasks among a theater's staff. The same type of problem might occur between the PSM and SM, or between the SM and ASM, or between the TD and SM. There is no correct answer for all theaters. What will work best for your theater?

Talk to the director's secretary about your feelings and discuss what is best for getting the show on most efficiently. If you fail to resolve the conflict, speak to the director and/or producer, and then abide by their judgment.

In all of the problems cited above, you will generally find that as the stage manager gains experience and reputation, more responsibility is given to him or her. As the stage manager moves on to other theaters, experience, reputation and clout carry along, and the stage manager knows enough to stipulate in advance what specific duties he or she will not surrender to, or take from, others on the staff.

Personal Equipment for Stage Managers

Besides your prompt script, what else do you keep handy? Actually, there is no end of little things to keep on hand to keep the show going, and it is amazing to see how the absence of a small thing at the crucial time can create havoc.

For instance, it hardly seems possible that responsible people would allow a shortage of pencils to delay a rehearsal. But it happens time and again in amateur as well as professional productions.

Consider Hildegard Knef's comments on the rehearsal of the 1954 Broadway musical *Silk Stockings:*

> Today was the first reading. The whole cast sat in a half-circle on the
> stage with their manuscripts in their hands, a paper cup of coffee

beside each chair . . . . Nobody had a pencil. Unbelievable that actors never have pencils at first readings. Henry, the stage manager, lent his and it went from hand to hand until finally Cy Feuer's temper snapped. "I'm well aware that you don't get paid till the opening but you could at least buy one little pencil . . . . We've wasted hours already." . . . I'd love to be able to invite a German student of Theatrical Science to attend rehearsals.

> from *The Gift Horse* by Hildegard Knef, translated by David Anthony Palastanga (McGraw-Hill Book Company: New York, 1971) English translation. Copyright © 1971 by Hildegard Knef.

Let us consider some items of personal equipment you are likely to need in running the rehearsal and the show.

Over a period of time you will find that you might be able to use one or two items in the mounting of one play and one or two items in mounting another. It is not mandatory that you own or buy these items. It is simply handy to collect things.

As the items accumulate with each successive play they'll overflow from your pockets and briefcase. You'll want a kit—a cardboard carton, tool box, or tackle box—to keep everything conveniently near you in the rehearsal area.

The items listed below are, for the most part, self-explanatory. Some of their uses have been mentioned already, and you are invited to imagine a likely use for the others:

Paraffin (When a tooth filling is suddenly lost, a small piece of
  paraffin may allow an actor to complete a rehearsal.)
Lighter flints and fluid
Matches
Paper clips
Sewing needles
Thread, black and white
Razor blade, single edge
Masking tape, two widths
Electric tape
Two-sided tape
Scotch mending tape
Safety pins
Straight pins
Hair pins
Carpet tacks
Tacks
One inch brads

Chalk
Pencils, many, #2
Pencil sharpener
Large eraser, art gum
Flashlight
Candle
Black ball point pen
Marking pens
Luminous paint and brush
Luminous paint solvent
Tape label maker
Graphite lock lubricant
Electric extension cord
Stop watch
Sixty minute timer
Ruler, 12"
Measuring tape, 50'
Architect's ruler, ½" = 1' scale
Tailor's measuring tape
Note cards, 3 × 5"
Oil, small can
Working bell and buzzer
Whistle
First aid kit
Change, $5 in nickles, dimes, and quarters
Duplicate keys to everything
Rubber cement
Plastic cement
Plasti-tak
Rubber bands
Tweezers
Magnifying glass
AC-DC current tester
Asbestos welding gloves (great for handling hot instruments)
Gel books
Cough drops
Throat lozenges and troches
Aspirin
Aspergum
Can opener
Salt, sugar, tea, coffee, powdered cream, boullion, packaged
    soup, honey, hot chocolate
Wash 'n Dri Towelettes

Paper towels
Paper cups
Nail file
Kleenex
Toothbrush and paste
Toothpicks
Dental floss
Comb
Mouthwash
Water heating element
Gummed reinforcements
Telephone extension
Dust cloth

You will enjoy those moments when you can dip into your kit and save someone, particularly yourself, a long walk.

Stage Diagrams

If you are starting to work in a new theater, you will want to check out the plant, record the information, be able to analyze and apply this to your production needs, and pass on that information in a convenient, usable form. The easiest way to do this is by making a series of diagrams.

Of course, if you've already done a show in this house, you should have all the information where it can be referred to quickly.

How big is your stage? Where are the sight lines? How high is the proscenium? Is there fly space and flying equipment? These are but a few of the questions that your *stage diagram* should answer.

Usually the stage wings and significant surrounding space—apron, stairs leading to the stage, backstage area, etc.—are drawn to scale. The scale of ½″ = 1′ is recommended, but any scale that is serviceable will do (see Figure 5-2).

When you have finished your drawing, list at the bottom the significant dimensions:

A. What is the width of the stage?
B. What is the depth (curtain line to back wall)?
C. What is the height of the proscenium arch?
D. What are the height, width, and diagonal measurements of the largest door through which scenery may pass to get from

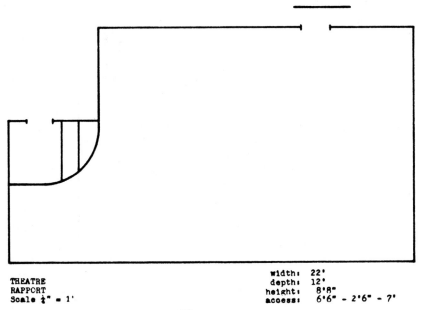

THEATRE
RAPPORT
Scale ¼" = 1'

width: 22'
depth: 12'
height: 8'8"
access: 6'6" - 2'6" - 7'

· **Figure 5-2** ·
Stage Diagram Drawn to Scale

an outside street onto the stage, or in from the scene shop to the stage?

This last measurement is significant because it limits the size of scenery and set pieces. Obviously, you can't use a set piece or section of scenery if you can't carry it onto the stage!

This diagram and list of important dimensions should be filed in your prompt script.

Some Applications:

A. The set designer is on a tight schedule and won't be in town until the second week of rehearsals. The director has planned essential entrance-ways and windows so that she could start blocking. Now the director asks you to send the set designer information which will allow him to start his plans without actually seeing the stage.

B. You go to a warehouse to pick up set pieces. The furniture dealer offers you one of several rugs that may not be cut. What size will you need? Of course you have that information with you and will not have to make another trip.

C. The set designer of a theater in the round presents his water color sketches for the next week's production at staff meeting. You ask how tall the boxy set pieces are. The set designer explains that they are 12 feet tall and that he knows they will fit through the entrances to the tent because he has measured them. You point out that they may fit through the 12½ foot entrances which you have also measured, but since the men who carry them can't very easily hold them a mere six inches off the ground, getting them in and off stage may be clumsy and therefore slow down the scene changes. You also point out that you will have to raise the microphones which hang at the aisle positions since they are only 10 feet off the ground.

The height of hanging microphones was in this case a significant dimension that you should have noted. The demands of a production sometimes determine which dimensions are most significant. If you are doing *Madwoman of Chaillot*, the stage trap dimensions become significant.

Note in example C above that both you and the set designer were anticipating problems on the basis of sketches and diagrams rather than waiting for set pieces to be built to see if they worked.

If your theater expects to be in operation for many years, you will want to make sure that many copies of more detailed stage plans are on hand for the use of transient set designers and technical directors (see Figure 5-3).

Fuse Boxes

Check the fuse box of your theater. Is there a diagram explaining what lines each fuse monitors? Are the fuses labeled in some way to show what's on them? If not, make a diagram or label them. Write on masking tape or use a tape tool. Is each fuse socket labeled with the size and type of fuse it should contain? It is important that this information be readily available. The diagram should therefore be posted near the fuse box if not on it.

Spare fuses of the correct size should be on hand.

Take the time to check all of the outlets in your theater. A current tester is a very inexpensive and handy tool to keep in your kit, (e.g., Circuit Master 90-550 Volt, AC & DC; Fordham Mfg. Co. No. 101).

Typical Problems:

A. One of the cast members, without asking permission, brings in an electric heater to warm up the dressing room. Soon all of the

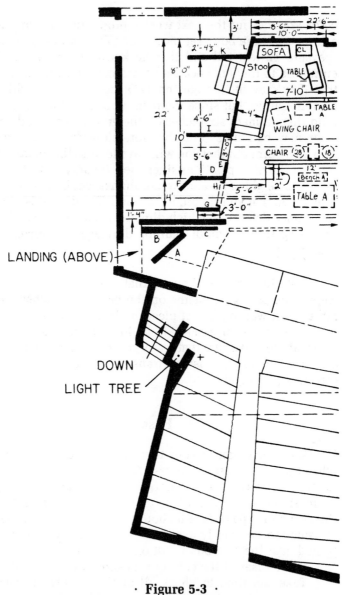

· **Figure 5-3** ·
Reproduced Complete Stage Diagram

lights and the heater are out. You are called on to restore current. Where, if anywhere, can the electric heater be replugged?

B. The lighting designer has completed her work and left for another production. The director now decides that he needs another lighting effect. The dimmer source line is loaded to capacity, yet

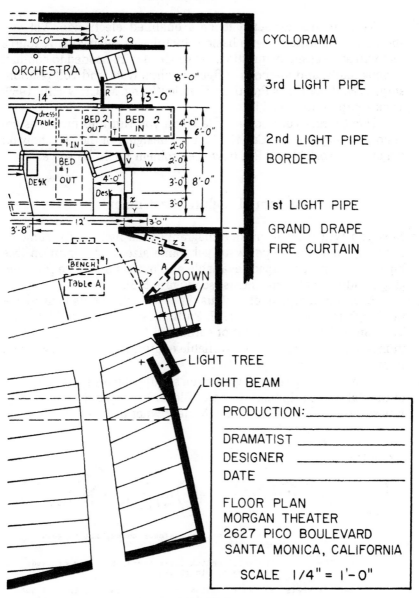

CYCLORAMA

3rd LIGHT PIPE

2nd LIGHT PIPE
BORDER

Ist LIGHT PIPE
GRAND DRAPE
FIRE CURTAIN

LIGHT TREE
LIGHT BEAM

PRODUCTION: _____

DRAMATIST _____
DESIGNER _____
DATE _____

FLOOR PLAN
MORGAN THEATER
2627 PICO BOULEVARD
SANTA MONICA, CALIFORNIA
SCALE 1/4" = 1'-0"

· **Figure 5-3** ·
(Continued)

another small dimmer will now be needed. Is there another circuit in the building with enough capacity to supply another dimmer?

C. The sound technician can't get the buzzer to work. A lamp is working from the same outlet. Can you help?

You are not expected to be a qualified electrician. Yet you should be comfortable with basic principles of electricity. A source that will answer many questions on gauge of wire needed to conduct various loads, and methods of figuring ohm, watt, and volt relationships is H. P. Richter's *Practical Electric Wiring*, McGraw-Hill, 1960. Tuck a copy into your kit.

Don't forget your contact file when you run into problems beyond your experience. Call the lighting designer of the last show on which you worked and ask how the problem might be solved.

Diagram of Lighting Instruments

Next you will want to make a diagram of the lighting instruments currently in place—type, watt, gel frame size, and condition (see Figure 5-4). Indicate space available and outlets available for plugging in additional instruments (see Figure 5-5).

A plastic template of various types of instruments is available from Lighting Associates, 7817 S. Phillips Ave., Chicago, Ill. 60649. You can make your own out of cardboard (see Figure 5-6) to assist in making rapid diagrams of available equipment and its placement in production (see Chapter Eleven).

While making your diagrams you should check on the condition of the lighting equipment (Chapter Eleven). Is it serviceable or will it need repair? Obviously, if the theater owner has rented your com-

1st pipe

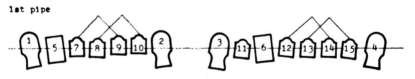

1-4 Lekos   750 watt, medium prefocus bases, all in good condition

5-6 PCs   400 watt, medium screw bases, #5 lense cracked, #6 focusing pin missing

7-15 Fresnels   500 watt, medium prefocus bases, all in good condition except #11 (#11 seems to have internal wiring problem)

Notes: No spare lamps for any instruments on hand! Only four twofers on hand as indicated.

     Ten cables run directly to board. No ceiling plugging locations.

· Figure 5-4 ·
Diagram of Lighting Instruments

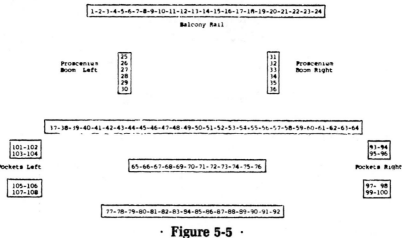

· **Figure 5-5** ·
Diagram of Plugging Locations

pany sixty instruments and ten are not working, or if three out of ten dimmers do not work, this must be brought to the producer's or management's attention. If you discover the limitations of your lighting equipment immediately, you will have time to repair, improvise, rent, or buy additional equipment. Don't wait until the tech rehearsal to find that instruments are out of order.

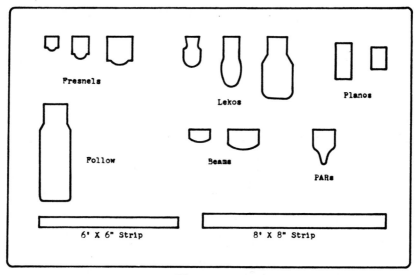

· **Figure 5-6** ·
Cardboard Template of Lighting Instruments,
Scale ¼″ = 1′

If the lighting designer and technicians are on hand, checking the equipment is their responsibility (see Chapter Eleven). But if they are not, as is frequently the case, you can save the staff and crew a lot of grief by checking out the equipment as soon as possible.

Information Packets

If your theater hosts, or has the desire to host, outside productions, you may hope to find on hand a "theater information packet" (see Figure 5-7). Or if you are helping to manager your theater, you may be asked to help develop such a packet.

This packet should include measurements of the stage, details of the technical capability, and other information of value to an incoming company.

The purpose of such an information packet is to allow touring companies and other production companies to determine whether or how they can use the theater. It also allows the stage manager and staff of an incoming production to solve many technical problems before ever setting foot in the theater.

The following pages show sample information sheets with typical detailed specifications on the capability of the theater for any company that might use it for a production. Along with the physical dimension specifications of the stage would be included some scaled stage diagrams such as the one shown in Figure 5–3, as well as diagrams of the rest of the theater building, and diagrams showing the draw-curtain plan or any other special feature of the theater. Along with the description of electrical capabilities might be a series of electrical diagrams if these show distinctive capabilities. A complete information packet would then go on to describe many of the accessory services available from related professionals who are likely to be part of production work in this theater. The accessory services described might include there:

—The availability of stage crew and help, whether regular theater staff or contracted from local area contacts, as well as standard pay scales for them.

—The availability of wardrobe assistants, costume people, laundry and cleaning facilities, dressing room space and equipment, and sanitary facilities.

—Information about customary curtain hours and customary audience preferences in attending matinees, weekday evening performances, etc.

—Contacts for news and media in the area to ease the publicizing process.

—Transportation facilities, local and interstate, passenger and freight.

—Hotel and restaurant services that have proven useful to theater companies.

—Information on ushers and house managerial services, ticket takers, etc.

The packet should also include full information on the seating capacity of each section of the theater, and a detailed account of parking facilities available.

· **Figure 5-7** ·
Typical Theater Information Packet Material

Theatre: LINDY OPERA HSE.   Date of inf.: March 1, 1961
City: LOS ANGELES   Source of inf.: HSE. CARPENTER
Tot. seat. cap.: 1320   B. off. phone: WE 7 3500
Year constr.: APPROX 1926   Owner: Mr. SIDNEY LINDEN
Address: 5215 WILSHIRE BLVD   Manager: WILLIAM A. McDONALD

STAGE SPECIFICATIONS

Proscenium height 50 ft.   Maximum trim height 58 feet.

Minimum trim height 68 ft.   Width 42 feet.

There are no unique sight line problems.

Depth: Curtain line to back wall is 24 feet.

Feet to curtain line is 4 feet 4 inches.

The apron is curved with a depth of 7 feet.

The distance from the center of the stage to the stage right wall is 56 feet.

The distance from the center of the stage to the stage left wall is 39 feet.

Describe obstructions, clearance, and/or stacking problems evaded by any of the following:

Picture screen NONE   Radiators NONE

Speakers NONE   House switchboard NONE

Columns or pilasters NONE   Legs and borders NONE

There is no permanent band shell.

The location of the pinrail is on the floor on stage right.

HEIGHT:
Floor to grid is 59 feet 3 inches.
Above grid is 8 feet.

HEIGHT:

Floor to weight loading floor is 31 feet.

The total no. of line sets is 41 counterweight.
The no. of line sets available for use is 41.
The no. of lines per set is 5 on 10 foot centers on grid.
The pull lines are 5/8 inch.

The arbors will take from 300 to 350 lbs. in weight.

The type of rigging used is 1 - 1 RATIO.

The length of battens/pipes is 50 ft., & there are 42 available.

The distance from curtain line to last set of usable lines is 23 feet 6 inches.

The distance from curtain line to first available set of lines is 6 inches.

*ENCLOSED IS A LINE PLOT OF STAGE

The stage floor is hardwood and laid on concrete and will take screws.
The stage floor is not raked.

DESCRIPTION OF DROPS AND LEGS AVAILABLE

Full set of legs -- full set of blacks -- 3 RT. legs, 28 feet high
3 borders, 8 feet high -- 1 drop - 28 x 50

Rigging of house curtain: a. Drop - operates from st. right
                           b. Traveler - operates from st. left

The house curtain is not motorized.

The house switchboard is located on stage right.
Roadshow boards may locate either on stage right or left.

The power available for portable switchboards is 500 amps., 120 volts AC. An additional power of 1000 amps. can be brought in.

The electric service is 3 wire, 220 phase - single - AC.

HOUSE SWITCHBOARD:
The type of control is auto transformer.
The number of dimmer circuits is 9.
The wattage per circuit is 6000.
The number of non-dim circuits is 2.
The wattage per circuit is 3000.

A roadshow can play off the houseboard.

· **Figure 5-7** ·
(Continued)

LOADING:
The loading door is located on stage left - the rear wall of the stage.
The width of the loading door is 8 feet.
The height of the loading door is 12 feet.
The door is truck level and two trucks can unload at one time.
The distance from the loading door to the stage floor is 2 ft.

A truck can back up to the door.
There are no parking problems.
The truck approach to the loading door is by the street.

*ATTACHED IS A LOCAL STREET MAP WHICH IS MARKED WITH THE LOCATION OF THE THEATRE.

LOCAL TRANSFER COMPANIES

Atlantic Transfer
10053 International Road
Los Angeles, California
776-1870

Local loaders are required. Rates are $25.00 per truck.

ORCHESTRA FACILITIES:
The maximum amount that the orchestra pit will accomodate is 40.

HEIGHT:
Pit floor to the house floor is 2 feet 8 inches.
Pit floor to the stage floor is 6 feet 3 inches.
Width from side to side is 41 feet 6 inches.
Depth from front to back is 12 feet 3 inches.

There are 40 music stands with light on hand.
The piano on hand is a Baldwin - Concert - 9 foot Grand.

There is a rehearsal room -- 50 feet x 30 feet - adjoining stage.
The orchestra room is located on stage left.

MUSICIANS:
Minimum requirements for musical shows are as set by local scales for individual types of presentations.
All non music be A.F. of M.
Local scale for performances is as set by local scales for individual types of presentations.

House lighting equipment can play off show switchboard.

A first balcony rail may be hung.
The distance to stage is 45 feet.
A second balcony rail cannot be hung.

Box booms can be placed in the house.
The distance to stage is 30 feet.

There is a spot booth and an area for a follow spot (s).
There are 4 power lines available -30 amps. - AC.
The area will accomodate 4 follow spots.
The distance to stage is 112 feet.

The connectors are straight male Hubbell.

The number of stage floor pockets is 5 - amps. - 20 - location 2L - 2R 1 USC.

Houselights are controlled from backstage and light booth.
They are on the dimmer.

The nearest available theatrical equipment rental service is 10 miles.

SOUND:
The house acoustics are excellent.
A sound system has not been necessary in the past.
Our theatre will permit a roadshow to use its own sound system.
Our theatre has its own sound system which is of monaural type.
The number of mikes is 10.
The type of mikes is Altec.
The gain is controlled from the aud. booth - auditorium left.
Our theatre has a standby amplifier and it also has a pre-amplifier.

There is a sound technician available at the theatre.

The roadshow's tape deck can be operated through our system.
The number of inputs - 8.
The impedance is for high and low impedance mikes.

We have an intercom from the:
a. stage manager to switchboard.
b. stage manager to stage left.
c. stage manager to stage right.
d. stage manager to fly floor.
e. stage manager to follow spots.
f. stage manager to front house.
g. stage manager to dressing rooms.

The stage manager can work from stage right.

· Figure 5-7 ·
(Continued)

71

· 6 ·

Expediting Auditions and Readings

In the process of auditioning actors for roles in plays it is desirable to make the actors comfortable and to move them quickly through an interview-audition procedure. In general, two areas are set up, one in which the actors may gather and wait, and a second in which the director, and sometimes producer, musical director, choreographer, and other staff members may interview and audition the actor.

To expedite the procedure you should insure that both areas are properly set up. There should be adequate light to read by, and comfortable seating. Access to restrooms should be provided for actors who wish to find a mirror and freshen up. If possible, it is a nice touch to set up a coffee/tea table to show hospitality and consideration for those who are trying out.

Since this may be a difficult time for many actors, you should make attempts to be a cheerful receptionist. You are usually the first person in the company that the actor is exposed to, and the actor starts to form an opinion of the company by the way you deport yourself. You should offer the same warm, friendly welcome that you would want to receive if you were the auditioning actor.

You will want to write down the actors' names as they arrive so that you can audition them on a first come, first served basis.

Working with Actors

You can't make theater without actors. The actor is the central ingredient in making theater happen. Audiences may come to theaters to see the work of stage managers, directors, and producers, but the only people who can communicate any of this to audiences, through ideas and emotions, are the actors. They are the only ones who can communicate this by themselves, and if necessary, they can get along without you. But you can't make theater without the actor.

So, regardless of your personal opinion of individual actors, you have to maintain a healthy respect for the function of the actor. And this healthy respect should be the bedrock of your relationship with cast members. As stage manager, yours is a support function. You are there to help actors, to help them get more out of rehearsal time, to help them concentrate on their task by having everything so well organized and running so smoothly that there is nothing to distract them from their work.

On the other hand, as the producer's foreman and the director's principal assistant, you are a supervisor of the actor's time and whereabouts. When a stage manager posts a schedule or announces a picture call, she or he must expect the actor to be there, just as a military commander who had given a direct order would. When a stage manager has to move backstage, to supervise a shift or for any other reason, cast members are expected to yield the right of way. During performances, cast members are expected not to speak to the stage manager unless they are spoken to (with the exception of informing the stage manager of a fire or some other imminent threat to life or safety or the continuation of the performance). Cast members should know that the stage manager is responsible for the smooth running of the performance, and out of respect for that function they should do their utmost to cooperate.

So the actor-stage manager relationship should be one of mutual respect and mutual cooperation. As in all human relationships, this may be difficult to codify further. However, in practice, I've found that it works out quite easily. Early in rehearsals actors realize that you are concerned with their welfare and comfort, that you are anxious to get the show on efficiently, and that you are quite obviously helping them. They see that what you're doing is all for the common goal of a better performance. And so they are willing and anxious to cooperate with you when you exert your authority.

Some comments on the stage manager's relationship with cast members were already made in Chapter Two.

Posting Notes for Readings

During casting calls most actors will ask the "person with the clip-board" for information. You should be able to refer everyone to the notes you have posted.

If you were an actor showing up for a casting call, what would you like to know about the production?

First, is there a part in it for you? Who's putting this play on? Why? Who's directing? What's the rehearsal schedule like? Where can you get a script? On what pages does the character you're right for appear? What pages will you be asked to read?

Try to anticipate what the actors would like to know and post that information in the lobby or waiting area where actors can read it before filling out audition forms.

Fact Sheet

Coordinate with the producer and publicist to get the basic facts up for the actors: who, what, when, where, and why. If possible, note on the fact sheet where the actors may obtain scripts (see Figure 6-1).

THE EMPEROR COMPANY
December 30

FACT SHEET

What/	A three act play about Nero, notoriously cruel and depraved Roman emperor (37 A.D. – 68 A.D.)
Who/	Hermann Gressieker – author George White – translator and adapter Lou Rifkin – producer Charles Rome Smith – director Lawrence Stern – production stage manager Norman Houle – set designer Hellene Heigh – publicist
Where/	Cahuenga Playhouse, 3333 Cahuenga Blvd. West (Barham exit of Hollywood Freeway) HO7 3936
When/	Opens February 7, to run on weekends, four week minimum. (See posted rehearsal schedule.)
Why/	To present the highly original and well-received German playwright to Los Angeles audiences and to showcase local talent. This is an Equity production under the Hollywood Area Contract.

· **Figure 6-1** ·
Production Fact Sheet for Auditioning Actors

THE RIGHT HONORABLE GENTLEMAN

CHARACTER DESCRIPTIONS

Sir Charles Dilke
    mid 40's, air of distinc-
    tion, natural command,
    enigmatic
          pp. 1-14, 16-21, 29-43;
              47-50, 55-67; 77-90.

Mrs. Ashton Dilke
    early 30's, kindhearted
    busybody, Dilke's sister-
    in-law
          pp. 1-7, 38-42; 55-57;
              83-85.

Mrs. Emilia Pattison (later
    Lady Dilke) mature, ele-
    gant, charming, quiet
    integrity & warmth
          pp. 7-14, 29-40; 81-90.

Mr. Joseph Chamberlain
    Statesman of Dilke's
    stature, at least med 40's
          pp. 10-19, 42-43; 49-54;
              77-90.

Mrs. Virginia Crawford (Nia)
    Vital, restless, intelle-
    gent, waspish, challenging
    manner, 22
          pp. 14-40; 50-54; 77-85.

Mr. Donald Crawford
    Late 40's, stiff, inhi-
    bited, slight Scottish
    accent, formal & pedantic
          pp. 21-27; 81-85.

Sir James Russel
    Distinguished, incisive,
    jurist, dry, mid 50's.
          pp. 32-41; 50-53.

Sarah Gray
    Handsome woman, reserved,
    Mid 30's, a decided cut
    above her station
          pp. 39-44.

Mrs. Rossiter (Lila)
    Mother of Nia, Maye, &
    Helen.
          pp. 51-56; 81-83.

· **Figure 6-2** ·

Character Descriptions for Auditioning Actors

Character Descriptions

How old are the characters? How much do they age during the course
of the play? Who played the part on Broadway? How does the author
describe the character? How does the director see the character?
Many actors do not have time or opportunity to read scripts and
study them before they come to readings. Sometimes the scripts are
simply not available to the actor until ten minutes before a reading.

SHOW BOAT

Principals	**$5 Parts**
Gaylord Ravenal	Rubberface
Julie	Jake
Captain Andy	Guitar Player
Queenie	Backwoods Men
Pete	Piano Player
Landlady	Barker
Old Lady	Carrie
Ellie	Jim
Magnolia	Dancer-Charleston
Vallon	Fatima
Windy	Mother Superior
Dahoney King	Jeb
Parthy Ann Hawkes	
Joe	
Steve	
Frank	
Kim (child)	

Should a production be sufficiently changed, either by cutting, re-writing or re-choreographing, to make questionable the category in which a particular part belongs, please consult with Equity immediately for a determination.

· Figure 6-3 ·
Equity Paid Parts Listing

You can help the actors adjust to this situation by lining up this information from script and director and posting much of the information the actors will need (see Figure 6-2).

Equity Paid Parts

Under some contracts, Actors' Equity Association, the union for actors, determines which parts will be paid or not paid. Under other contracts, Equity allows producers to pay chorus members small additional fees to handle small roles. Post the paid parts list if applicable (see Figure 6-3).

Suggested Readings

You may wish to post a list of readings from the play with which the actors may audition. It sometimes expedites casting calls if actors can read in pairs, or even three at a time. Otherwise you may be called upon to read with the actors (see Figure 6-4).

Rehearsal Schedule

If the rehearsal schedule is ready, post it. Otherwise you might add a paragraph to the fact sheet indicating the anticipated pattern of

THE EMPEROR COMPANY
December 30

SUGGESTED READINGS

Seneca	monologue I 1-2
	w/Nero III 8-11
	w/Burrus II 9
	w/Nero, Agrippina II 6-8
Nero	w/Actis I 11-18
	w/Poppaea II 10-15
	w/Seneca III 8-11
	w/Seneca, Agrippina II 6-8
Agrippina	w/Nero I 2-4 & 19-21
	w/Seneca, Burrus II 6-8
Burrus	w/Seneca II 9
	w/Seneca, Agrippina I 10-11
Actis	w/Nero I 11-18
Poppaea	w/Nero II 10-15
	w/Nero, Seneca II 16-21
Messenger	w/Seneca, Nero II 25
Paulus	w/Seneca, Nero III 1-7
Thrasea	w/Lucanus, Seneca III 12-14
Lucanus	w/Thrasea, Seneca III 12-14

· **Figure 6-4** ·
Suggested Readings for Auditioning Actors

rehearsals. ("We will be rehearsing for four weeks, afternoons and evenings, Monday through Friday." "We expect to rehearse week nights from 7:30 to 10:30 P.M.")

Audition Form Format

If pre-printed audition forms (see Figure 6-8) are not available, you should post a format and examples of the information that the company requires (see Figure 6-9).

Callback Schedule

If many actors are called back to read for several parts, you may want to set up a schedule so that actors may read in groups, showing how they play to one another. The callback schedule would not

THE EMPEROR COMPANY
January 4

CALLBACK SCHEDULE

Time	Nero	Actis	Seneca	Poppaea	Paulus
4:00	Nathan Hanek	Betty Ray	Earl Olsen	Liz Victor	Ronald Penny
4:15	John Heyman	Linda Mook		G. Merriman	Ed Marko
4:30	Barton Carton			G. Quentin	
4:45	Bill Cannon	Liz Bullard	Br. Matthews	Dol. MacRae	
5:00	Glen Colmar	Anita Morrel	Ray Anderson	Jean Scott	Mike Delgado
5:15	Erik Douglas	Darlene Gainsborough	John Hammond	A. Shelton	H. Feinberg
5:30	Richard Presby	Manuela Keeney		Abig. Perry	

· **Figure 6-5** ·
Callback Schedule (Not Normally Posted)

normally be posted for actors, as it is not necessary for them to know who else is being considered for the part they want. It is helpful for you so that you can manage the callback period carefully (see Figure 6-5).

Thorough preparation for casting calls shows cast members from the outset that you are in total command of the situation, anticipating everything.

Accepting Résumés

In the course of casting calls, especially in professional theater, many actors and actresses will submit their résumés. These résumés generally consist of a picture or several pictures in various costumes and poses (composites), and written information giving physical measurements, credits in features, TV, and on the stage; and agent's name and phone number (see Figures 6-6 and 6-7).

The purpose of a résumé is to help the director recall and contact the actor after the reading. In a production involving amateur actors, it is wise for a manager to secure information comparable to the résumé coverage, and keep those notes in convenient form to help the director recall the actors in tryouts.

When you accept a résumé, look it over carefully. For amateur actors, try to secure basic résumé information. For professionals, ask the actor if she or he still has the same agent, and if she or he can still be reached at the same numbers. Agents and phone numbers change rapidly, and it is important to make sure that the essential entries are up to date. Be sure to note on the résumé the part that the actor reads for.

PAM CLINE
555-3756

Height: 5'7"   Hair: Brown   Eyes: Blue
Weight: 125   Range: 15-35

SCHOOL PLAYS

"Taming of the Shrew"—   "Valley of the Dolls"—
                    Bit Part   Neeley O'Hara
"Take Her She's Mine"—   "Androcles and the Lion"—
            Liz Michealson   Makeup
"The Crucible"—   "Celebration"—
        Student Director   Crew

COMMUNITY THEATRE

"The Springs"—   "You're a Good Man Charlie
            Costume Designer   Brown"—
            (original musical)   Lucy
"Call Me Madam"—   "Play it Again, Sam"—
                Governess   Linda
"Lovers and Other Strangers"—   "House of Blue Leaves"—
                    Joan   Corrina
"Joe Egg"—   "Except for Susie Finkle"—
                     Pam   Mike

NIGHTCLUBS

Toured nine months / Los Angeles area / variety act (singing,
dancing & comedy)

· Figure 6-6 ·
A Sample Résumé

Sometimes the staff will want to look over the actor's résumé (or your comparable notes) before the actor is ushered in to read. This allows them to review the actor's background and judge his or her experience level before meeting him or her. In some other theater situations the actor may be judged solely on appearance and reading, and résumés or preliminary notes are intentionally ignored.

After the show has been cast, don't throw away the résumés or notes. If the résumé picture is an 8 × 10" glossy print, it may be

Photos by Edd Linskey

· **Figure 6-7** ·
Composite of Photos to Accompany a Résumé

useful to the company publicity person as part of a publicity release or for posting in the lobby. Information on the résumé might be useful to you, the publicity person, or others. Keep the résumés of those not cast also. You might have to replace a cast member suddenly. When casting your next show, you just might remember someone right for a role by flipping through your collection of résumés.

PLAYLAND THEATRE

AUDITION FORM   DATE_____#_____

ADDRESS:_____ AGE:_____SEX:_____

NAME:_____PHONE:_____

        ACTOR ☐   SINGER ☐   DANCER ☐
           COLOR   VOICE   VOICE

HT.:_____ WT.:_____HAIR:_____EYES:_____TYPE:_____RANGE:_____

THEATRICAL UNION MEMBERSHIP:_____

THEATRICAL TRAINING & EXPERIENCE:_____

_____

_____

NAME & PHONE OF AGENT:_____

ARE YOU PREPARED TO SING IN THE ENSEMBLE?_____

SOCIAL SECURITY NO._____

LAST NAME   FIRST   MIDDLE (Print)

Address   City/Zip

Phone Numbers (Home, work, service, other)
Equity, SAG, AFTRA, AGVA, SEG, Other
Circle Union Membership

Agency, Agent   (His phone)

Height, Weight, Color Eyes Color Hair

RECENT CREDITS:

STUDIES:

CURRENT COMMITMENTS:

· **Figure 6-8** ·
Printed Company Audition Form Cards

If you save résumés for future productions, you will want to make some simple evaluation of the actor's ability and code the résumé. Your code might be: (1) excellent, exciting actor, (2) capable actor, (3) barely competent, (4) no talent; (A) well suited to the part, (B) possible for the part, (C) not suited for the part.

The value of such a code is that in invitational readings for future productions you would not call the 4's to read, and would start with the 1's. The letters, along with the names of the roles they read for, might remind you of the actors' physical types.

Controlling Scripts

During the casting call you are responsible for controlling scripts. If you have not already numbered your scripts, now would be a good

```
LAST NAME, FIRST MIDDLE (Please
print caps)

Address, City, Zip

Phones (Home, Work, Service,
Other)

Union membership (SAG, AFTRA,
AEA, SEG, AGVA, other)

Agency, Agent (his phone)

Height, Weight, Color eyes,
Color hair

Social Security Number
```
(front)

FORMAT

```
Recent Credits




Studies
```

Have you filled out a card? The

information requested will help

us remember you, cast you, and

reach you. Thank you!

```
Current Commitments
```
(reverse side)

(front)

SAMPLE

```
FLEGGLE, FRED FIGLEAF

117½ Marrow Bone Drive, LA 90037

555 8763 (home) 555 4588 (days)
555 3000 (serv)

Equity, SAG, AFTRA

Talent Ltd., G. Leech (555 7756)

6'8", 176 lbs., Grn eyes, Brn
hair

492-82-9175
```

```
SHOWBOAT Captain Andy
DEATH OF A SALESMAN
  Willy
LILI (MGM) Clown
UNTOUCHABLES Mafia member
BREAKING POINT Pencil
  Salesman


Fyodor Lermontovich
Studio (NYC)
Neighborhood Playhouse
(Grand Forks, ND)



Tape Bob Hope Show
Sept. 2
Tour with American
Ballet Company starting
Jan. 4
Work afternoons 3-5 PM
```

· **Figure 6-9** ·
Posted Model-Examples for Audition Information Cards

time to do so. Jot down the names of the readers and the script numbers as you issue them. As the actors depart the interview area, be sure to reclaim the scripts and cross off their names.

Actors will beg to take home scripts in order to prepare for callbacks. You must frequently advise these actors that scripts are needed for auditions. You should be prepared to point out where scripts are available.

Obtaining Information

During auditions, at the first reading, and every time a newcomer joins your cast, crew, or staff, you will want to obtain information that you and other members of your staff can use. It is convenient to gather this information on cards (3 × 5″ or 4 × 6″) or on standard sized pre-printed information sheets.

The information/audition card may be preprinted (see Figure 6-8), or you may post an explanation of the information you want and the format you want it in, and distribute blank cards (see Figure 6-9).

The former method is preferable, as you are more likely to get serviceable results. Whichever approach you use, it is best to check each card as it is completed to insure that it is legible and that both sides have been completed.

The following entries deserve special attention:

Age Range:

Some actors do not feel it necessary that you know their ages. If you ask for the range that they feel they can portray on stage, they do not feel pinned down. (You are welcome to your own opinion, and discreetly keep it to yourself.)

Rather than asking for the age range, you might offer the following multiple choice: (1) child, (2) ingenue, (3) mature. This offends no one (except the "aging ingenue").

Union Affiliation:

An actor who is a member of any of the performers' unions (AEA, SAG, AFTRA, or AGVA—discussed in Chapter Eighteen) may be prohibited by the union from performing in any non-union production. In auditioning for showcase productions and no-budget, non-union productions, actors have been known not to state their union affiliation on their audition cards in order to work. It is the producer's responsibility to check or face union sanctions.

When a preprinted audition form is used, an area may be set aside ("Do not write below this line.") for results of questions that the director or casting director will want to ask during interviews (see Figures 6-10 and 6-11).

The information cards or forms should be clipped to the actor's photo or composite. In school theaters, be sure to have the actors write their schedules of classes on their audition forms.

```
                                    THE ST. GENESIUS PLAYERS

                                    THE ODD COUPLE


        C A S T I N G


        NAME _____  PHONE _____

        ADDRESS_____

        HEIGHT_____WEIGHT_____EYES_____HAIR_____

        AGE RANGE _____

        UNION:    AEA   SAG   SEG   AFTRA   AGVA   Other:_____
                  (circle any to which you have ever belonged)

        AGENCY, AGENT, PHONE (if any):_____

        ACTING EXPERIENCE:  Use reverse side of this form to list
                            recent credits if you are not sub-
                            mitting a resume.


        Do not write below line. _ _ _ _ _ _ _ _ _ _ _ _ _ _ _

          Felix                     smokes

          Oscar                     poker

          Speed                     goal

          Murray                    schedule

          Roy                       SM

          Vinnie                    St. G?

          Gwendolyn

          Cecily
```

· **Figure 6-10** ·
Full-length Audition Form

Controlling Forms

The first cast meeting after casting calls and callbacks is frequently a readthrough of the script. You should take advantage of a time when all the cast are present by getting the paperwork done. Take a few minutes of cast time to review the cast rules and to take care of the required forms. If you fail to get it all done at once, you will have to run after individual cast members to distribute and collect forms, and this can be time-consuming.

Plan this paperwork session ahead of time by grouping forms

WORKSHOP APPLICATION

TALENT

NAME:_____

ADDRESS:_____

TELEPHONE NO:_____

UNION AFFILIATION:_____

    A.E.A._____   AGVA_____

    SAG _____   C.E._____

    AFTRA_____   OTHER_____

ACTOR _____
DIRECTOR_____
PLAYWRIGHT_____
ST. MANAGER_____
DESIGNER_____
TECHNICIAN_____
SINGER_____
DANCER_____
CHOREOGRAPHER_____
PRODUCER_____
MUSICIAN_____
OTHER _____

PROFESSIONAL BACKGROUND: (LIST ANY ADDITIONAL CREDITS ON REVERSE SIDE)
(RESUME & PICTURE, IF AVAILABLE)

TRAINING: Where and with whom have you studied?

CHECK SESSIONS YOU ARE INTERESTED IN ATTENDING:

_____ LECTURE SESSIONS

_____ WORKSHOP SCENES: Assignments, observations, critiques

_____ DIRECTING CLASS

_____ PRODUCTION: Panels, Budgeting, Stage Manager, Scenic Designer, Lighting, Etc.

_____ (Please do not write below this line) _____

· **Figure 6-11** ·
Model of Workshop Application Form

for each actor into a packet. Make sure that you have plenty of pens and pencils on hand. Each packet might include:
Cast keeps:

1. Rehearsal schedule,
2. Company rules,
3. Cast list (see Figure 6-15),
4. Guides to hotels, restaurants, points of interest (if cast is from out of town).

You need returned:

5. Biographical data form (see Figure 6-13) (check with your publicity person),

EQUITY LEAGUE WELFARE TRUST FUND

PLEASE PRINT OR TYPE						BLUE CROSS
PROFESSIONAL NAME AS LISTED WITH ACTORS EQUITY	LAST NAME		FIRST NAME		MIDDLE INITIAL	
HOME ADDRESS	NUMBER AND STREET OR AVENUE		CITY, TOWN, VILLAGE		STATE	ZIP CODE
DATE OF BIRTH	MONTH DAY YEAR	SEX		SOCIAL SECURITY NO.		FOR OFFICE USE ONLY
MARITAL STATUS		DATE OF MARRIAGE	MO. DAY YR.			
NAME OF SHOW IN WHICH EMPLOYED						
EMPLOYER'S NAME AND ADDRESS						
DATE OF YOUR FIRST REHEARSAL	MONTH DAY YEAR	TYPE OF EQUITY CONTRACT				

LIST BELOW NAME OF SPOUSE AND UNMARRIED CHILDREN UNDER 19
(Please Remember You, The Member, Must Pay For Your Dependents Coverage)

NAME (IN ORDER OF AGE)	RELATION TO YOU		DATE OF BIRTH		
	WIFE	HSBD.	MONTH	DAY	YEAR

SIGNATURE

EMPLOYEE'S WITHHOLDING EXEMPTION CERTIFICATE

FORM W-4 (Rev. July 1963)
U. S. Treasury Department
Internal Revenue Service

Social Security Account Number ....

Print full name ....

Print home address .... City .... State ....

EMPLOYEE:	HOW TO CLAIM YOUR WITHHOLDING EXEMPTIONS
File this form with your employer. Otherwise, he must withhold U. S. income tax from your wages without exemption.	1. If SINGLE, and you claim your exemption, write "1"; if you do not, write "0" ....
	2. If MARRIED, one exemption each is allowable for husband and wife if not claimed on another certificate
EMPLOYER: Keep this certificate with your records. If the employee is believed to have claimed too many exemptions, the District Director should be so advised.	(a) If you claim both of these exemptions, write "2"
	(b) If you claim one of these exemptions, write "1"
	(c) If you claim neither of these exemptions, write "0"
	3. Exemptions for age and blindness (applicable only to you and your wife but not to dependents):
	(a) If you or your wife will be 65 years of age or older at the end of the year, and you claim this exemption, write "1"; if both will be 65 or older, and you claim both of these exemptions, write "2" ....
	(b) If you or your wife are blind, and you claim this exemption, write "1"; if both are blind, and you claim both of these exemptions, write "2" ....
	4. If you claim exemptions for one or more dependents, write the number of such exemptions. (Do not claim exemption for a dependent unless you are qualified under instruction 4 on other side.) ....
	5. Add the number of exemptions which you have claimed above and write the total .... [ ]
	6. Additional withholding per pay period under agreement with employer. *See* Instruction 1 ..... $

I CERTIFY that the number of withholding exemptions claimed on this certificate does not exceed the number to which I am entitled.

(Date) ...., 19...... 640—16—77780-1 (Signed) ....

· **Figure 6-12** ·
Forms That Professional Cast and Crew Must Complete

6. Costume size form (see Figure 6-14) (check with your costume designer),
7. Blue Cross form (if Equity company—see Figure 6-12),
8. Welfare Coverage form (if Equity company),
9. W-4 form (if paid company),
10. Life Insurance form (if Equity company).

BIOGRAPHICAL DATA

Information requested below will be used for program
notes and publicity releases. Use reverse side to
complete comments if space below is not sufficient.
Thank you.

NAME _____ ROLE _____

Education:

Military service:

Theatrical training:

First stage appearance:

Credits:

Most recent stage:

Most recent film:

Most recent TV:

Current commitments (stage, film, TV):

Family:

Hobbies:

Highlight to date of your career:

Career ambition:

When did you come to Los Angeles? What brought you?

If you wish to add any unusual personal facts or viewpoints
which might aid in publicity, please use reverse side.

· Figure 6-13 ·
Model of Biographical Data Form

If you have time, print the actor's name on each form before you
distribute them. Then make sure that you get back the forms you
need. The actors usually want to take them home. They may insist
that they have the information written down at home and they can

<u>COSTUMES</u>

The costume department needs to know your measurements.
Please mark them on this sheet and return it to the
stage manager. Thank you.

NAME _____ ROLE _____

HEIGHT_____ft._____inches   WEIGHT _____lbs.

<u>men only</u>   <u>women only</u>

jacket size _____   bust _____

shirt _____   waist _____
    (neck) (sleeve)
                                  waist to floor _____
waist _____
                                  hips _____
inseam _____

shoes _____

sox _____

hat _____

· **Figure 6-14** ·
Model Costume Size Form

copy it if you will just allow them to take the forms home. Don't.
You may never see the forms again. Insist that they fill out as much
as they can, that you must have all forms back before they get up
from the table. Have your tailor's tape handy for those who don't
remember their costume sizes. Tell them that you will call them at
home for the information they can't remember.

"I have my biography at home."

"My agent fills these in."

"I'm covered by my wife's insurance."

"I always forget how many of my husband's children by his
first wife I'm supposed to claim."

Actors, like most other people, don't like to fill out forms. You
must plead, cajole, and remain pleasant.

THE TORCH-BEARERS   CAST

		HOME	WORK	SERVICE
Mr. Fred. Ritter	Albert Alvarez 1058 Bramercy Dr.	753 3691 (Jerry Rosen Agcy	870 5414 - 274 5861)	752 7975
Mr. Huxley Hossefrosse	Ben Blahzay 3916 Melrose	232 5756 (William Barnes	389 7726 - 273 0205)	none
Mr. Spindler	Charles Corn 12113 Redondo	268 6612 (Ted Cooper	231 1961 - 654 3050)	399 7171
Mr. Ralph Twiller	Dave Dumpling 161 S. Berendo	758 0058 (no agent)	292 5352	752 7975
Teddy Spearing	Earl Eastman 355 Douglas	665 1039 (GAC	none - 273 2400)	none
Mr. Stage Manager	Frank Farley 3607 W. 3rd	732 9444 (Coralie Jr.	778 3557 - 663 1268)	none
Mrs. Paula Ritter	Gina Glass 232 S. Serrano	567 6743 (Kurt Frings	652 7934 - 274 8881)	334 0101
Mrs. J. Duro Pampinelli	Helen Harvey 1510 S. Vermont	665 1605 (no agent)	none	none
Mrs. Nelly Fell	Ida Isely 2136 McPherson	221 2074 (Kumin-Olenick	295 1781 - 274 7281)	752 7975
Miss Flor. McCrickett	Judy Jennings 5716 Aldama Rd.	936 2325 (no agent)	627 4554	none
Mrs. Clara Sheppard	Karen Kirsten 3130 W. 11th	870 5079 (Kendall Agcy	none - 274 8107)	334 0101
Jenny	Louise Lehrer 139 E. 27th	877 2232 (Mishkin	754 3024 - 274 5261)	292 1333

· **Figure 6-15** ·
Cast List for Duplication and Distribution

Check each return form on the spot to make sure that it is complete and legible.

Preparing a Cast List

The ability to reach any actor immediately is a function of prime importance to you. The cast list is an invaluable tool in that function. The list should include the character, full name of the actor who plays the character exactly as that actor wishes to have the name appear in the program, address, home phone, work or business

THE TORCH-BEARERS   CAST LIST/check List

		HOME	WORK	SERVICE
Mr. Fred. Ritter	Albert Alvarez 1058 Bramercy Dr.	753 3691	870 5414	752 7975
		(J. Rosen Agcy - 274 5861)		
Mr. Huxley Hossefrosse	Ben Blahzay 3916 Melrose	232 5756	389 7726	none
		(Wm. Barnes - 273 0205)		
Mr. Spindler	Charles Corn 12113 Redondo	268 6612	231 1961	399 7171
		(Ted Cooper - 654 3050)		
Mr. Ralph Twiller	Dave Dumpling 161 S. Berendo	758 0058	292 5352	752 7975
		(no agent)		
Teddy Spearing	Earl Eastman 355 Douglas	665 1052	none	none
		(GAC - 273 2400)		
Mr. Stage Manager	Frank Farley 3607 W. 3rd	732 9444	778 3557	none
		(Coralie Jr. - 663 1268)		
Mrs. Paula Ritter	Gina Glass 232 S. Serrano	567 6743	652 7934	334 0101
		(Kurt Frings - 274 8881)		
Mrs. J. Duro Pampinelli	Helen Harvey 1510 S. Vermont	665 1605	none	none
		(no agent)		
Mrs. Nelly Fell	Ida Isely 2136 McPherson	221 2074	295 1781	752 7975
		(Kumin-Olenick - 274 7281)		
Miss Flor. McCrickett	Judy Jennings 5716 Aldama Rd.	936 2325	627 4554	none
		(no agent)		
Mrs. Clara Sheppard	Karen Kirsten 3130 W. 11th	870 5079	none	334 0101
		(Kendall Agcy - 274 8107)		
Jenny	Louise Lehrer 139 E. 27th	877 2232	754 3024	292 1333
		(Mishkin - 274 5261)		

Overlay grid columns: Contract, 8 x 10's, W-2, Blue X-GHI, AVAIL. TUES., Program Notes, Picnic, Pick up July

· **Figure 6-16** ·
Duplicated Cast List with Overlay Grid for a Checklist

phone, service number, agent's name and agent's phone number (see Figure 6-15).

Check for accuracy with each cast member before duplicating.

In rare cases actors will want to have their home phone and address withheld from all but you. Check this, too, before duplicating and distributing.

You never seem to have enough cast lists. Each cast member wants one so that she or he can contact other cast members (and send Christmas cards). The costume designer needs one. The publicist needs one. The payroll clerk needs one. The union insists on one. The program editor needs one. And as soon as you have given out your last copy, you find that there is still another person who needs one—the assistant director, the assistant stage manager, the doorman, the receptionist, the box office, or the sign painter.

You can't go too far in obtaining extra phone numbers at which you can reach an actor. Ask for any other numbers at which he or she can be reached when not at home or at the theater. Note these numbers on your copy against the emergency situation when you will have to reach that actor in a hurry.

You will find a few good uses for a well-designed, complete cast list. One should be posted near your home telephone. Another should be indexed into your prompt script for handy reference during rehearsals. You can use still another copy, with a grid overlay (see Figure 6-16), as a check list. Every time you have a distribution to make, you can check off each cast member to insure that everyone was told about a pickup rehearsal, a cast picnic, or an invitation to see a matinee of another show.

Be sure to store a copy of each cast list for your personal files. This is the only list that has both home phone and home address, information you won't readily have available if you save only a program.

In a musical stock situation with only a one week rehearsal period, you may not know all of the casting until the second day of rehearsals, which is only a few days before the printer needs that information in order to have programs for opening night. In such a case, it is desirable to run off lists with just the character name so that you may fill in cast members' names on the spot as casting is finalized, and hasten the information to the needy (see Figure 6-17).

You will also need a complete list of the staff and crew, with their addresses and telephone numbers. A grid overlay on such a list makes a handy coordination form to insure that you get all schedule changes and other necessary information to every member of the staff and crew.

Conducting the Deputy Election

At the first meeting of an Equity company, or the first rehearsal following casting at which the entire cast is present, you should conduct the election of the deputy. The deputy is that cast member

SHOW BOAT

OLD LADY ON LEVEE	
QUENNIE	*Bertha Powell*
PARTHY ANNE HAWKS	
CAPTAIN ANDY	*Marvin Miller*
ELLIE	
FRANK	*Dean Barlow*
JULIE	*Beverly Alvarez*
GAYLORD RAVENAL	*Alan Gilbert*
MAGNOLIA	*Kate Miller*
JOE	
WINDY	
STEVE	
PETE	
IKE VALLON	*Lou Boudreau*
BACKWOODSMAN	
BARKER	
FATIMA	
DAHOMEY QUEEN	
LANDLADY	
ETHEL	
MOTHER SUPERIOR	
KIM	
JAKE	
JIM	
MAN WITH GUITAR	
DOORMAN	
MISS SO-AND-SO	
MISS THINGAMABOB	
HEADWAITER	
ANNOUNCER	

· **Figure 6-17** ·

Production Cast List with Characters in Appearance Order

who will represent her or his fellow union cast members in all union business.

You should not serve as deputy.

The union normally mails the official election form to you when

DEPUTY ELECTION SHEET

　　　　The Stage Manager shall conduct the election and there shall be no person present at these proceedings who is not employed under an Equity contract (for this production). A Deputy may be elected by voice vote or, if more than one member is nominated, by secret ballot.

We, the undersigned Equity members, engaged under a standard form of Equity contract and constituting a majority of the cast of the (cross out inapplicable classification)

　　　　　　　Principals
　　　　　　　Ensemble Singers
　　　　　　　Ensemble Dancers

of the_____company

located at_____

under the management of _____

first day of rehearsal being_____ and opening on _____

do hereby elect_____ as Deputy

on this date_____19 _____

_____　　_____

_____　　_____

_____　　_____

_____　　_____

_____　　_____

_____　　_____

_____　　_____

_____　　_____

_____　　_____

_____　　_____

_____　　_____

· **Figure 6-18** ·
Election Form for Actor's Equity Deputy

your name is supplied to the union. If you do not receive the form prior to your first rehearsal, call the nearest Equity office (see Figure 6-18).

　　Take the time to read the official statement of election policy slowly and deliberately.

Secret ballots are desirable in large casts. This process slows the election enough to give voters time to think. In small casts, members usually reach accord in an open discussion of who might best serve. Formality is not as important as thoughtfulness. Causing cast members to reflect, rather than simply "get it over with," is a matter of tactful persuasion.

Time to conduct this deputy election, and subsequent union meetings, should the need arise, out of paid rehearsal time, is guaranteed to union actors in their contract.

First Cast Meeting or Readthrough

We have all seen trite first reading scenes in the movies in which the cast sits around a barren, coffee-stained table under a bleak work light. Why must it be this way?

I know one stage manager who brings from home a freshly pressed table cloth and a bouquet of flowers to place on the first reading table. It's a nice touch and it starts the cast off with the warm thought that someone went out of the way to make things a little better.

· 7 ·

Budgeting

Keeping a record of your expenses is the very least that is expected of you in the area of budgeting. If you pay any money out of your pocket to further a production, whether it be a dime for a phone call to a late actor or the C.O.D. charge for a prop delivered to the theater, make a record of it, and, if possible, get a written receipt.

You may want to use an expenditures form (see Figure 7-1) and attach your receipts to it. Keep the form in your prompt script so that it is with you when you need it. Periodically you will turn in the receipts for reimbursement.

In some instances it is more convenient to set up a petty cash fund, from twenty-five to one hundred dollars, depending on needs. When it has been spent, turn over the receipts to the business manager or the box office treasurer, who can advance another twenty-five to one hundred dollars, or whatever sum has been arranged and budgeted.

In some companies a purchase order must be obtained from the business manager before anything can be bought.

In other cases it may be necessary for you as manager to control funds for the technical director, the costume designer, the property master (see Chapter Ten), and other backstage personnel. To make sure that each does not spend beyond the total budgeted for the production, you might need to use a purchase order system: any staff member must ask for a purchase order *before* buying. You must then check the budget to see if this particular expenditure is within rea-

EXPENDITURES

_____ production of "_____" _____
dates

Supplier	Item(s)	Purchased by	Date	Cost
1				
2				
3				
4				
5				
6				
7				
8				
9				
10				
11				
12				
13				

Page ____ of ____   Prepared by _____

LAWRENCE STERN
Production Stage Manager
555-3719

· **Figure 7-1** ·
An Expenditures Record to Keep in the Prompt Script

son, and then approve or disapprove by giving or by denying a purchase order.

A typical budget for a one-week musical stock production might be (see Figure 7-2):

Lumber	$65.
Paint	$30.
Hardware	$20.

98

NAME OF PRODUCTION *Camelot*

P.O. NO.	$65 Lumber	$30 PAINT	$20 HD. WARE	$15 FAbriCS	$10 RIGGING
500					
501					
502					
503	53 12				
504					
503			25 71 O.K. pd		
505					
506					
507		18 07			
508					
509					
510					
511					
TOTALS	53 12	18 07	25 71		

Grand Total ($215 budgeted)
$173.02

· **Figure 7-2** ·
A Typical Production Budget Sheet

Fabrics	$15.
Rigging	$10.
Electrics	$10.
Tools	$ 5.

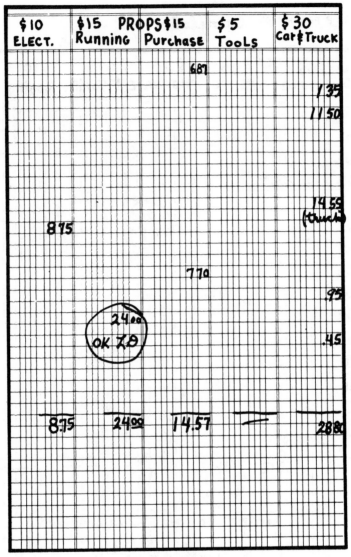

$10 ELECT.	$15 Running	PROPS $15 Purchase	$5 Tools	$30 Car & Truck
		6.87		
				1.35
				11.50
				14.55 (truck)
8.75				
		7.70		
		24.00 OK LO		.95
				.45
8.75	24.00	14.57	⟋	28.80

· **Figure 7-2** ·
(Continued)

Props
    Running $15. (expendable)
    Purchase $15. (permanent)
  Car (gas, oil) $15.
  Truck (rental) $20.

Example:

The technical director calls you from the lumber yard to say that the materials required to carry out the scene designer's plans will cost $98. Should you issue a purchase order?

Review the budget for this show and other shows this season. There's $65 allotted to lumber. But, being familiar with the scene design and the show, you also know that there will be no flying of scenery or actors, or effects that require rigging. So you can add the rigging allocation of $10. You should also be aware of the budget situation for the season: tools have already cost $7.50 over the budget because of a lost sabre saw; the last two shows were under budget by $10 and $15, respectively, in lumber, and three of the four coming shows have been staged before in past seasons; therefore, since most of the scenery is stored, they should come in under budget. Sifting these factors, and perhaps some others, while the tech director waits on the phone, you might go-ahead and give the purchase order number.

Or you might be under strict orders to clear all over-budget items with the business manager or other higher budget authority. In this case, you might have to ask the scene designer to streamline the design and bring it into line with the budget.

For a more extensive look at theater accounting practices, see Chapter Six of *School and Community Theater Management*.

· **8** ·

Rehearsal Procedures

Working with the Director during Rehearsal

As the closest assistant to the director, one of your most important functions will be to assist in getting the most productive results out of the time allotted to each rehearsal. To do this well it will be important to maintain a clear understanding of the director's function and a working relationship that will help his or her aims to be carried out smoothly.

The director is responsible for interpreting the playwright's work through the cast with the help of the staff. It is the director's artistic concept of the play that the cast, staff, and crew work to obtain.

When casting has been completed and rehearsals are underway, the director goes about her or his work in phases.

In the first phase the director insures that each cast member understands the character to be portrayed. This is accomplished at initial readings and in private discussions between the director and the actor. The director continues to influence characterization as reflected in line interpretations and business throughout the rehearsal period.

In the second phase, the director blocks—tells the actors where and how to move on stage and how to handle props.

Next, the director works on pace—the timing of lines and business, of scenes and acts. He or she imparts pace to the play the way an orchestra conductor imparts tempo to a symphony, one scene *presto*, another *moderato*.

In the last phase, the director works on polishing the interaction of characters with sets, with props, and most important, with one another.

The final quality of the performance is the product of all four phases of the director's work.

(In amateur theater, work sometimes does not go beyond the first two phases by opening night. Work on characterization consists of the actors learning their lines, and blocking means that they don't trip over one another. In professional theater, when a director is unable to progress beyond the first two phases, we call him or her a "traffic cop.")

The stage manager's functions in support of the director are twofold. First, she or he helps to expedite the rehearsals so that the director and cast will have as much time as possible to work on pace and interaction. Setting rehearsal furniture, taking blocking notation, and warning actors for their entrances during rehearsals are examples of the duties implied by this function.

Second, the stage manager accepts the responsibility for relieving the director of all concern for the mechanics of production so that the director may concentrate on bringing about an artistic interpretation of the script. Calling all sound and light cues, scheduling crew calls, and informing the director of progress on the sets are examples of the duties implied here.

The stage manager does not have any voice in the artistic interpretation of the script and must not intrude into this area. When prompting, for instance, he or she must not offer an interpretation of the lines to the actors.

What happens then, if the stage manager notices during a rehearsal that one actor is addressing a line to a second actor that the playwright obviously intended for a third actor? The mistake is repeated at the next rehearsal. Still the actors and director miss the obvious.

The stage manager should make a note in the prompt script and call the error to the attention of the director after the rehearsal and out of earshot of the cast. Let the director take remedial action.

Sometimes the stage manager observes very basic mistakes in direction. For example, focus is drawn away from an actress's important lines by an actor moving upstage of her during her speech. The stage manager observes that the director is oblivious or condones this at rehearsal after rehearsal. What should the stage manager do?

The stage manager calls such items to the director's attention, privately and tactfully.

Now let's take it to extremes. The stage manager notices during rehearsals that the director is demanding a light, comedy tone from an actress in a speech that simply won't work that way. It throws her fellow cast members off and it ruins the whole impact of the scene. What does the stage manager do?

The stage manager should exercise very careful judgment in deciding whether or not to discuss the matter with the director confidentially. I advise great caution until you get to know and understand the director. Certainly the stage manager should be extremely proficient in his or her own area before offering a director advice in another.

Although the stage manager does not participate in the creative interpretation of the script, he or she does make a conscientious effort to identify and understand the director's interpretation so that he or she may retain it, if called upon to do so, in keeping the show in hand during a long run (Chapter Sixteen) or blocking replacements and rehearsing understudies (see the end of Chapter Sixteen). Again, in these last mentioned duties, it is the director's intent that the stage manager strives to retain; the stage manager does not impose his or her own artistic interpretation.

Preset Diagrams

As soon as the scene designer decides where the sets and set pieces are to be located, you should make a diagram that will allow you to place those sets (or indications of sets) and set pieces (or rehearsal substitutes) exactly where they should be (see Figure 8-1).

As frequently as placement changes in the course of rehearsals, you must update your diagrams.

When it is decided which props will be *discovered* (found on the set at the rise of the curtain), you should add these props to your diagram with exacting specifications on just how the props are to be set (i.e., the label on a bottle should face upstage, the envelope is to be placed under the telephone with the address up and the flap open and pointing downstage).

The purpose of the preset diagram is to allow you to make a visual inspection prior to every rehearsal and performance. You must insure that every part of the set, all set pieces, and all props are in exactly the position that the cast expects to find them. This ritual is one of your most sacred duties.

The preset diagram differs from a diagram of the stage (Chapter Five) in that it includes indications of sets and props, and it need not be drawn to scale. The preset diagram may be the same as a

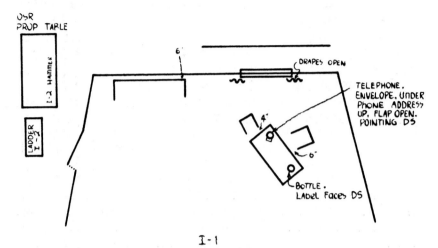

I-1
· **Figure 8-1** ·
Preset Diagram of Set and Props

scene shift diagram (Chapter Twelve), but the shift diagrams are placed in the crew area to help brief the crew, whereas preset diagrams are placed in your prompt script.

Examples:

A. The property mistress is late. You know where everything goes from your diagram. You set the props in her absence and rehearsal is not delayed.

B. The crew, in setting for Act II, forgets to move a table on stage.

During the intermission you check your diagram for Act II, realize that the table is not in place, and remind the crew.

C. An actor omits the business of closing the drapes on the set in Act II.

Checking your diagram for Act III you realize that the drapes are supposed to be discovered closed. You make the adjustment.

Actors become very dependent psychologically upon the exact placement of set pieces and props. Their timing for business is dependent on this placement. Adjusting to misplacement puts a strain on them, and sometimes it throws them off completely.

Your preset diagram should extend to the wings and include all stacked set pieces and props that are offstage. You must check their presence just as carefully as the units on stage.

Example:

A ladder and hammer, used as a set piece and prop in Scene 2, are borrowed for practical use in the shop and not returned. The items are not preset for Scene 1. If the crew waits until their cue for the Scene 1–2 fast change to discover that the props are missing, the change will be delayed. Your inspection of the offstage sets and props avoids this type of incident.

Rehearsals away from Your Stage

When stage time is not available for rehearsals and scenes must be rehearsed in other areas, preset diagrams, drawn to scale, allow you to lay out the exact dimensions of the scene using measuring tape and masking tape and/or spare rehearsal furniture to indicate flats and doors. Physical barricades used to indicate flats are better than tape. Actors tend to move closer to the taped lines or even step over them. They later feel cramped when they get onto the actual set. Your care in setting up the makeshift rehearsal area saves the time and energy of the cast in reblocking on the actual set.

Your Rehearsal Call

Usually you should arrive in the rehearsal area thirty to forty minutes prior to the rehearsal call, depending on how much work must be done to ready the area.

Besides arranging sets and props according to your present diagram, you should check on working conditions. Sweep the stage and dust the rehearsal furniture, if necessary, and make whatever improvements you can in ventilation, temperature, and lighting.

You should also prepare a work area for yourself and the director. Usually you will place a desk with two chairs in front of the apron. (Some directors prefer to use a music stand to hold their script as they remain standing during rehearsals.) Is there adequate room for your prompt script, the director's script, scratch paper, pencils, and refreshments? Insure that there is satisfactory lighting so that you may follow your scripts comfortably.

Now, is everything ready to start rehearsal at the minute it is called? Or will the cast have to stand around fifteen minutes waiting and/or adjusting things and not really rehearsing? Fifteen minutes of pre-rehearsal work by you can save two or three hours of cast time at every rehearsal. These hours saved and devoted to the quality of the final production are one of your very valuable contributions to the production process.

You should try to anticipate the entire course of the rehearsal and have all working materials at hand so that you may be stationary or at the director's side throughout. As the director's closest assistant, you must be able to devote your full attention to the rehearsal, because it is your busiest and most demanding work period. You have many duties and a few run concurrently:

A. Calling all sound and light cues and special effects pinpointing cues,
B. Taking blocking notation,
C. Prompting,
D. Warning,
E. Maintaining order,
F. Spiking set pieces,
G. Timing.

Calling and Pinpointing Cues

From the very first rehearsal you should call every light, sound, and special-effect cue. You should do it with such regularity and accuracy that no cast member ever doubts for a second that you will miss a cue during the production.

No matter how many times the director reruns the same scene, you always call the cues.

At first you go by the script. You ring the phone at the place indicated by the script and the place where you inserted your light pencil rough cue (discussed in Chapter Three). But during rehearsals you discuss the exact pinpointing of the cue with the director. Perhaps the director wants the phone to ring two lines prior, and the actors to allow it to ring twice in order to heighten suspense as to which of the actors will answer the phone. Or the director decides that she or he doesn't want the first phone ring to come at the end of the actor's line, but three words from the end so that the actor may cross to the phone on the last words of his line. Now the cue is specific. You should caret the exact point in your script. Later, just prior to the technical rehearsal, or during it, you will mark the exact cue with bold marking pen.

It is handy for you to have a bell/buzzer device in your kit (see Chapter Five) to provide some basic rehearsal sound effects. If you don't, simply call out, "Phone," "Doorbell," "Auto horn," or whatever sound is called for.

Similarly you should call all lighting effects to which the actors must react. You call "Curtain," and/or "Lights," at the beginning and end of every act.

You will also call the beginning, and sometimes the end, of all special effects: "Fog rolls in," "Vase rises from bookcase," "Rain begins," "Rain ends."

You should call all cues *resolutely*, letting the cast know that you know your business and are self-assured.

Taking Blocking Notation

Recording the movement of the actors helps to expedite rehearsals. With a written record of where they move on their lines, you are able to remind them when they forget. You will also use this notation to block in replacements and conduct understudy rehearsals (see Chapter Sixteen).

Normally you simply observe the initial blocking that the director gives the actors. You do not start to take blocking notations until the blocking starts to gel.

There are several systems for making such notation.

Method I

The stage is divided as shown in Figure 8-2. Blocking notations using this method might read:

XDR—The actor crosses to the down right area of the stage.
XLC—The actor crosses to the left center area of the stage.

Method II (for theater in the round)

The stage is divided as shown in Figure 8-3. The stage is thought of as a clock, with the orchestra pit at 12 o'clock, and then divided into four concentric circles numbered from the audience to the center of the stage. Blocking notations might read as follows:

X3.2—The actor crosses to the second ring at 3 o'clock.
X11.1—The actor crosses to the first ring at 11 o'clock.

Method III

All notations are made, regardless of the shape of the stage, with reference to the destination of the actor and the number of steps she

For a large stage:

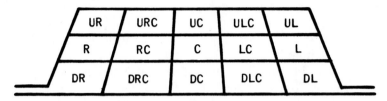

C – Center of the stage

D – Down (toward the audience)

U – Up (away from the audience)

R – Right (actor's right facing the audience)

L – Left (actor's left facing the audience)

For a small stage:

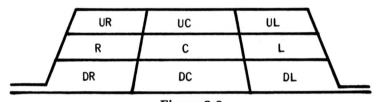

· **Figure 8-2** ·

Divisions of Proscenium Stage for Blocking Notation

or he takes in the direction of that destination. Blocking notations might read:

> X door 2—The actor takes two steps toward the door.
> X Pat 5—The actor crosses five steps toward Pat, another character.

With this type of notation it is not possible to understand from reading a single entry where on stage the actor is located. This disadvantage should be countered by using extensive "French-scene" diagrams described below.

Method IV (Combinations)

Prior methods are combined. Blocking notations might read:

> X DR door—The actor crosses to the down right door.
> X2 DR door—The actor takes two steps toward the down right door.

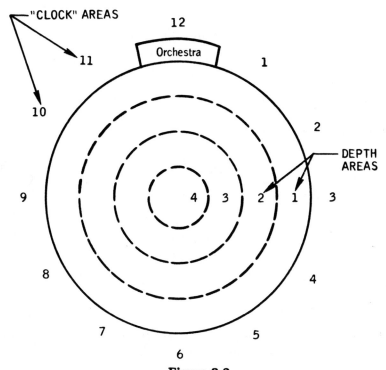

· **Figure 8-3** ·
Divisions of Round Stage for Blocking Notation

> X2DR—The actor takes two steps toward the down right
> area.
> X3.2 door—The actor crosses to the door in the 3.2 area.
> X2 3.2 door—The actor takes two steps toward the 3.2 door.

The best method is the method that works best for you.

Most often the actors move on their lines, that is, they cross while delivering a line of dialogue. They frequently start to move at the beginning of the line and stop moving with the last word of it. So when you make a blocking notation adjacent to an actor's line, it automatically indicates that the actor is moving on the line.

If an actor is blocked to move on another actor's line—not usually the case—this must be indicated. For these instances, and for the purpose of "French-scene" diagrams, it is convenient to have a symbol for each actor:

> Constance—C
> Irene—I
> George—G

111

Now, if George moves on Irene's line:

> Irene: One or two?   *G XDR table*

Or if two or more actors move at the same time:

> Constance: I won't insist.   *XDL; I XDR; G XULC*

(On Constance's line she crosses down left, Irene crosses down right, and George crosses up left center.)
    What if the actor moves before or after his or her line but not on another actor's line?
    Use carets:

> Constance: ∧I won't insist.   *XDL*

This indicates that Constance starts her cross prior to her line and finishes it with the end of her line.

> Constance: ∧∧I won't insist   *XDL*

These carets indicate that Constance begins and ends her cross prior to her line, but not on another actor's line.

> Constance: I won't ∧insist. ∧*XDL*

She starts her cross with the word indicated and completes the cross after the line.

> Constance: I won't insist. ∧∧*XDL.*

She begins and ends her cross after her line.

Blocking notation is not an exact science. Some stage managers find that they can remember where and when an actor moves without precise notation. Others rely very heavily on notation and longhand notes (see Figure 8-4).
    After you have observed the first few rough blocking rehearsals, you will start to make your notations, realizing that the blocking is not yet set (permanent). It is best to take notation in light pencil. If you do not care to erase, you may make changes in columns at the side of the original blocking:

> Constance: I won't insist.   *XDL / XULC / XRC*

Note to Props: Large, very dusty books

80   THE IMPORTANCE   [ACT II ✓

Miss Prism. That would be delightful. Cecily, you will read your Political Economy in my absence. The chapter on the Fall of the Rupee you may omit. It is somewhat too sensational. ∧Even these metallic problems have their melodramatic side.   **XC**

   Ex UL

[Goes down the garden with DR. CHASUBLE.]

> *Cecily [picks up books and throws them back on table.]*∧Horrid Political Economy! Horrid Geography! Horrid, horrid German!

Rises
XR2
Ent R2

ENTER MERRIMAN *with a card on a salver.*

Merriman. Mr. Ernest Worthing has just driven over from the station. He has brought his luggage with him.

Cecily [takes the card and reads it].∧"Mr. Ernest Worthing, B 4 The Albany, W." Uncle Jack's brother! Did you tell him Mr. Worthing was in town?   **XM**

Merriman. Yes, Miss. He seemed very much disappointed. I mentioned that you and Miss Prism were in the garden. He said he was anxious to speak to you privately for a moment.

Cecily. Ask Mr. Ernest Worthing to come here.∧I suppose you had better talk to the housekeeper about a room for him.   **XL3**

Merriman. Yes, Miss. [MERRIMAN goes off.]   **Ex R**

Cecily. I have never met any really wicked person before. I feel rather frightened. I am so afraid he will look just like everyone else.

ENTER ALGERNON, *very gay and debonnair.*
∧He does!   **Ent R**
   turns R

Algernon [raising his hat]. You are my little cousin Cecily, I'm sure.

Cecily. You are under some strange mistake.

· **Figure 8-4** ·
Blocking Notation as Entered on Prompt Script Page

Using columns may be advantageous. When a director wants to go back to an earlier blocking, you will be able to tell the actors how they used to move.

After a few rehearsals when the same blocking is repeated, it is safe to assume that the blocking is set. A director may still change all or part of the blocking after this point, but it is set in so far as the director expects the actors to repeat their movement unless he or she changes it. The time when this happens varies with the director's technique. Some directors rough block at home, using diagrams of the stage and tokens for actors. They bring in their own notation of projected blocking and start early rehearsals with very firm blocking.

Other directors allow cast members to drift at will as they recite their lines, and then try to arrange the drifting, sometimes called organic blocking.

When you feel that the blocking is set, you should start to prompt on blocking.

Example A:

An actor says: "I know I was supposed to move on that line but I've forgotten where."
You: "Your cross is down left."

Example B:

A director says to an actor: "You're not supposed to be there when Sam enters."
You advise the director (not the actor): "He missed his cross down left three lines back on 'Hark, here comes the king' ."

In general, in the prompting of blocking, you should advise the director rather than the actors. If you observe actors not following their blocking, you whisper to the director without interrupting the flow of the scene. Let directors decide if they want to stop and bring the error to the actor's attention, or if they want you to call the error to the actor's attention later, during a break or after the rehearsal, or if they want you to change your blocking notation in order to take advantage of what the actor has done instinctively.

A very common occurrence is actors taking their crosses on the line following their cross line. The cross line triggers their memory too late. But they get where they are supposed to be in time not to upset the overall effect of the scene. This error can usually be corrected by calling the actor's attention to it after the scene is over. If you place a light penciled caret in the margin with an appropriate symbol, this will remind you of what the actor did wrong.

Constance: I won't insist. *XDL* *<LX*

When you have brought the late cross to the actor's attention, during the break or after rehearsal, erase the caret and symbol.

While taking blocking notation you should make production notes (I use the upper right corner of my prompt book page) on (1) blocking that will require special lighting, and (2) light and sound cues that will be dependent on blocking.

Example A:

The director decides that an actor will sit on the apron and recite a poem with the curtain closed to cover a scene change. You realize that this will call for at least one additional lighting instrument that was not in the lighting designer's original plans. You make a note. After the rehearsal you tell the lighting designer and you change your light plot. You also place new cues in your prompt script.

Example B:

The director decides that the nurse will rise and cross to a table to examine a knife before she hears a bell that summons her offstage. Formerly the cue for the bell was the doctor's line to the nurse. You realize that the cue for the bell is now a visual one rather than an oral one, so you make this change in your prompt script immediately.

French-Scene Diagrams

Within a scene there may be many "French-scenes." Every time a character enters or exits, a new French-scene is begun (after the conventional scene designations in classical French drama). A French-scene is that part of a scene or act in which the number of characters is constant.

The director usually starts or resumes rehearsing from the beginning of a French-scene. You may find it quite helpful to make small diagrams of the position of the cast at the beginning of each French-scene (see Figure 8-5).

If the director says, "Let's take it from the top of page 83 where Fran enters," the cast members will probably not remember where they are supposed to be for Fran's entrance. If you review your blocking notation just prior to Fran's entrance, you may eventually be able to determine where they are, but it will take time. But if you have made a diagram, you can say immediately (from Figure 8-5), "Al is seated on the couch facing down left, Ralph is looking out the window, and Alice is standing down right center facing down left."

As there are frequently many French-scenes in every act, you may expedite your diagraming with a cardboard template of the set and set pieces (see Figure 8-5). At the top of every prompt book page on which a character enters or exits, you simply copy your scene diagram. Jotting in the positions of the cast then takes very little effort.

Spiking Set Pieces

It is very important to the actors' movement on stage that set pieces be in exactly the same place at every rehearsal and performance. To

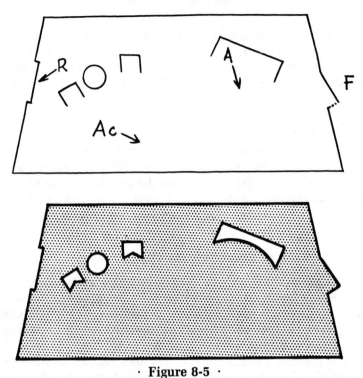

· **Figure 8-5** ·
"French-Scene" Cardboard Template and Scene Diagram

insure this, you not only check your preset diagrams, but also *spike* the set pieces, that is, you mark their position on the stage floor. Then if moved, accidentally or intentionally, the set pieces may be returned to exactly the same location.

Spiking is usually done with masking tape placed on the stage at the upstage end of the set piece, thus out of sight of the audience.

Spike your set pieces as early in the rehearsal process as practical.

When many scenes are to play in the same area, it becomes necessary to code the spike marks—to write on the masking tape which set piece plays there during which scene. Next to one tape marked "II-2 table" there might be another tape marked "III-7 chair."

Frequently shifts must be made so fast that stagehands do not have time to read the tapes. In these cases the tapes should be color coded, painted a certain color for each scene.

Or if the changes are to be made in blackouts, it may be helpful to paint the spike marks with luminous paint. The stage lighting will usually "heat up" the luminous paint so that it will glow during blackouts. If you are using luminous paint in areas where it is not

116

hit by stage lights, you can heat it up by shining a spot or sunlamp on it at close range for a few minutes prior to performance.

Prompting

Prompting procedure is determined by the director. You should ask the director privately, prior to rehearsals, how he or she wants the cast prompted. How close are the actors to be held to the lines in the script? Letter perfect? Or may they paraphrase as long as they get the sense of the line? How are the actors to call for lines? When and how are you to review lines with actors? Ask the director to brief the cast at the outset of rehearsals on just what he or she expects in the prompting process.

The few words on the subject might go like this: "Our stage manager has been instructed to hold you very close to the script. If you deliver a line and our stage manager calls out the correct one, repeat the line as he gives it, without breaking character, and carry on. Do not argue about changing the line. See me before or after rehearsals about any possible line changes. Our stage manager will also approach you during breaks and after rehearsals to cite lines or cues that were missed. Please do not argue. Simply repeat out loud the line cited and then say, 'Thank you.' Call for lines by saying 'line,' and in no other way."

Some directors insist that the cast be held letter perfect to the script, particularly if the playwright's reputation is great. They allow their casts greater latitude with the works of lesser-known playwrights. Some directors feel that they must update plays and encourage their cast members to experiment with, and modernize the dialogue.

Some directors insist that the stage manager throw the exact line whenever an actor hesitates or paraphrases, as well as when an actor calls for a line. Other directors want lines thrown only when the actor calls for them or when the cast jumps out of sequence. But they want all errors in lines brought to the attention of the cast during breaks or after rehearsals.

Some directors want cast members to say "line" when asking for a line. Others want them to snap their fingers but otherwise to remain in character. Some directors do not want their actors to call for lines at all. Some set a date in the rehearsal schedule after which actors are not to call for lines. Many directors resent any other remarks that actors throw when calling for lines, such as, "Oh, I always forget that one."

Talk it over with your director. If she or he does not give specific instructions to the cast explaining the prompting interaction expected, start out in the way you feel is best, and apply her or his criticism of your prompting technique as you go along.

To prompt efficiently, read the script to yourself, mouthing the words as the actors recite them. That way you are right there with them. Actors appreciate getting their line immediately after they call for it. If they and the director have to wait while you search for the line, then you are delaying the rehearsal.

When you prompt, give the actor the line in a clear, resolute, but emotionless tone of voice. Do not interpret the actor's line for him or her.

Be sure to make line changes in your prompt script as they are decided upon. Prompt the new lines as if they were the old lines.

As you prompt, draw a caret in the margin to indicate every line that was delivered improperly. Use a code to indicate the type of error. Work in light pencil.

C — called for line
P — paraphrased
BB — bobbled
L — late (cite cue to actor)
PR — pronunciation
J — jumped cue
H — handle—added extra word not in script prior to line
S — sequence, jumped out of

Use any code that works for you.

At the next break or after rehearsal, go to each actor, point out the missed line, and ask the actor to read it aloud. It is not necessary to say why you marked the line unless you are asked. Then erase the caret and code (see Figure 8-6).

Most professional actors are grateful for this service. If you should meet with resentment ("That's exactly what I said." "I know I missed it. You don't have to tell me."), say, "Thank you," politely, and walk away. Try it again at the next rehearsal and see how the actor accepts your help more graciously. When the actors are convinced that you are trying to help them, they are appreciative.

If there is an intentional pause prior to, or during a line, you should mark your script with an inverted caret (V) at the pause point so that you are reminded not to prompt there (and don't panic on opening night).

Sometimes it is convenient to write out line cites during rehearsal so that you can hand each actor a list of lines that need to

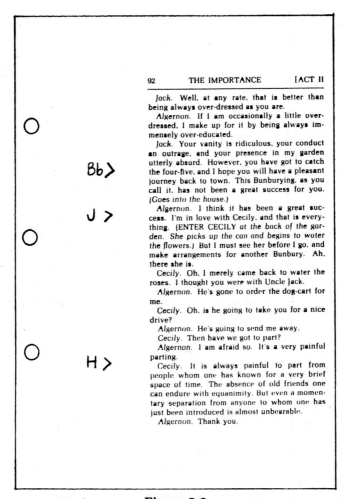

· **Figure 8-6** ·
Prompting Cites, Lightly Penciled on Inside Script Margin

be reviewed. This allows you to dismiss the cast faster after rehearsal, rather than hold them while you flip through pages of the script. If the director habitually holds the cast after rehearsals to review notes with them, you might use that same time to cite lines, doing it as unobtrusively as possible, and not interfering with the director's notes.

Getting up on lines is basic to any production. You helped establish deadlines for line memorization in making up the master calendar and rehearsal schedule. Now, how can you help the actors meet those deadlines? Are you willing to run lines with them before or after rehearsals? Can you arrange extra pre-rehearsal sessions for cast members when they can help each other by running lines? Can you assign a gopher to run lines with an actor who is offstage?

Start prompting with gusto just as soon as cast members are willing to put down their scripts. Let the cast know that you mean to help them get up on their lines quickly and accurately. It is easier to start working hard than to start leniently and then apply pressure after the cast has gotten into sloppy habits.

If you can make every actor feel that you are earnestly trying to help, rather than criticize, your prompting technique is good.

Prompting during a performance is a matter of the director's policy. Once a production has opened it is generally considered very unprofessional to prompt, and actors are expected to ad lib their way out of any situation.

Warning

During rehearsals actors may wander out of the rehearsal area. If they leave, they must always check out with the stage manager to say where they are going. ("I'm going to get this sewn up in costumes." "We're running lines in the lobby.") They should also check in with the stage manager when they return (see Chapter Three, "Actors and Their Entrance Cues").

You must think ahead. Which scene will the director work on next? You must warn wandering actors to be ready to appear. Waiting for an actor to be summoned so that a rehearsal can continue wastes a lot of time. If you observe your entrance warns (see Chapter Three and Figure 3-9) you can avoid such delays.

If an actor is on the premises and rehearsal is delayed while waiting for that actor to appear, the fault is yours.

Sometimes an actor will be summoned only to find that the director wishes to rerun the scene prior to her or his entrance. It is better that a single actor be inconvenienced than that several be hung up by her or his absence. When you work at mounting a few plays with the same director, you will develop a sixth sense as to whether the director will press on or rerun.

If possible, don't leave your post to summon a wandering actor. Send a gopher or another actor.

During performances you are not responsible for warning actors for individual entrances, but you are responsible for warning the crew about impending shifts and the orchestra about musical cues, as necessary. (See Chapter Three, p. 33, for discussion of exceptions.)

Maintaining Order

A director should never have to ask for quiet working conditions that will allow him or her and the cast to concentrate on their work. You should be aware of any noise or other disruptions and try to remedy the situation.

Try personal contact. Approach the noisy offender and explain, eyeball to eyeball, that rehearsals require silence from those who are not on stage, that it is a matter of courtesy.

Do not hesitate to shout, "Quiet, PLEASE!" if personal contact fails.

Some people have greater tolerance of noise levels than others. If you can read Christopher Fry during an air raid, but your director gets shell shock from seats squeaking, try to sympathize with his or her problem and hold the cast down to the level he or she can tolerate.

Giving Rehearsal, Publicity, and Costume Calls

The last official voice that every actor should hear as she or he leaves a rehearsal is yours, giving the next call, whether that call is for a rehearsal, publicity meeting with a TV interviewer, costume call at a supply house across town, or conference with the producer.

It should be standard procedure that every actor check out, after rehearsal or performance, with the stage manager. This might simply mean a cheerful "Goodnight," to which you might answer with an equally informal, "See you at ten tomorrow." That informal "ten tomorrow" is an order to appear at 10 o'clock sharp.

It is not enough to publish, post, and distribute rehearsal schedules. You must give the calls in person, face to face. You must then mentally or physically check off each cast member; if anyone left early and failed to check out with you, you must phone that individual to give the call.

If you are working with a large cast, divided into principals, chorus, and dancers, or other major groups, you may wish to use a special callboard.

The term *callboard* has come to mean a bulletin board where any information, including the next call, can be brought to the attention of the cast. *Special callboard* is used here to mean a board display with only the next call (see Figure 8-7). Rather than placing it on the general callboard, it is effective to place the special callboard by itself near the exit through which the cast must leave.

121

YOUR C A L LFOR

TUES. July 14
(DATE)

	TIME	PLACE
PRINCIPALS		
Frank *	10:00	TenT
Julie *	10:30	Music Room
Ravenal	10:30	Costume Shop
All Others	10:30	Tent
SINGING ENSEMBLE		
BOYS	Off	
GIRLS	11:00	Chorus Room
DANCING ENSEMBLE		
BOYS	11:00	Costume Shop
GIRLS	11:00	Chorus Room
LOCAL CHORUS		
BOYS	5:30	Costume Shop
GIRLS	5:30	Costume Shop

＊SPECIAL APPOINTMENTS

Frank	Publicity Lunch	12:00	Florentine Room
Julie	Hairdresser	6:00	Claire's 140 W. 2nd

· **Figure 8-7** ·
Special Callboard Format, for Next Upcoming Calls

The special callboard form can be covered with plastic, glass, or even a plastic film wrap so that the blanks may be filled in with crayon and then erased with a rag.

When photo calls are scheduled in the rehearsal area, whether for publicity, cast souvenirs, or the theater scrapbook, it is often helpful to post a picture schedule (see Figure 8-8).

The publicity person usually decides who is to appear in the pictures. But to save time in posing the shots, you might want to pre-select emotional peak scenes from the script. During the call you can then throw a line before the emotional peak and have the cast

PICTURE CALL

Thursday night after performance pictures will be taken.
Please remain in costume and change for subsequent shots.

1. Entire cast (curtain call order) and crew.

2. III-2: "So I'll say goodnight..." - Arlene, Jonas, Terry

3. III-1: "...because I'm going to get married." - Arlene, Sandy, Rita, Larry

4. III-1: "My arms, my lips..." - Larry, Rita, Sandy

5. II-3 : "I'm going to be frank with you, Pa." - Jonas, Dave, JoAnne

6. II-3: "We going to be here that long?" - Dave, JoAnne, Terry

7. II-1: "I want to go to a hotel." - Jonas, Arlene

8. II-1: "He don't look like no Cary Grant to me." - Dee, Sandy, Norma, Jonas, Rita

9. I-3: "Then start going out on dates again." - Arlene, Jonas

10. I-2: "Stop trying to fix me up with all your friends." Shirley-May, Jonas, Terry

11. I-2: "Rosalind, do me a favor." - Terry, Vicky, Jonas, JoAnne

12. I-2: "Rosalind, you know my brother Jerry." - Vicky, Jonas, Terry

13. I-1: "I'm in trouble now, Ma." - Arlene, Rita

14. I-1: "Will you get dressed and go to school." - Arlene, Rita, Sandy

· **Figure 8-8** ·
Picture Call Schedule

pick it up in character. If someone will shout freeze when they come to the peak line, this process will usually result in an interesting tableau.

It is often necessary for the photographer to tighten the shot by moving the actors closer to one another than they normally appear in that sequence. But reposing and rerunning still saves time over the unplanned approach of deciding in front of the camera just what poses are appropriate.

If the picture call follows a runthrough or dress rehearsal or

T A K E   M E   A L O N G

RUNNING ORDER

ACT I

I-1   OUTSIDE MILLER HOME

   Townspeople
        "Fire Machine"

   Fire Chief, Nat, Essie, Art, Tommy, Mildred
        "Oh, Please"

   Lilly
        reprise: "Oh, Please"

I-2   MACOMBER HOUSE

   Richard, Muriel
        "I Would Die"

   Macomber

I-3 CARBARN

   Sid, Voices
        "Sid, Ol' Kid"

I-4   STREET (Played In Aisle)

   Art, Sid

I-5   MILLER HOME

   Essie, Lilly, Tommy, Mildred, Nat, Richard, Macomber
        "Staying Young"

   Art, Sid
        "I Get Embarrassed"
        "We're Home"
        "Take Me Along"

I-6   PICNIC

   Sid, Carter, McDonald, Nat
   "For Sweet Charity"

· **Figure 8-9** ·
Running Order on a Large Board, Easily Legible

performance, it is desirable to start with poses selected from the last scene of the last act and work backwards so that cast members are saved an unnecessary costume change.

Posting a picture call and picture schedule well in advance

allows cast members to plan for the session in terms of shaving, hair style, makeup, costumes, and time.

Posting the Running Order

The running order is a list, in production sequence, of the scenes, giving the place of the scene, the cast members in the scene, the songs or dance numbers (if any) in that scene, and special cue lines (see Figure 8-9). You should post it on the first day of rehearsal or as soon thereafter as possible, and update it as necessary.

The function of the running order is to help remind cast members when they appear next.

Why is this necessary? Shouldn't every cast member know when he or she appears next?

Sometimes it is very confusing. In a one-week rehearsal for a musical stock show, the chorus may have rehearsed their songs in a chorus room, their dances in a rehearsal hall, and many will not have gone through the show in production sequence until the "put together," possibly the day before dress rehearsal, and only two days before opening night. So, as the chorus members dash from the stage to the dressing room, they need to have some easily accessible reference to answer the questions, "What do I do next?" and "Which of my eight costumes do I change into?"

In the rewrite phase of a new musical, the chorus might come in for half hour call to find that the running order has been drastically changed. The finale will be sung as the opening number, the show done as a flashback, and the principals will reprise the finale at the final curtain with the chorus humming the bridge from the wings. Then, the next night at half hour call, the chorus learns that the finale will be sung at the second act curtain and that they will reprise their Act I, Scene 2 hit song as the finale. Their actual performance sequence will vary from day to day. So in addition to briefings from the staff, they need a written running order that they can refer to in haste.

The running order should be BIG!, possibly two feet wide by three feet tall, and carefully lettered so that it is easily legible. It should be placed along the path from the stage to the dressing rooms so that cast members don't have to detour to read it. It should be well lighted. It should be in the same place from the time it is posted until closing night, so that cast members don't have to search for it.

If there is a blackout within a scene to denote time lapse, a "false blackout," this should be noted on the running order so that cast members will be forewarned not to enter on that blackout for the following scene. A song or line that occurs after the time lapse blackout should be listed so that cast members will have an accurate cue for their entrance blackout.

All reprises should be carefully designated as reprises so that there is no confusion as to whether the song or the reprise is the cue. This is a particular problem when the song and the reprise occur within the same scene.

To make the entries on your running order immediately discernible, write your song titles in one color or style of script (e.g., letters underlined), the names of the scenes in a second color or style (e.g., large capitals), the cast members involved in a third (e.g., small capitals), and special notes about cue lines and blackouts in still another (e.g., cursive script). A work of art is not your goal, but any scheme that will help cast members to decipher the running order quickly is helpful.

You must call all revisions to the attention of the cast and discuss the problems incurred by changes with them.

Typed copies of the running order should be placed in the crew area and on the callboard. You are very definitely responsible for alerting all crew members (props, lights, scene changes, costumes, etc.) to changes. The crew is not expected to decipher and apply a revised running order without a briefing from you and your immediate close supervision.

When changes in the production sequence are made, the running order should not be done over, but revisions should be cited with bold marking pen so that cast members can pick out the changes without studying the whole running order.

Summer stock running orders rarely parallel the New York productions as reflected in published scripts, so the running order must be coordinated with the staff before it is posted.

Timing of Rehearsals and Performances

You should carefully time each scene, and sometimes critical parts of scenes. The purpose of timing during rehearsals is to help the director know what the total playing time is, and to let the box office and house manager know what time the show will be out and what time to expect intermissions. The purpose of timing during performances is to keep track of the pace of each scene and act.

Using a stopwatch is desirable, but an ordinary watch with a sweep second hand may be used.

Start to time scenes just as soon in rehearsal as the scenes are run without interruption. At the end of each rehearsal, advise the director of the running times. Tell him or her not only how long the scenes took, but how long it took last time they were run, and the shortest time in which they were run.

As soon as every scene in the play has been timed once, give the director some projection of the total running time.

During the run, time each scene at every performance. You will find that running time of each scene varies from performance to performance. Sometimes it's audience response; sometimes it's actors who are not picking up their lines or are adding pauses. Sometimes a bit of business will vary in time. There are many reasons for differences in the timing of scenes. If the director is "with the show" (attending performances regularly or even periodically), judgment as to why the times vary may be left to her or him. If the director has left the show, or if the show is on the road, then it is your responsibility to evaluate the running times and take appropriate action (see Chapter Sixteen).

If you index a weekly time chart (see Figure 8-10) into your prompt script, you will be easily able to make the necessary comparisons and have the information readily available to your staff.

In most theater situations you will be responsible for the timing of blackouts and intermissions. You must direct the blackouts and the backstage aspects of the intermissions just as carefully as the director directs the scenes. Some of the factors in a blackout or intermission are changes of sets, striking and/or setting of props, change of position of actors, changes in costumes, patching of the lighting board, re-geling of instruments, etc. (see Chapter Eleven).

During a blackout, audience attention wanders. Perhaps the first 10 seconds of a blackout are consumed in applause and/or mental reaction to what has just happened. After that, coughing, fidgeting, and conversations indicate that the audience is no longer involved with the scene that is past. The longer that the audience is left in darkness, the harder it is for the actors in the following scene to regain the audience's attention, emotional focus, and/or intellectual concern.

So it is very important that you be able to organize the proceedings during blackouts to make them as short as possible. Some directors insist that no blackouts be longer than 20 seconds. During the technical rehearsal and subsequent dress rehearsals, you must

WEEKLY TIME CHART

PRODUCTION **The Bunny** WEEK OF **OCT. 10, '53**

	Tues Dress	Wed Dress	Thur opening	Fri	Sat early	Sat late	Sun
Announced Curtain	8:00	8:00	8:30	8:30	8:00	10:30	8:30
Actual Curtain	8:06	8:14	8:41	8:35	8:04	10:31	8:36
I-1	8:14 / 8	8:22 / 8	8:48 / 7	8:43 / 8	8:12 / 8	10:40 / 9	8:45 / 9
Blackout	8:14 / :30	8:38 / :16	8:48 / :25	8:43 / :20	8:12 / :20	10:40 / :20	8:45 / :20
I-2	8:29 / 15	8:39 / 17	9:03 / 15	8:58 / 15	8:27 / 15	10:54 / 14	9:00 / 15
Blackout	8:30 / :35	8:39 / :30	9:04 / :30	8:59 / :30	8:28 / :30	10:55 / :30	9:01 / :30
I-3	8:47 / 17	8:55 / 16	9:19 / 15	9:14 / 15	8:44 / 16	11:10 / 15	9:16 / 15
Intermission	9:09 / 22	9:07 / 12	9:30 / 11	9:25 / 11	8:53 / 9	11:20 / 10	9:26 / 10
II-1	9:25 / 16	9:23 / 16	9:46 / 16	9:42 / 17	9:10 / 17	11:36 / 16	9:42 / 16
Blackout	9:26 / :48	9:24 / :45	9:47 / :40	9:43 / :35	9:11 / :35	11:37 / :35	9:43 / :30
II-2	9:37 / 11	9:34 / 10	9:56 / 9	9:52 / 9	9:29 / 9	11:46 / 9	9:52 / 9
Blackout	9:37 / :25	9:34 / :25	9:56 / :25	9:53 / :30	9:29 / :25	11:46 / :25	9:52 / :25
II-3	9:57 / 20	9:53 / 19	10:14 / 18	10:11 / 18	9:39 / 19	12:04 / 18	10:10 / 18
Total Running Time	1:27	1:26	1:20	1:22	1:24	1:21	1:22

· **Figure 8-10** ·
Chart Record of Running Time

ask to run, rerun, and if necessary, choreograph blackouts until you and the director are satisfied that they are run in minimum time.

During the rehearsals you should also time certain of the sound effects and special effects to figure out the length for your plots.

Example:

You realize during a rehearsal that an alarm bell sound effect must last long enough to cover an actor's business of opening a safe, ransacking it, and escaping through a window, and it must also last long enough to cover the entrance of two other characters, their reaction, and the closing of the curtain. How long should a tape of that alarm bell effect be? During the rehearsals you carefully time the business and either make a production note in your script or add this timing to your sound plot. Then at the sound session you are prepared to say, "We will need at least three minutes of the alarm bell on tape."

Keeping a Rehearsal Log

The rehearsal log is a very brief diary of what happened or failed to happen at rehearsals. You should always be able to answer the question, "How did we come to this state of affairs?" with specifics. It is not always possible to remember the specifics unless you keep notes. It is convenient to tab your log into your prompt script.

Entries in the rehearsal log should include date, cast members who are late or absent, cast changes, the scene or scenes that were blocked or run, the number of times these scenes were run, delays and causes of delays in rehearsals, failure to run a scheduled scene, and any significant occurrence out of the ordinary—e.g., an accident, failure to meet a deadline, or mechanical failure of equipment (see Figure 8-11).

If you have the opportunity to help critique a production, your rehearsal log will be an invaluable asset (see Chapter Nineteen).

Submitting Rehearsal Reports

In some companies the producer or top management may require a daily written report from the stage manager. This report usually requires the same information that you would want to keep in your log, but in a more formal format (see Figure 8-12). If you were to keep a copy of this report, you would not have to keep a log, as the same purpose would be served.

Note that in the rehearsal report, under the heading "Engaged/Dismissed," you are expected to indicate those cast members who joined or left the company. The payroll department and Equity must be notified in these cases.

In some companies the stage manager is also required to submit a report to Equity (see Figure 8-13).

Accident Prevention and Reports

You must always be alert to situations that might cause accidents: set construction materials left on stage or backstage, materials left perched precariously on ladders and on flats, nails and boards pro-

REHEARSAL LOG

Sunday, May 28   - Read through script (Mike, Will, Jackie out).

Monday, May 29   - Read through again, made a few revisions (Jackie still out).

Friday, June 2   - Blocked Act I to p. 17.

Saturday, June 3   - Started 15 minutes late. (Dick claimed shooting wound up late.) Blocked remainder of Act I.

Sunday, June 4   - Jackie, Dick only - script changes.

Monday, June 5   - Jackie, Dick only - blocked their scenes in Act II.

Tuesday, June 6   - Billy only. Worked him through all blocking as Eric's replacement.

Wednesday, June 7 - Ran Act I twice. Sound session after rehearsal. (Steve was late but no delay in rehearsal.)

Thursday, June 8   - Blocked Act II (except Jackie, Dick scenes.)

Friday, June 9   - Attempted to integrate sound but amplifier went out. Ran Act II twice.

Saturday, June 10 - First runthrough, integrated sound cues.

Sunday, June 11   - Polished Act I, ran five times.

Tuesday, June 13   - Ran Act II twice. Dick, Pandora out so rehearsal suffered;did not run Dick-Jackie scenes (Dick was shooting, Pandora's husband in auto accident.)

· **Figure 8-11** ·
Rehearsal Log with Typical Entries

truding upstage of flats which might tear actors' costumes or skin, wires not secured on which to trip, sharp edges on corners in dark areas backstage, etc. The list is endless.

Check flying cables, whether or not you have immediate plans

COMPANY *J. Gill*

STAGE MANAGER's REHEARSAL REPORT FORM

PLACE: *Loft*   DATE: *Aug. 13, '69*

CALL: **7:30**

SCENES: **I-4**
      II-2

Rehearsal started: **7:30**
Lunch/Dinner break: —
Rehearsal resumed: —
Rehearsal ended: **10:00**
Rehearsal time: **2:30**
Overtime (if any): —

Expenses:
—

Engaged/Dismissed:
—

Injuries:
Dinah Left Early —
see report

Absent/Excused:
AL — still out sick

Late:
—

Remarks: **Good work done on both scenes despite AL's absence. — Dinah did well before she left.**

Laurence Stern
Stage Manager

· **Figure 8-12** ·
Rehearsal Report Format

to use them, to be sure they will hold under strain. Twist the cables open to check the condition of the inside. If rotten, replace.

It takes constant vigilance to prevent carelessness and inconsideration from turning into serious accidents.

You should encourage all members of the staff, cast, and crew to report unsafe conditions to you, and you should take immediate steps to correct them.

Most large or long-established theaters are covered by accident insurance as a form of protection against suit by actors or patrons for accidents that occur on the theater premises. Most insurance companies want to have the same information about any accident that occurs (see Figure 8-14).

If your theater does have such insurance, make sure that you have accident report forms on hand.

In the event of an accident, whether or not your theater has

Stage Management

STAGE MANAGER'S WEEKLY REPORT

Location: _____ Week Ending: _____

Name of Theatre: _____

Violations by Actor

1. List the name of the Actor.

2. Type of violation (lateness for half-hour, altering direction, etc.

3. Indicate in column 1 if sufficient explanation given so that violation should be considered excused (E for excused, U for unexcused)

4. Has the Actor been spoken to about this type of violation before? Indicate in column 2 (R for repeated, 1 for the first time, 2 for second time, etc.)

NAME	VIOLATION	COLUMN 1 2

Violations by Manager

1. List only violations by Manager which he has not corrected after being informed by you, the Deputy or Equity.

Signed:_____
Stage Manager

7/29/68 Rev. 4/72   USE REVERSE SIDE FOR REMARKS   PO-5

· **Figure 8-13** ·
Report Form to Actor's Equity

insurance, obtain all of the information required in the illustration and write a brief narrative of what happened. Ask the individual involved to write his or her own brief narrative, and have him or her sign it.

No matter how many copies of the accident form are required by the insurance company, make one additional copy for your files.

Keeping a Do-List

A *do-list* (talk of redundant definitions!) is a self-kept list of things that you need to do. It is usually kept on your clipboard, but might just as practically be attached to the inside front cover of your prompt

EMPLOYER'S REPORT
OF
INDUSTRIAL INJURY

STATE OF CALIFORNIA
DEPARTMENT OF INDUSTRIAL RELATIONS
DIVISION OF LABOR STATISTICS AND RESEARCH
P. O. Box 5971, San Francisco, Calif. 94101

Every question must be answered fully to avoid further correspondence. FAILURE TO FILE IS A MISDEMEANOR SUBJECT TO MAXIMUM FINE OF $100.
(Labor Code, Sections 6407-6413)

Every work injury to an employee which causes disability lasting longer than the day of the injury or which requires medical services other than first aid treatment must be reported within five days after the injury. If the injury results in death, a report must be made by telephone or telegraph directly to the Division of Labor Statistics and Research not later than 24 hours after death.

	DO NOT WRITE IN THIS COLUMN
EMPLOYER	
1. Name (Give name under which concern does business)	Case No.
2. Office address (No. and Street) (City or Town)	
3. Nature of business (Manufacturing shoes, retailing men's clothes, trucking for hire, etc.)	Employer No.
INJURED EMPLOYEE	
4. Name Soc. Sec. No.	
5. Address (No. and Street) (City or Town)	Industry
6. Age 7. Sex: Check (√) Male Female 8. Check (√) Married Single	
9. Number of hours worked per day ; per week . Number of days worked per week	Age
10. Wages: $ per hour, or $ per day, or $ per week. (If earnings at irregular rate, such as piece work or on commission basis, enter actual average weekly earnings for convenient period not to exceed one year.)	
11. If board, lodging, or other advantages furnished in addition to wages, give estimated value $ per day, or $ per week	Sex and Marital Status
ACCIDENT	
12. Place of accident (No. and Street) (City or Town) (County)	Weekly Wage
13. On employer's premises (Yes or No) 14. Department	
15. Date of accident (Yes or No) 16. Hour of day A.M P.M. 17. Did injury result in disability beyond day of	
accident? (Yes or No) 18. If yes, give date last worked 19. Was injured paid in full for	County
this day? (Yes or No) 20. If injured in a mine, check (√) accident location: Surface Mill Underground Shaft	
CAUSE OF ACCIDENT	
21. Occupation (job title)	Accident Date
occupation? Check (√) Less than 6 months ; 6 months to 2 years ; over 2 years 23. What was employee doing when accident occurred? (Describe briefly such as loading truck, operating drill press, shoveling dirt, walking down stairs, etc.) 22. How long employed by you at this	
	Occupation
24. How did the accident happen? (Describe fully, stating whether the injured person fell, was struck, etc.; give all factors contributing to accident. Use other side of report for additional space.)	Accident Type
	Agency
25. What machine, tool, substance, or object was most closely connected with the accident? (Name the specific machine, tool, appliance, gas, liquid, etc. involved)	Agency Part
26. If mechanical apparatus or vehicle, what part of it? (State if gears, pulley, motor, etc.)	
27. Were mechanical guards, or other safeguards provided? (Yes or No) 28. Was injured using them? (Yes or No)	Mech. Defect
29. What do you recommend for preventing this type of accident? (State the specific preventive measures that can be taken by employer and workers. Do not say: By being more careful. Specify what should or should not be done)	
	Unsafe Act
NATURE OF INJURY AND PART OF BODY AFFECTED	
30. (Describe in detail the nature of the injury and the part of the body affected. For example amputation of right index finger at second joint, fracture of ribs, lead poisoning, dermatitis of left hand, etc.)	Personal Defect
31. Name and address of physician	
32. Name and address of hospital	Nature of Injury
33. Has employee returned to work? (Yes or No) 34. If yes, give date 35. At what wage? $ per	
36. Did injury result in death? (Yes or No) 37. If yes, give date	Location
38. In case of death, give name and address of nearest relative	
	Extent of Injury
39. Name of workmen's compensation insurance carrier	
	Insurance Carrier
Firm name Date of this report	
	Report Lag
Signed by Official position Signature	
Filing of this report is not an admission of liability. ". . . No report of injury required to be filed by an employer or an insurer by this chapter shall be admissible as evidence in any adversary proceeding before the Industrial Accident Commission." Labor Code, Section 6413.	Coded by

FORM 5020 REV 5 87484-801 10-71 10M △ OSP

· **Figure 8-14** ·
Accident Report Form

script. Anyone who has ever made out a shopping list can write one, and anyone who has ever made out a shopping list will appreciate the necessity for one (see Figure 8-15).

Your do-list should always be with you. Whenever staff, crew,

133

Wednesday

1. Touch up staples reflecting lights

2. weight bottom of flaps swinging in draft.

3. Call Norman on plans for ramp

4. Get sack of wheat paste.

5. tell Nick he won't be needed Friday night

6. Call photographer for schedule

<u>remind Chuck</u>:
1. mortar & pestle
2. Bring in III revisions
3. Call Ray 7:00 PM

· **Figure 8-15** ·
Manager's Daily Do-List and Reminder Checklist

or cast tell you anything that requires an action on your part, you should make a note of it. Any change of schedule should be noted so that you can figure out the consequences and deal with them. You will also want to note information that must be relayed to other staff members. Do not trust to memory. There are simply too many things to be done.

Writing something on your list implies that you will take care of it or see that it is taken care of. It is reassuring to a director to see you make a note when he or she asks for something.

Take time at the end of each day to review your list and to assess what must be done first tomorrow and what may be delegated to others.

Keep a special area for notes for the director. In doing so you will be functioning not only as the director's assistant but as the director's secretary. When the director promises to do something—bring in a prop, contact a scene designer with whom he or she has worked in the past, write a letter of introduction for a cast member who will be going to New York—jot down a note for him or her. After rehearsal, present your notes with tact. Obviously, if the director does not appreciate this, discontinue. You'll find most directors grateful.

Avoiding Rehearsal Problems

I'll take a few paragraphs here to throw in a little philosophy—the Gospel according to Stern—very little and not too deep:

My "Discipline of the Theater" theory is an oversimplification and may be stated very briefly: The play exists *only* on stage when the curtain is up. Prior to performance, the play exists *only* in the mind of the director, and *everyone* works to realize his or her concept.

In reality, this theory never quite works. Still, I feel that it is the premise on which everyone should work, and it is a premise that serves stage managers well in deciding what their words and deeds should be.

Play production is a process of compromise. From the first casting audition, the director may find that an actor brings forth an aspect of characterization that is superior to her or his original concept. Or, she or he may find that no actor really lives up to that concept, so the best available actor is cast. Either way, the original concept is changed. Compromise.

During rehearsals the director attempts to bring forth from the cast his or her concept. Actors experiment in early rehearsals and present the director with their concepts. Further compromise.

The scene designer talks to the director to understand the director's concept of the play and then supports the director by designing a set that will put the director's concept on the stage. It is the same with the costume designer, the lighting designer, sound designer, and all of the other creative people concerned with the production. In reality there are further compromises as the designers try to turn the director's inspired or approved concepts into reality.

The stage manager is concerned with this process because the inevitable compromises are sometimes preceded by confrontations that disrupt rehearsals or pre-production work and/or demoralize cast members.

Sometimes problems arise between the producer and the director. In theory the producer is responsible for obtaining the materials and personnel to make the play happen. He or she generally hires or selects the director. Thereafter, the producer is supposed to work to realize the director's concept along with everyone else. But the producer hires the director and can usually fire the director. In commercial theater the producer is concerned with possible loss of great amounts of money if the director's concept does not pay off. In theory, the producer should discuss and evaluate the director's concept before hiring her or him; once the producer has hired, he or she should go with the director.

In practice, however, the producer feels that his or her powers should allow him or her to influence the director, not only as to general concepts, but also with respect to specifics. So there are many incidents of producers directing over the director's shoulder—pulling strings in casting, changing designs that the director and designers have agreed upon, demanding that changes in the director's realm be made up to the very last minute.

Even if the producers do not subscribe to my oversimplified theory, they should honor some ethics of supervision:

1. The authority of any supervisor should not be diminished before his or her subordinates.
2. A person can only follow the dictates of one supervisor.

Translated into theater practice this means that a director and producer should never discuss their differences of opinion in front of cast members, staff, or crew. Once their differences have been ironed out, all resulting changes should be announced by the director. They should not be prefaced with any disclaimers, such as, "I don't feel this way, but due to circumstances beyond my control . . . ." If the director can't say firmly, "I have decided that . . . ," then she or he should firmly announce, "I have quit and it's up to the producer to provide another director."

As stage manager, if you should observe that producer-director conflicts during rehearsals are demoralizing cast members or disrupting rehearsals or work calls, you should call the director and producer aside and tactfully request that their disputes be resolved in private. It's psychologically hard to back down in public, but significantly easier to listen to reason and change one's mind in private.

Theater is not a democratic process in which the producer and director debate and then resolve their differences by a vote of the cast.

It is always preferable to anticipate such problems and to discuss problem solving procedures at early staff meetings before they erupt into rehearsal delays.

Playwright at Work

What happens when the playwright is present? The play still exists in only one place prior to the curtain's rise—in the director's mind. I know this sounds improbable, and I've never met a playwright who could accept it. But once the playwright commits her or his work to paper and the producer turns it over to the director, the play is a concept in the director's mind.

Of course, some changes can and should be made as the playwright and director see the play come to life. But the playwright should go through the director privately to work on changes and should not communicate directly with the cast. The director should also suggest changes to the playwright privately.

I have seen playwrights angrily interrupt rehearsals because an actor paraphrased a line. I have seen casts thoroughly demoralized by director-playwright conflicts during rehearsals. If you are going into any production in which the playwright will be allowed in the rehearsal area, please discuss in advance with the director, playwright, and producer what procedures will be used to resolve disputes, and particularly *where* disputes will be handled—in private and outside the rehearsal area, I hope.

I have the greatest respect for playwrights. None of us could work without their words and ideas. But I believe that if they cannot accept the principles above, they should write novels or greeting cards, or direct their own plays.

[Another rule that I would like to see accepted by playwrights, I have the decency to put in brackets because I know that this is a book on stage management and not on playwriting or directing: Every director should have the right to cut 5 percent of a playwright's lines without negotiation. There isn't a play by Shakespeare, Eugene O'Neill, Arthur Miller, Tennessee Williams, or Neil Simon that could not survive a 5 percent cut easily. It's hard for playwrights to see this.

[I find that inexperienced playwrights become emotionally involved—love!—with their every word, article, and comma. Directors bring a different perspective to a script. Experienced directors know instinctively when action is bogging down in verbage, when a scene is not playing. They don't need to wait for audience reaction to know.

137

[When it comes to discussions or arguments between playwright and director, the playwright can always rationalize every syllable that he or she has committed to paper. "It reveals character." "It'll get a laugh." "It advances the plot." "It foreshadows." The playwright knows all the good writing craft reasons why every word is immortal. The director knows only that those immortal words don't play.

[If the playwright doesn't trust the director enough with his or her baby to allow the director to change the diapers, he or she ought to find another director.

[But this is not a book on directing or playwriting, and stage managers do not make rules for the relationship between directors and playwrights; they only make things run smoothly by getting an understanding of what the rules are, and insuring that everyone knows them.

[Sometimes actors approach a playwright to ask if they are giving the playwright the interpretation of the role he or she wants. Actually the actors are looking for reassurance or seeking praise. The playwright launches into a discussion of characterization, completely confusing the actor, not only by giving specifics that conflict with the director's but also by talking an entirely different language. Playwrights should have a stock of supportive generalizations to offer insecure actors: "I really appreciate all the hard work you are putting into this production." "I really admire the way you take direction." "I'm very well pleased with the way the director is interpreting my work and the way the cast is supporting her interpretation."

[The best time for the playwright to clarify his or her intent is when he or she is writing the play. If it isn't in the script, he or she shouldn't expect his or her presence at rehearsals to put it on the stage. If he or she must have contact with the cast, he or she may give extensive notes at an early reading. But when the director and cast are in blocking, pacing, and polishing rehearsals, all further changes and clarifications should be discussed between the playwright and the director privately and then any agreed upon changes should issue from the director.]

A "no more changes" deadline should be established at an early staff meeting. Additionally, playwrights should understand that the later changes are made in rehearsals, the less chance there is for a polished performance.

Stage managers who are new to their work or are working with a new company should raise the issue of change procedures at the very first production meeting to arrive at an understanding among director, producer, and playwright. Tell them that you or your fellow stage managers have had bad experiences in the past and that you want to prevent future problems by getting procedures spelled out in advance. If the playwright, producer, and director can't agree, or if you can't live by their agreement, find another job.

· 9 ·

Keeping the Cast on Time

You are (of course) personally so punctual that it is hard for you to understand those who are late. Your mental clock is ten minutes ahead of real time. You always feel that if you are not ten minutes early for an appointment, you're late. You know that you are being paid to think ahead. You plan ahead with master calendars and schedules. You work ahead of others, arriving at the theater before the staff and cast to open up and prepare for rehearsals and performances. You are never late. With that kind of orientation, and with punctuality so deeply infused into the fiber of your being, you find it difficult to comprehend how an actor can possibly show up twenty-two minutes late for a rehearsal. Yet it happens.

When an actor does arrive late, the rehearsal should not come to a halt while that actor is questioned. You should tell the late actor what page of the script you are on, or the scene if you are off book, and ask the late actor to take her or his place. The late actor should be advised not to apologize, but simply to get to work. If the late actor is not in the scene, you should tell her or him which scene will be worked on next, and ask the late actor to go over lines until she or he is needed.

Under no circumstances should you allow other cast members to sit around to wait for a late actor. Urge your director to do the scene that was scheduled. Either throw the missing actor's lines or have another cast member or understudy read the part. Make use of the time as best you can. Perhaps the director will allow you to check

141

your visual display of characters and select a sequence that can be rehearsed without the missing actor. If there is only one actor present on time, regardless of the minimum number needed to do a scene, start working with that one actor. It is important to the play, to the on-time actors, and to the late actors that work be in progress from the minute that the rehearsal was called!

At the end of the rehearsal period, you should discuss tardiness with the late actor, privately. First, especially in a professional situation, you should turn to your log in the presence of the actor and write the number of minutes that he or she was late. Ask the reason that he or she was late, and write it also. Then ask him or her to sign the log. In any case, confront him or her politely with the facts and ask if the rehearsal schedule was clear and if he or she understood what time he or she was expected. Ask him or her if there is anything you can do to help overcome the cause of the tardiness. Ask him or her if he or she needs to be called prior to the next rehearsal. If necessary, review the importance of rehearsal time, the fact that twenty-two minutes of tardiness represents over two hours of lost rehearsal time in terms of complete cast interaction, that not only the tardy actor but all of the other actors in the scene suffer, and ultimately the quality of the play suffers. Stress the positive factors, that early arrival at rehearsals allows the actor to review lines and to run lines with other actors, that the director is going for the kind of polished performance that needs every possible minute of rehearsal time, and that since this is also the tardy actor's goal, you know that you can count on future cooperation. In short, make it absolutely clear that you care, that it is important to you that actors be on time.

In professional theaters steps may be taken against habitually tardy actors through their union, but in both union and non-union situations you should try to educate and stress the positive rather than threaten and punish.

Directors should not have to discuss tardiness with actors. They should be able to rely on you in this matter.

Sign-In Sheets

As early as dress rehearsals, sign-in sheets should be posted. Cast members should be reminded to initial in, until they get into the habit (see Figure 9-1). Initialing prevents actors from placing a check mark in the wrong block. If they initial the wrong block, the error can be traced. Alternate lines of the sign-in sheet may be set up in different colors or in different indention patterns; this makes it easier to find the correct space to initial.

Please ~~Initial~~ In !

ALBATROSS

SIGN IN

	TUE	WED	THUR	FRI	SAT	SUN
Frank ALETTEr						
Jenny Gillespie						
Pauline Meyers						
Lee Meriwether						
James H. Sweet						
FRanKLin Smith						
MarGe Redmond						
Paul Bryar						
Katy Freehan						
Dick Ramos						
Ellen Webb						

· **Figure 9-1** ·
Sign-In Sheet for Cast Members

The sign-in sheet saves you work. It allows you to see if the cast is there by looking in only one place. If anyone has not initialed in by half hour call, you must check the dressing rooms. Then you must phone those who are late.

Placement of the sign-in sheet on the callboard insures that cast members will be close enough to the callboard to read any urgent new information that has been posted.

If you have a cast of two, you may elect not to post a sign-in sheet. If you have a cast of one hundred, you may elect to turn the sign-in sheet over to a gate man or stage door guard and have that individual check in the cast. You would still check with that individual for tardiness.

Calling any actor who has failed to sign in by half hour call (see below, "The Calls") is an important responsibility. Nothing should get in the way of your carrying out that duty.

Examples:

During a three-month run the home of an habitually late actor was frequently called. His wife always answered the phone and told the stage manager that the actor had left for the theater. When the actor arrived, the stage manager explained that he had called his home. The actor complained that the stage manager was needlessly alarming his wife, who would worry about traffic accidents until he called her to reassure her that he'd arrived safely. The stage manager's complaint that he was late and the actor's complaint that the stage manager was needlessly worrying his wife were frequently voiced—until the evening that the stage manager called and woke him up!

Opening night of a musical five principals and the director were late for half hour call. None responded to the stage manager's phone calls. The stage manager assumed that they were on their way. At fifteen minute call they were still not there. The stage manager alerted the house manager and the producer. Then a chorus member remembered that one of the principals had mentioned that they were going out to dinner before the show. The restaurant was called. They had been there and left—thirty-five minutes ago. At five minute call they had still not arrived. Now the producer and the house manager were pacing the lobby. An audience of 1,400 awaited, completely unaware that they were missing quite a drama. At curtain time there were still no principals and no word from them. The producer's guidance was, "Stay calm," but he was clearly upset. How could such a thing happen? Why hadn't they called? The stage manager was numb.

At seven minutes past curtain the principals and director arrived. Blocked road, train accident, waited to clear road, hemmed in by other cars, no way out, no phone or house visible to horizon.

At thirteen minutes past curtain time the overture began.

And that was the night that one of the bit players who lived next door to the theater overslept and missed his one line. The stage manager had failed to call him.

In a situation of complete pandemonium, don't fail to carry out your basic duties!

During the run of any production, if an actor is late for half hour call, she or he should be reminded that the half hour prior to performance is meant to be used by the actor to get into costume, makeup, and character, and to relax in order to store up energy for the performance.

Actors sometimes argue the necessity of being at the theater one half hour prior to curtain. They claim that they can get into costume, makeup, and character in seven and one half minutes, they can relax at home, and they have plenty of energy. Then too, they don't like to wait back stage because it's musty, crowded, etc.

144

Regardless of such arguments you should continue to expect punctuality. Call every time the actor is late and use whatever methods you can to convince the actor to be at the theater for half hour call.

Should an actor who drives for forty-five minutes to get to the theater still have the same call as other cast members? Should you call that actor's home forty-five minutes prior to curtain to assure yourself that the actor is on the way? What if that same actor does not appear until fifteen minutes into the first act?

Should another actor who does not appear until the third act be granted a late call? Should an actress who puts on her makeup and costume at home to avoid using the overcrowded dressing room be allowed to sign in after half hour call?

These are but a few of the practical questions that will come up. To answer them you must ask yourself: Can I help insure that this actor will get to the theater on time? Can I insure that the cast will not be rushed in putting on makeup, getting into costume and into character? Can I assure myself that I will have adequate time to call actors and still carry out my other pre-curtain duties?

If an actor is ever granted a late call, the call should coincide with a period of time that you have free to check on his or her arrival.

The Calls

Calls—announcements of the time to the curtain—are given in order to alert cast members to how much time they have before the play begins. The traditional calls are:

Half hour, please.
Fifteen minutes, please.
Five minutes, please.
Places, please.

The first three calls are given thirty, fifteen, and five minutes prior to the announced curtain time. The "places" call is given after the house manager has turned the house over to you and when you are ready to run the show.

Notice that "please" is a part of the call. Don't omit it.

It is traditional that all cast members acknowledge your calls with a cheery "Thank you." If cast members are unaware of this custom, you might bring it to their attention.

In some cases the curtain will be delayed—last minute rush at the box office, bad weather, traffic and parking problems, late arrival of theater parties, etc. The house manager might ask you to hold the curtain for five, ten, or fifteen minutes. You should relay these holds to the cast with an additional call of "Five minute hold, please." If possible you should explain to the cast the reason for the delay.

At intermissions the calls are "Five minutes, please," and "Places, please."

Do not rely on a one-way speaker system from your work area to the dressing rooms to give the calls. You not only run the risk of mechanical failure, but you lose that bit of contact with the cast.

A two-way communications system is only slightly better because mechanical failure is immediately noticeable and cast members have a chance to respond. But a face-to-face exchange is much better.

Only if it is absolutely impossible for you to give the calls should you assign this duty to an assistant or call boy. But this is not a task that should be delegated. This is one of your more important duties.

If you cannot greet and chat with each cast member as that cast member arrives at the theater, you have all too little contact. The call itself is not sufficient. There has to be a little dialogue between you and cast members. The subtext is, "Are you all right? Can you give a good performance tonight? Are you overtired? Did you get too sunburned? Did you have too much to drink? Do you have a stomachache?"

There is very little that you can do to relieve the pains and suffering of the acting condition. But some hot coffee, a few aspirins, and some kind words can go a long way in boosting cast morale to performance level. If you are effective, you can make just a few words and a friendly, sympathetic smile serve as a mental rubdown.

Under normal conditions you are not expected to give calls or warns for individual actor entrances once the act has begun. Actors are expected to listen for their cues in the wings, or if available, on dressing room monitors.

There are exceptions.

Example:

A big name personality who had played the same role in hundreds of theaters in the round across the country had become so indifferent to the script and local variations in blocking, that he had to be led out of his dressing room by the hand, pointed down the correct aisle, and pushed on cue. He also had to be retrieved as he exited, whenever and wherever he chose, and led back to his dressing room, as he could never remember where the dressing room was. The stage manager assigned the big name a "seeing-eye gopher."

If you are a new stage manager, do not worry about gaining the respect of the actors. Just assume that you already have it. You do have it by virtue of your title and you will earn it by virtue of your work. Respect is reciprocal. The more you give, the more you can count on getting back. As soon as the actors realize that you respect them, you will also gain their utmost cooperation.

· 10 ·

Department Management
and Property Management

The Manager as Supervisor

Stage managers are called upon to work with, coordinate the efforts of, and/or supervise many theater workers—the builders on the "premises of illusion": set designers, lighting designers, technical directors, master carpenters, lighting technicians, crew members, costume designers, property masters, and others.

To do this, (1) they must first be knowledgeable about their work. They must understand the technical aspects of making theater. This they gain through observation and study.

Next, (2) they must understand their personal relationship to co-workers. As stage managers move from theater to theater, from educational to community to professional levels, they find the titles and relationships of the builders changing frequently. At one theater the set designer is the technical director. At another, there is no technical director, and the stage manager and set designer work together in supervising the construction and painting of sets. At still another there are both a resident scene designer and resident technical director, and the latter supervises both the stage manager and the master carpenter.

Despite the wide range of job titles and descriptions, and the

149

deviations in the chain of command, stage managers quickly find out who does what and who reports to whom by observation and through conversations with the staff (see Chapter Five).

Once she or he determines which of the staff are directly responsible to her or him, (3) she or he exerts control over their work. She or he acts as the foreman for the producer or management, coordinating their work through the master calendar and the schedules she or he distributes. She or he personally oversees their work as necessary.

Getting along with subordinates and managing their work is an art form in itself. Stage management is certainly a proving ground for this art. Here are a few simple recommendations for supervising subordinates:

(a) Take time to give your instructions with great clarity, making sure that you are understood, or that the director's or producer's intention, which you are passing on, is understood.

(b) Give instructions in bite size portions. Don't give a gopher twenty things to do. Give one, and when it's finished, then give the next.

(c) Don't give an individual more work than you feel confident he or she can accomplish. If you expect that he or she will need more labor or more time than immediately available, explain that you only expect him or her to make a start on the work.

(d) Deliver instruction with calmness and self-confidence.

(e) Follow up on the work you assign, checking on problems and reviving interest in projects as necessary by showing your interest and appreciation. Re-emphasize goals when the enthusiasm of your subordinates is flagging.

(f) Whenever you assign work, remember that the responsibility for its completion remains with you.

Additional comments on getting along with others and supervising department heads may be found in Chapter Two.

Supervision of Department Heads

In the course of your work you are likely to be supervising the property manager, but you may also be asked to supervise a few other department heads—sometimes the costumer and sometimes the technical director.

If so, during the rehearsal period you will want to see that the department heads (a) are working, (b) are on schedule, and (c) have not run into any "insurmountable" problems.

(a) Department heads and their assistants don't usually punch clocks. But if they are not there to do the work, the production will not be able to open on time. You informally make the rounds to see if the staff is at work. It may occasionally mean rousing a late sleeper or providing transportation for someone with an unreliable auto. When you make the rounds, you chat about progress on the current production.

(b) Falling behind on the schedule sometimes means that a department will need more staff. Can you send over an assistant, some apprentices, or your gopher to help the shop wire on the ornamental grapes that light up? Or will you have to approach the business manager because the costumer insists on another union costume technician at union wages in order to accomplish the costume work on time?

(c) Problem solving is frequently the same as listening well. If every department head feels able to express her- or himself to you, he or she will air "insurmountable" problems. In doing so, he or she will usually come up with the solution. If you should observe that the department heads themselves are largely the cause of their own problems, you keep this to yourself and praise their solutions.

By asking questions (What if . . .? What would happen if . . .?) rather than imposing solutions (You should . . . .) or placing blame (You should have . . . .), you tactfully get department heads to feel that they are in command of the situation, and the commander usually works harder than the guy who is merely following orders.

In supervision, tact can usually get it done.

Property Management and You

Regardless of theater level, the function of the property person remains the same—to get the props. Your usual function is to supervise. To do this you should know all aspects of property management.

In union theaters, the property person is paid for services. In community, educational, showcase, and children's theater, the property person is usually an unpaid volunteer. Some people do not consider working on props particularly exciting or glamorous. It calls for someone who is methodical and persistent.

Finding and motivating a competent property person is a problem that plagues many theaters. Sometimes when a property person cannot be found, you find yourself either working as property person or retaining overall responsibility for props and dividing the prop work among the staff and cast.

Whether supervising or doing it yourself, you should appreciate the importance of having props available for rehearsals.

Just as soon as the actors set down their scripts, having memorized their lines, they should be able to pick up their props. Using props early in the rehearsal period allows the cast and director to experiment and to develop suitable business. This is highly desirable as it may add immeasurably to the quality of the production.

Conversely, not having props on time leads to serious problems.

Examples:

Scenes may have to be reblocked because an actor did not allow enough room for his imagined sword.

The leading lady sneezes through opening night because of the bouquet. The wadded-up newspaper used as a rehearsal prop did not affect her allergies.

Property Person's Checklist

To help determine the extent of the property person's responsibilities, you might review the following:

Before Rehearsals

Before rehearsals will the property person

1. Be responsible for hand properties?
2. Be responsible for set pieces? Which ones?
3. Be responsible for obtaining transportation to pick up and return all props?
4. Coordinate with the director, scene designer, and producer to assure appropriate props?
5. Insure that set pieces arrive on time for the take-in?
6. Obtain hand props as soon as possible in order to give actors maximum rehearsal time to work with them?
7. Provide temporary rehearsal props for unusual or costly props which cannot be obtained until later in the rehearsal period?
8. Give a written receipt to lenders of props and set pieces? Note on both the original and carbon copy the condition of the prop and the intended date of return?
9. Coordinate with the producer, through the stage manager, prior to rental of expensive props?

10. Be able to give _____ hours per week for _____ weeks to this work?
11. Need assistance (an assistant property master)?
12. Report to the stage manager any difficulties that he or she encounters in sufficient time to avert a last-minute rush?

During Rehearsals

During rehearsals will the property person

1. Attend rehearsals to make notes of additional props, where and how props are used, which actors use them, and from which entrance they come on stage?
2. Bring in large boxes and label them by act or scene as necessary in order to store the props?
3. Set props for each scene fifteen minutes before rehearsal is scheduled?
4. Lock up or otherwise secure all props after rehearsals?
5. Draw maps of prop tables and post them on or above the prop tables off stage to insure quick, accurate checks of all props prior to rehearsals and performances?
6. Make maps of locations of props in each scene so that he or she can change or supervise changes of props between scenes?
7. Draw diagrams on stage surfaces (tables, bars, mantels, etc.) to indicate exact placement of props?

Prior to Performance

Prior to the performance will the property person

1. Check presence and condition of all props, and report to the stage manager? (usually forty-five minutes prior to performance)
2. Replace expendable items (water in pitcher, tea in booze bottles, telegram that gets crumpled, etc.) prior to each performance?

During Performance

During the performance will the property person

1. Change properties on the stage between acts as needed?

After Performance

After the performance will the property person

1. Check for return of all props to the property tables?
2. Store props between performances, providing secure storage for expensive props?

After Production

After the production will the property person

1. Clean or repair borrowed items to insure good will for future borrowing?
2. Obtain receipts for return of items borrowed, give notes of thanks, and thank contributors personally?
3. Be financially responsible for all lost props?
4. Keep a list of sources, and the types of props that can be borrowed from each, as an aid to future productions?
5. Write a critique of his experience, emphasizing problem areas, in order to help the next property master?

Although it is desirable, it is not necessary that the property person do everything reflected in the questions above. Rather than review the above list with the property person, you might want to give her or him just a few items at a time, or as much responsibility as you feel she or he can accept at one time. A new property person might accept more and more responsibility gradually but might balk if presented with the whole range.

It is necessary, however, that you and the property person come to a clear understanding of the property person's exact duties.

Property Forms

The two forms, "Borrowed Items," and "Acknowledgment of Borrowed Items (Returned)," may be used by the property person to control props (see Figures 10-1 and 10-2). When she or he picks up a prop, the property master fills out the "Acknowledgment" form and gives it to the lender. She or he then notes on the "Borrowed Items" form the program credit line that is expected and other information. When she or he returns the prop, she or he picks up the "Acknowledgment" form.

BORROWED ITEMS

_____ production of "_____"   _____

dates

Item(s) Borrowed	Date Received	Borrowed From*	Date (to be) Returned
1			
2			
3			
4			
5			
6			
7			
8			
9			
10			
11			
12			
13			

*include company name, address, phone no., extension, and personal contact!

page___of _____   Prepared by _____

LAWRENCE STERN
Production Stage Manager
555-3719

· **Figure 10-1** ·
Property Master's Control Form and Record of Borrowed Items

Receipt forms, found in most stationery stores, may be used in place of the forms above (see Figure 10-3). One receipt and a carbon are made out for each borrowed prop. The carbon is issued to the lender and retrieved when the prop is returned. The original is kept by the property master.

In some cases it is easier to use the prop plot (Figure 3-8) as a control form. If many copies of the prop plot can be duplicated, then they may be posted on prop storage boxes, placed on prop tables, and even given to cast and staff as reminders of the props they have pledged to bring in.

The cost of all props which must be purchased by the theater should be carefully recorded on the property person's expense sheet

```
ACKNOWLEDGMENT OF BORROWED ITEMS (RETURNED)
```

The following items, loaned to the_____production

of "_____" were returned on _____
                                                date
by _____in satisfactory condition:

1.

2.

3.

4.

5.

6.

7.

8.

9.

10.

11.

12.

13.

14.

15.

Received by:
name_____

position_____

```
LAWRENCE STERN
Production Stage Manager
555-3719
```
company_____

· **Figure 10-2** ·

Acknowledgment Form for Borrowed Items

(see Figure 7-1). For bookkeeping purposes, the property person might be asked to record expendable and permanent items on separate sheets.

Program credits and/or complimentary tickets are sometimes given for the use of props. Be sure to check the producer's or management's policy and coordinate with the program editor. In some cases the lender definitely does not want a program credit. Be sure to clear this with the lender.

As soon as props are used in the rehearsals, you should remind the cast to cooperate with the property person by returning all props to the prop tables when they are carried off stage as part of the actor's business. Otherwise the property person finds her- or himself searching the dressing rooms and even the pockets of costumes.

As a safety factor, you are usually responsible for, and must

Great American Theater
Date Nov. 24 19 63 No. 3873
Received Of Shiker Bar Furnishings Inc.
Address 1038 Bluedale Road
1 finished bar, 2 bar stools $
For 3" scratch Upstage End
HOW PAID | BALANCE DUE | to be returned Jan. 11, P.M. by us.
5X 820 Rediform | | By Eric Spelvin, PM

Great American Theater
Date Nov. 24 19 63 No. 3873
Received Of Shiker Bar Furnishings Inc.
Address 1038 Bluedale Road
1 finished bar, 2 bar stools $
For 3" scratch Upstage End
HOW PAID | BALANCE DUE | to be returned Jan. 11, P.M. by us.
Rediform | | By Eric Spelvin, PM

· **Figure 10-3** ·

Receipt Form Acknowledgment for a Borrowed Item. Note: Original is kept by the property master and duplicate is issued to the lender. Both copies should specify the date of return and the condition of the prop.

carefully supervise, the firing of blanks, even though the weapon is a prop.

When the property person is also responsible for certain of the set pieces—those which will be bought, borrowed, or rented, as opposed to those which will be constructed—you must make absolutely certain that all staff members know which set pieces they are responsible for.

· 11 ·

Supervision of Lights

You have checked all fuse boxes and circuit capacities, all lighting equipment and plugging locations (Chapter Five), you have worked out all light cues at the technical rehearsal (Chapter Thirteen), and you are ready to light up for the first performance. But before every performance, a light check must be run before the audience is admitted to the house.

To conduct this check, you normally ask the master electrician or lighting technician to bring all of the instruments used in the show to full. You then inspect the instruments to make sure that none are out. You must also see that the instruments are still properly focused. To do this you bring up one area of the stage at a time and check the effect against your area lighting diagram (see Figure 11-3). Then you check the focus of each special effect instrument.

If *gel frames* are changed in the course of the show for special effect lighting, you must inspect to make sure that the correct gel is set for Act I. (For instance, one spot may be used to produce both a bright sunlight effect flooding a window in Act I, and a moonlight effect at the same window in Act III by changing a gel frame during an intermission. You should inspect, as part of your light check, to make sure that the right gel is in place for Act I.)

The complete inspection of lights must be finished early enough to allow time to correct deficiencies without delaying the entrance of the audience. How long would it take you to bring in the ladder, set it up, trace a short in a cable, repair the short, and strike the

159

ladder? That amount of time should be allowed between light check and the opening of the house. Yes, it means an early call for you and the lighting technician at every single performance.

Do you have on hand spare lamp bulbs ("bottles") of the appropriate base type and wattage for your instruments? Do you have on hand appropriate repair parts and tools?

Here are a few examples of mishaps that properly conducted light checks would have avoided.

Example A:

On Sunday mornings a small theater in Hollywood was used by a religious sect for meetings. During one meeting a screen was hung to show a movie—from the yokes of two instruments set for a performance that night. The stage manager later supervised the light check and found all of the instruments to be working. But he did not check focus against his area diagram (Figure 11-3). Result: an actor who was to give his final monologue illuminated by a single spot, delivered his speech in virtual darkness while a nearby table was lit beautifully. The actor could not move into the light without mounting the table.

Example B:

In another incident, the light check was habitually late, conducted after the audience was in. The stage manager peeked through the curtains (extremely unprofessional) from his work area backstage to check the anti-pros (see Glossary), even though he could not replace burnt out lamps at this point without working over the heads of the audience. Then he checked instruments behind the curtains. Finding that one instrument on the first pipe was not working, he hurriedly brought in a ladder, checked the instrument by cross plugging, and concluded that there was a short in the cable. Quickly he replaced it with a spare cable and called "places." Unfortunately the play began with a coronation parade of the cast from the rear of the house. As they approached the proscenium, the curtain was to open revealing the throne. The stage manager cued the curtain. It opened two feet and stopped!

In his haste, the stage manager had run the replacement cable through the curtain rope. Subsequent repair had to be done in full view of the audience while the coronation parade looked on.

Example C:

The house lights dimmed, an actor delivered the first line of the script, and the director's voice came from the back of the theater:

"We don't have any lights. Check out the problem and let's back it up and start again."

The stage manager had not only forgotten to perform the light check, he had failed to insure that the dimmers were on. The house, on a separate dimmer, went out all right, but when the lighting technician brought up the dimmer handles for the first light effect, there was no light. The first actor to speak was to start in darkness, taking his cue from a sound effect. When the lights failed to come up, the actor continued, assuming that the lights were late. So the director had to stop the show from the back of the house.

Embroider this on your sampler: an ounce of leisurely inspection prior to the opening of the house is worth tons of rushed repair.

In addition to conducting a thorough light check prior to half hour call, you must check each lighting effect immediately after you give the cue. (This will be discussed in Chapter Fourteen again.)

If you are fortunate enough to be working in a booth in back of the audience, you will have a good view of every effect. But if you are in the wings, you must arrange for a view, resorting to peepholes or mirrors if necessary.

If the cue is not immediately followed by the anticipated effect, you must be programmed as follows:

1. Don't panic.
2. Did the technician recognize and execute the cue you gave?
3. Is there a mechanical failure?
4. Is there anything you can do to alleviate this problem? If yes, do it. If no, restrain yourself.

In the case of a mechanical problem that cannot be immediately corrected, the most important principle to remember is the most basic and obvious one, that the audience must see the actors.

Example:

You give a cue to bring up an area. The area comes up slowly to full and the dimmer fuse pops. The actors who took their cue from the burn-in (first glow of the elements), continue their lines in darkness. What should you do? Answer: give the actors any light you can, short of shining your flashlight at them from the wings. You might bring up adjacent areas in the hopes that the actors will find some of it or gain from the spill. You might throw on the work light. At last resort you might even have to bring up the house lights. If and when the actors have enough light to continue the scene, then see if you can replace the fuse.

The continuance of the play takes precedence over the quality of the lighting.

Preparing a Lighting Sheet

Prior to the technical rehearsal, you should prepare written instructions for the individual who actually pushes the dimmer handles—the board man.

In a union theater the lighting technician is usually the master electrician, a member of the International Alliance of Theatrical and Stage Employees (IATSE).

In a union theater the lighting technician is sometimes referred to as the board man or light tech. Sometimes you will be asked to serve as light tech, but this is not desirable. You should give the cues and should not actually handle the equipment.

The light tech does not need the entire light plot that you prepared to analyze the lighting problems of the play. He or she simply needs to know which dimmers to work for which cue, which direction, how far and how fast. You will probably want to tell him or her through the use of a lighting sheet (see Figure 11-1).

On your light plot, "light cue #9" may call for lights to come up in a small area around a doorway. To achieve this, the light tech will have to push up dimmer handles 6 and 13. The lighting sheet entry might look like this:

Col. One	Col. Two	Col. Three	Col. Four
9	6, 13	↑ 10	Bump up

Column one is the cue number. (It is advisable to reserve numbers one through fifty for light cues and number the sound cues from fifty-one up. This prevents confusion in warning and cuing.)

Column two tells which dimmer handles are to be moved. Dimmer handles are frequently labeled, each numbered or designated by the area or effect it controls, i.e., "Doorway special." The name or number of the dimmer is written on masking tape and placed beneath the dimmer handle.

In column three the arrow indicates the direction the dimmer handle is to move and the number ten tells how far it is to move. Many dimmers are graduated from zero to ten, with ten being full intensity, but there are other systems.

The fourth column indicates how fast the cue is to be executed.

You usually guess at your entries for columns three and four prior to the technical rehearsal, based on your observations at re-

LiGHTiNG   **SHOWBOAT ①**

Check RAMPS Off
House ↓ ½
CondUctors SPot ↑

{ House ↓ O
{ Conductors Spot ↓ ← trail

1 BlUE GEN ↑ **7**
   BLUE X RayS **7**

1a PooL 7 ↑ 8
_____

1b Pool I ↑ 8
_____

PooL 7 ↓ O **THEN POOL 1 ↓O**

1c 1,2,3,4,5 ↑ 5 VERY GRadUAL faDE
   OCs ↑ 5
   AproNS ↑ 5
   PiNK GEN ↑ 4
   ~~Pools~~ ↓O ←When you can

1d Blue GEN ↓ O ⎤
   Blue X RayS ↓ O ⎥
   1,2,3,4,5 ↑ F ⎬ X FaDE VerY SLow
   OCs ↑ F ⎥
   ApRONS ↑ F ⎥
   PiNK GEn ↑ F ⎦

2 Ramp, AisLe, PooL 7 ↑ F

· **Figure 11-1** ·
Lighting Sheet Instructions for Technicians,
Extracted from Light Plot

hearsals. During the tech the director approves or refines each cue and you insure that the light tech makes corrections on the lighting sheet. At this point you rarely update your light plot; instead you write final cue factors in bold marking pen on each final horizontal cue line in your prompt script (see Chapter Fourteen and Figure 14-2).

Leave room between entries on your light sheet so that additional cues may be written in during the tech. If you number ahead (instead of during the tech) you will have to use fractions to indicate additional cues, i.e., "Warn 9½."

Several cues which happen in a fast sequence should be numbered as a series:

Col. One	Col. Two	Col. Three	Col. Four
9a	6, 13	↑10	Bump up
9b	1, 2, 3, 4, 5	↑ 8	Fast
9c	6, 13	↓ 8	Imperceptibly

There is no time to give warns between cues. So you warn once with, "Warn series nine," and give your cues as, "Go A, go B, go C." When the light tech sees a series cue, he or she knows that he or she must execute the whole series without taking time to check each single cue between each execution.

The light tech usually takes the speed of the cue from your hand signal; that is, he or she moves the dimmer handle at the same speed as you move your hand in giving the cue. Entries in column four simply prepare the light tech for the speed that will be expected. Some commonly used terms are:

Bump up	Up as fast as possible, opposite of a blackout.
Fade up	Gradual.
Cross fade	Take two cues simultaneously, one coming in, one going out.
Lag fade	Start first cue, take second as soon as the first is perceptible.
Fade in (7)	Move dimmer handle on a count of seven.
Imperceptible fade	Move dimmer handle so slowly that change in effect is not noticeable.
Blackout	Take out as fast as possible.

Whatever words communicate your exact intentions to the light tech are the right ones to use.

Entries in column four should correspond to the notes that you write in bold marking pen on the final cue lines in your prompt script to remind yourself of the desired effect.

Rather than using sheets of paper, some light technicians prefer to work from a deck of 3 × 5″ note cards with one cue, or a series cue, on each card. You might discuss this with the lighting technician prior to making out the lighting sheet.

In some cases the lighting designer will prepare the lighting sheet if he or she is provided with the light plot or a script and thereby knows all of the cue lines and numbers. In some cases the lighting technician can prepare his or her own light sheet or deck during a tech call preceding the tech rehearsal, or even during the technical rehearsal (see Chapter Thirteen). If you do not actually write out the lighting sheet, you must insure that it is done properly.

Re-Geling Plans/Lighting Schedule

You've just finished your light check, found one lamp out in an instrument and one gel in a special effects instrument so faded that it needs to be replaced. So you climb up the ladder to remove the old lamp, find out what size it is, climb down the ladder, find a replacement lamp and climb back up the ladder to put it in. Then you climb up the ladder to get the gel frame from the light instrument, climb down the ladder, hold the gel frame over the gel sheet, cut out the new gel, and climb up the ladder to replace the frame. Right?

Wrong. You completed your re-geling plan/lighting schedule at the beginning of the season and you know the watts, base types, and gel sizes of every one of the seventy-eight instruments without climbing the ladder to find out. Your re-geling plan/lighting schedule is indexed into your prompt script (see Figure 11-2). And you have gel patterns (see Figure 11-4) so that you don't need the gel frame as a pattern. You can take your replacement gel and lamp up the ladder the first time and save yourself a trip.

The main purpose of the re-geling plan is to enable the lighting designer to tell the lighting technicians what color gels to put into what instruments. This form will expedite the turnover between shows. So you want to be sure that the form is on hand and filled in up to date.

You are usually responsible for supervising re-geling for productions that run longer than the life of the gels, so it is desirable that you review the form with the lighting designer.

Area Lighting Diagrams

The area lighting diagram (see Figure 11-3) shows the areas on the stage where the instruments are focused. It may be expanded with

page _____ of _____ pages

RE-GELING PLAN / LIGHTING SCHEDULE

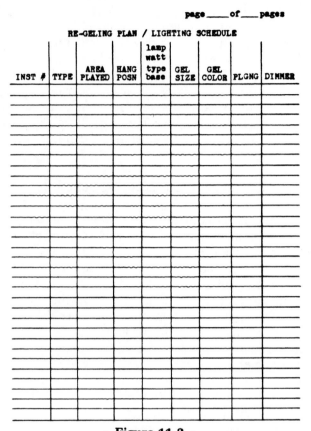

INST #	TYPE	AREA PLAYED	HANG POSN	lamp watt type base	GEL SIZE	GEL COLOR	PLGNG	DIMMER

· **Figure 11-2** ·

Format for Re-Geling Plan/Lighting Schedule

notes and diagrams to remind you where certain focusing is critical, e.g., the lighting designer wants an instrument shuttered so that the light is exactly on a door frame and there is no spill on adjacent flats.

In re-geling instruments, or during other work near instruments, technicians sometimes accidentally jar the instruments out of focus. Sometimes an instrument is simply not tightened sufficiently when initially focused and slips over a period of time. The area lighting diagram helps you to prevent such occurrences from affecting the quality of lighting in a performance.

The lighting designer usually makes a complex area lighting diagram for her or his own purposes. You can use the lighting designer's, or copy the important aspects of it. But for the sake of your familiarity with the lighting design, it is better if you make your own and then review it with the lighting designer.

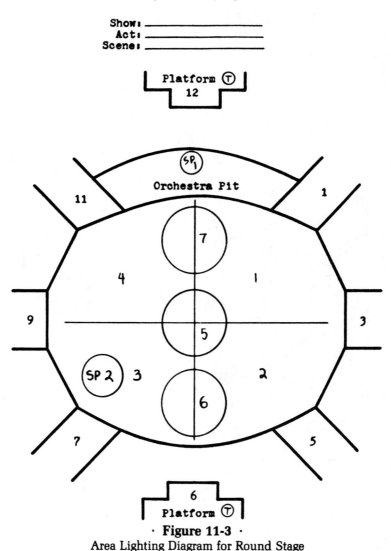

· **Figure 11-3** ·
Area Lighting Diagram for Round Stage

Gel Patterns

Gel patterns are usually made of cardboard (see Figure 11-4). They are cut to the size of the gel frames used in your instruments. If you have spare gel frames on hand for all the different sizes used in your instruments, you may use the spares as patterns. The advantage of cardboard patterns is that you can easily write on them the numbers of the instruments that take that size. The cardboard patterns are also easier to handle.

SHEET METAL FRAME
(for 500 watt fresnels)

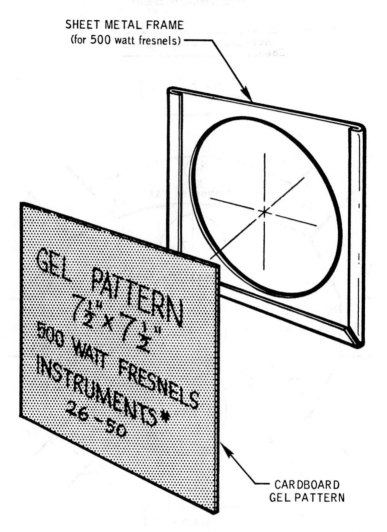

CARDBOARD
GEL PATTERN

GEL PATTERN
7½" x 7½"
500 WATT FRESNELS
INSTRUMENTS *
26 - 50

· **Figure 11-4** ·
Gel Pattern Template with Complete Labeling

· 12 ·

Supervision of Shifts

Find a way, when working in the round, to coordinate a stage crew of fifteen in making scene shifts, striking an average of five props and eleven set pieces and setting as many—in thirty seconds—in the dark—every twelve minutes—for one hour and thirty-five minutes—for a total of fourteen shifts. This is the type of logistical problem that can make managers lose sleep and eat aspirins.

Shift Plot Charts

A shift plot chart (see Figure 12-1) is a device that will help you in planning and supervising scene shifts. Although this technique (and this example) is primarily applicable to productions in the round, it may also be used for complex shifts in any theater. The chart may be posted in the scene dock and prop area so that the crew may use it as a self-briefing aid.

Notice that the top row lists the scenes, the second row lists the cue that precedes the shift, and each row beneath describes an individual crew member's responsibility in each shift.

Make your shift plot chart BIG so that it is easily readable. Allow 2½″ high by 3″ wide rectangles for each separate entry. This allows you to make corrections conveniently by posting halves of 3 × 5″ notecards over entries that must be changed.

Take Me Along – Act II	II-1 Barroom	II-1 BALLEt	II-2 & 3 Miller Home
Warn CUE	PRESET	he reads book in bed. Thus spa Kezara- Thustra Blackout	Ballet Ends... Blackout
George Ray IATSE 1	↓7 (4:00) Strike piano, set birdcage(2) SET Bikbox(9)	1st ↓ 5 Set Bird(your) Strike piano (w·Bill) ↑5	1st ↓1 SET DESK (2:00) strike Footpot(3) 1↑
Dennis IATSE 2	↓7 set bar (10:00) Strike porch(7) ↑7 W/Harold	1st ↓ 11 Strike Bar w/ Harold ↑↓ 11	1st ↓ 5 SET Porch (5:00) W/HAL ↑7
Harold IATSE 3	↓7 10:00 Set bar (w Dennis) Strike porch(7) ↑ 7 W/Dennis	2nd ↓ 11 Strike bar w/ Dennis 11↑	2nd ↓ 5 SET porch (5:00 W/Dennis ↑ 7
BILL C.	↓7 w/Mike set Piano stool Strike chair (2:00 To Rch Hall	2nd ↓ 5 strike piano w/George 5↑	3rd ↓ 7 SET Window st. (6:00) Strike chairs ↑ #1
MIKE	↓7 (1:00) set 2 chairs Strike Table (3) To Rch Hall	1st ↓ 1 Strike Table ↑1	3rd ↓ 11 SET, TABLE (11:30) & chair ↑7
Wally	GATE TENT	2nd ↓ 1 Strike 2 chairs ↑	2nd ↓ 11 SET Chair (12:00) ↑↓ Flyman Drop BKT.
WAYNE	GUARD INSIDE TENT	SET Dry ice IN Bucket (9:00)	3rd ↓ 11 SET STEPS (11:00) ↑ 11

· **Figure 12-1** ·
Shift Plot Chart for Several Crew Members

Notice that each entry gives the following information (for an "in the round" production):

A. Aisle traveled to reach the stage (e.g., 1st down 11; the number 11 means the aisle at 11 o'clock if the stage is compared to the face of a clock with the orchestra pit at 12 o'clock).

B. Order number on which to travel (e.g., 1st down 11; if a

II-4 BEDROOM	II-5 & 6 BEACH	II 7 & 8 Miller Home	AFTER PERFORMANCE
"Staying YOUNG" reprise BLACKOUT	HEllo, Operator PHONE Light out	SCRUMPTIOUS! Short: 9:00 reprise BlackOUT	WHEN AUDIENCE OUT
2ND ↓ 1 (2:00) STRIKE DESK W/WAYNE ↑1	3rd ↓ 1 set log ctr. ↑7	1st ↓ 1 SET DESK (2:00) WITH John ↑ 1	STRIKE LAMP (4:30) UNPLUG
2ND ↓ 7 SET PLATFORM W/HAROLD (Ctr.) ↑5	1st ↓ 11 STRIKE PLAT. W/HAL ↑ 7	1st ↓ 5 strike log w/Hal ↑ 5 During SCENE Move Trolley into posit.	strike lamp (11:30) UNPLUG
3rd ↓ 7 Set PLatform W/Dennis ↑5	1st ↓ 3 Strike PLatform W Dennis ↑7	2nd ↓ 5 Strike Log ↑ 5 Move Trolley To Position	STRIKE PLUG (11:30)
4th ↓ 7 set bed open. W/Mike Strike F.Place ↑7	2ND ↓ 7 SET FIREPLACE (9:00) ↑ 11 ⌐	2nd ↓ 5 set window seat (6:00) ↑ 5 Pull Trolley	
1st ↓ 7 Set bed w/ Bill Cook ↑ 7	1st ↓ 11 (11:30) set table & Chair (11:0) ↑7 AFTER WINDOW SEAT IN	↓ 11 strike F.Place (9:00) Pull ↑ Trolley 11	unplug (11:30)
4th ↓ 1 Strike Log ↑ 1	3rd ↓ 11 (11:00) set Steps ↑ 11 ⌐	↓ 11 SET LAMP (11:00) Plug in ← STRIKE TABLE(11) ↑ 11 ⌐	
1st ↓ 1 strike chair ↑1	3rd ↓ 7 Set 6:00 lwr. rail w/HAL ↑7 ⌐	↓ 11 Set small. plg. (11:30) strike chair ↑ 11	

· **Figure 12-1** ·
(Continued)

crew member is preceded by two others she or he is "3rd down aisle"). Controlling order helps you to choreograph the change.

C. Set piece or prop carried on and location it is to be placed (e.g., "Set table at 11:00"). The location designator is not an exact one, but is used to refresh the runner's memory when used in conjunction with "before and after" diagrams described below.

D. Set piece or props to be struck, and destination if other than

the scene dock and prop area (e.g., "Leave at top of aisle 11 for use in Sc. 5").
E. Aisle to exit.
F. Order to exit is designated rarely—when more than one large set piece must move up the same aisle, or when fast traveling light pieces must precede slow moving heavy pieces to expedite the shift.
G. If more than one crew member handles a single set piece, the names of the other crew members working on that unit are listed so that each crew member knows with whom she or he is to work (e.g., "with Roy").
H. If errors were made at any performance, you may put special cautions in an entry rectangle (e.g., "Watch out for hanging mike hit on opening night"). Other cautions might concern a false blackout or the rapid succession of two cues (e.g., "Hustle back to prop table for next shift").

Normally you wait until the take-in (see below) to make up the chart, because you must know for certain exactly where the set pieces will play. Since the chart takes so much time to make, it is advisable to lay it out in advance, filling in the first column (crew members), the top row (scenes), and the second row (cues) well in advance of the take-in.

At the *take-in* (see below), you see all of the set pieces on stage for the first time. You should handle each piece. How much does it weigh? Should more than one person be assigned to carry it? Can it be picked up easily, or should handles be added? Should wheels be built onto it, or can it be moved on a dolly? Can it be carried in some other way than intended—upside down, sideways? Should it be cut in two, carried down in sections, and fastened together during the shift? Does it have sharp protruding edges that might be a safety hazard?

At the take-in, you also make changes in your scene diagrams to indicate the exact placement of each set piece as determined by the set designer. There may be still more changes during the dress rehearsal, and you must continue to update your diagrams and call changes to the attention of the crew via the chart.

Immediately following the take-in you should be ready to make your chart. The best way to do this is by using cutouts of paper for the set pieces. Actually move the paper set pieces as you calculate who should move what and when. It is a fairly complex problem and errors are easy to make.

When there is time and money to allow for a crew rehearsal, all of the errors may be worked out by repeating shifts until they are "greased." (Also see below, "Crew Briefing.") But, as often happens, when crew rehearsal and dress rehearsal are simultaneous and the producer must justifiably use all available time for the cast and orchestra which the audience will see and hear, rather than for the crew, which the audience should not see or hear, shifts must be corrected and "greased" by debriefing, that awkward process of trying to talk through what happened and visualize what changes should be made. The shift plot chart and the scene diagrams are invaluable in this process.

What sometimes happens in a union situation is that after Act I and part of Act II have consumed the entire dress rehearsal call, the producer opts to finish the rehearsal by putting the cast and orchestra on overtime; but she or he sends the union crew members home in order to save money. You then carry out the remaining shifts with any hands available, and find yourself in the unenviable position of running some of the shifts with actual personnel involved for the first time on opening night—briefing union crew members during the scene for their moves at the end of the scene. Can you imagine the pressured chaos? The preciseness and accuracy of your shift plot chart are really significant factors in running those "no rehearsal" shifts.

The chart should be posted prior to the first crew rehearsal and each member of the crew should jot down her or his moves from the chart so that she or he does not have to check the chart between each scene shift. This can save a lot of walking if she or he has two consecutive moves up and down an aisle that is 180 degrees away from the aisle leading to the scene dock.

If you desire, you may issue each crew member a complete strike/set order (see Figure 12-2). This order would take the place of the individual crew member's notes and theoretically make it unnecessary to post the shift plot chart. Unfortunately, this type of strike/set order gets lost or left in other pants. Then the crew member has to have some reference from which to copy. So you still need the chart.

Take-In

Coordinating with the scene designer and technical director, you share in supervision of the *take-in*.

The take-in is a procedure in which all of the set pieces and scenery are brought from storage, the shop and the scene dock, and set up on stage for the first time. This allows the scene designer, technical director, and you to assess your progress and problems in turning the scene designer's sketches into illusion.

TAKE ME ALONG

SET/STRIKE
ORDER for George Spelvin (IATSE 1)

ACT SCENE CUE	ENTER	SET/STRIKE/DO	EXIT
Preset		Set desk 2:00 Lay trolley track.	
I-2 "Oh, Please" reprise!!!!! blackout	First down one	Set porch rail 3:00 Strike desk 2:00 with Wayne	Up One
I-3 "I wish we still belonged to England." blackout	Second down Five	Set Lamp 4:30 PLUG IT IN!!!!!!!!!!! Strike porch rail (to rehearsal hall, not scene dock)	Up One

· **Figure 12-2** ·
A Set/Strike Order with Typical Entries

Your responsibility is to get enough hands out to move the scenery quickly so that the take-in may be completed as soon as possible without wearing out the participants. As usual, many hands make light work.

Your work during the take-in has been described above as part of your preparation for making the shift plot chart (Figure 12-1). Again, you must personally handle all of the set pieces and scenery so that you know what problems your crew members will encounter.

Crew Briefing

Generally you brief the whole crew prior to their first rehearsal. A handout to the crew is helpful in passing on important points that you've learned from experience (see Figure 12-3).

ATTENTION CREW

1. Shake hands with your new crew members. The crew is a team. Everyone must know everyone else - and be able to depend on him.

2. Think of the stage as a clock. The orchestra pit is at 12 o'clock. Aisles 1, 3, 5, 7, 9, and 11 are relative - one o'clock, three o'clock, etc.

3. The Shift plot chart and diagrams of "before and after" positions of all props, set pieces and scenery are located above and on the prop table. Study them at your conv. If you don't understand, ask the SM, George Spelvin, or IATSE crew chief, Nate Spelvin, to explain it to you.

4. Follow these rules PLEASE!
   A. Don't run.
   B. Crouch at the bottom of aisles behind sight lines anticipating the blackout noiselessly.
   C. Watch out for audience moving on blackouts.
   D. Don't hit hanging mikes with tall units.
   E. Stay out of the tent when not doing your thing.
   F. Stash all props and units in scene dock prior to intermission and after show so that audience can't trip over them.
   G. Move pointed units base first so as not to stab audience members.
   H. Don't mingle with audience during intermission.
   I. Don't call attention to yourself.
   J. No talking or noise while you work or wait.
   K. Report any accident to the SM.

5. Please wear black polo shirts and black <u>full</u> length pants. Black tennis shoes and sox are available (free) from the costume mistress.

6. Maintain a clear aisle of 2' in front of the prop table. Don't set any units on that area painted yellow.

7. Report any damage to any prop or unit to the property master or crew chief as soon as practical.

8. Check each night for red markings on the shift plot chart. Changes in your strike/set duties are indicated by the entire rectangle outlined in red. Study the change and discuss it with the crew chief. Red X's indicate errors made;red cautions advise you how to prevent repetitions of the error.

9. You are expected to check in with the gate man at 7:45 pm SHARP! Don't be late. In case of emergency, call the theater, 268 3558, and leave a message with the box office.

· **Figure 12-3** ·

Handout of Instructions to Crew

A. Introduce crew members to one another and explain that you expect them to work as a team.
B. Cite general problems.
   1. Audience moving during blackouts.
   2. Hitting mikes with set pieces.
   3. Too much talking among crew during scenes distracting audience.
   4. Necessity of crew members staying out of tent or backstage area during scenes.
   5. Necessity of having all props, set pieces, and scenery in the scene dock prior to the show, during intermissions, and after the show so that everything is out of sight of the audience, and not a safety hazard.

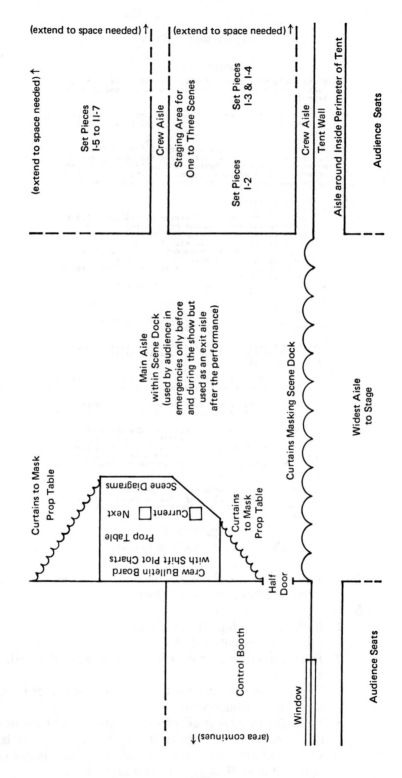

(extend to space needed) ↑

(extend to space needed) ↑

(extend to space needed) ↑

Set Pieces
I-5 to II-7

Crew Aisle

Staging Area for
One to Three Scenes

Set Pieces
I-3 & I-4

Set Pieces
I-2

Crew Aisle

Tent Wall

Aisle around Inside Perimeter of Tent

Audience Seats

Main Aisle
within Scene Dock
(used by audience in
emergencies only before
and during the show but
used as an exit aisle
after the performance)

Curtains Masking Scene Dock

Curtains to Mask
Prop Table

Scene Diagrams

Next   Current

Current   Next

Curtains
to Mask
Prop Table

Prop Table

Crew Bulletin Board
with Shift Plot Charts

Half
Door

Widest Aisle
to Stage

Control Booth

Window

(area continues) ↑

Audience Seats

176

C. Explain clock system (for round theater) or stage areas if necessary, set diagrams, and shift plot chart.
D. Review safety rules.
  1. Don't run.
  2. Pointed set pieces should be moved base first so as not to spear audience members.
E. Review dress and behavior expected of crew.
  1. Don't mingle with audience.
  2. Don't call attention to self.

Scene Dock

The scene dock is the area in which sets and props are stored while waiting to be placed on stage (see Figure 12-4).

During the first crew rehearsal you should delegate the responsibility for arranging the scene dock. Perhaps the crew chief or a particularly alert crew member can do it. Depending on the space inside the scene dock, the arrangement of scenery and set pieces must be controlled so that everything is accessible when needed. If a crew member needs a set piece that is blocked by other units, she or he must climb over the other units and unnecessarily expend time and energy. The person placed in charge of arranging the scene dock should supervise the placement of returning sets just as carefully as you supervise their placement on stage.

Here are the factors to consider in designing your scene dock:

1. The main aisle within the scene dock should not be wider than the widest aisle down to the stage, but just as wide.
2. The width of the set piece staging areas should be just slightly less than the widest aisle.
3. The smaller aisles within the scene dock should be just wide enough for crew members to stand in.
4. Lines delineating the set piece storage areas should be painted on the ground.
5. Curtains masking the scene dock should open to the width of the widest aisle to the stage.
6. The scene dock should be as close as possible to the control booth so that the stage manager and crew chief can communicate rapidly.

· **Figure 12-4** ·
Scene Dock Layout

7. Set pieces for Act I, Scene 1 may be stored outside of the tent and then brought into the main aisle of the scene dock if there are to be rehearsals on stage. Otherwise they may be preset for the next performance after the audience departs.
8. Depending on the size and number of set pieces, they may have to be stored as far away as the shop or other storage areas and then rotated into the scene dock during scenes.
9. Although outside of the main tent, the scene dock should be covered in case of rain.

Shift Inspection

During the shift, you or your assistant should be on stage to supervise. If possible, do not assign yourself anything to carry in the shift. Keep your hands free to cope with emergencies. Attach your flashlight to your belt. Follow the crew onto the stage. Stay out from under their feet and watch carefully what they do. Check the placement of scenery, set pieces, and props. Make sure that every item from the previous scene is struck. Check that all actors who are to be discovered are in place. Check that all crew members have left the stage. For a round-theater production, signal the booth, usually by blinking your flashlight from the stage that you are ready for light and sound. Dash offstage or up the aisle as the scene commences. You should be the last person to leave the stage before the performance resumes.

Do you think you can do all of that in less than thirty seconds? Practice.

Scene Shift Diagrams

Diagrams of every scene can help if there are many scene shifts and many crew members. These diagrams are a visual aid that will help prepare crew members for their journeys down and up the aisles in a theater in the round (see Figures 12-5 and 12-6) or offstage to the scene dock. These sketches allow crew members to check their next move and refresh their memories as to the exact location and specifications for the placement of props, set pieces, and scenery.

You should post these diagrams in the crew area so that only two at a time are visible. Rotating your diagrams in "current" and "next" positions, rather than posting all of the diagrams at once, avoids confusion.

Show: **ShowBoat**
Act: **I - 1**
Scene: **The Levee**

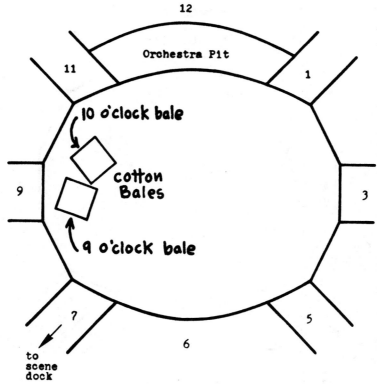

· **Figure 12-5** ·
Scene Shift Diagram: First Scene

Example:

The following discussion refers to a theater-round production in Figures 12-5, *Showboat*, Act I, Sc. 1, The Levee, and 12-6, *Showboat*, Act I, Scene 2, The Kitchen.

The shift from Scene 1 to Scene 2 calls for the dropping of the hanging unit, the striking of two cotton bales, and the setting of a stool, table, and chair—not considering props. How will you assign your crew to accomplish this one shift? Study the diagrams for a moment.

Here are some considerations:

A. If there is an experienced flyman on the crew, she or he should drop the hanging piece.

Show: **Showboat**
Act: **I-2**
Scene: **THE KITCHEN**

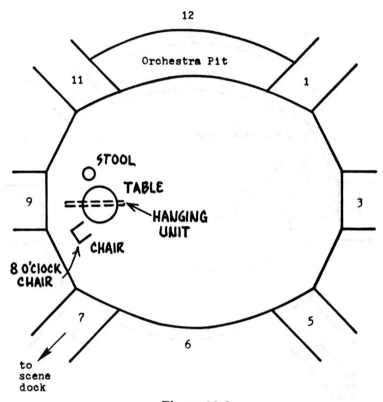

· **Figure 12-6** ·
Scene Shift Diagram: Second Scene

B. Since the table is large, two men should be assigned to it
   and it should move down aisle 7, the widest aisle and the
   aisle closest to the scene dock, thus eliminating carrying
   the table around the outside perimeter of the theater.
C. Since there are so few pieces to be moved, it will not be
   necessary for one crew member to set and strike a piece.
   Usually the fewer crew members used for a scene the better,
   as they have a tendency to run into one another in the dark.

In this case a stool is to play where a cotton bale is now set. If
one crew member is assigned to set the stool and strike the cotton

bale, she or he has to do the following: (1) run the stool down the aisle, (2) set it down, (3) pick up the cotton bale and move it aside, (4) pick up the stool and put it in place, (5) pick up the cotton bale and run it up the aisle. Yes, the move could be made this way, but evaluate the time and noise factors.

Or, you might have two crew members take care of the above cited units, with an empty handed striker going first to pick up the cotton bale ahead of the crew member who sets the piece that goes in its place. The striker might creep halfway down the aisle prior to the blackout and have the bale well off stage by the time the setter got her or his piece down to the stage.

Or, you may have the chair setter, not the crew member carrying the stool, place the chair at 8 o'clock and strike the 9 o'clock bale, to be followed by the crew member who places the stool. (Note that it is the 9 o'clock bale, not the 10 o'clock bale, that is blocking the placement of the stool. A set piece is designated as the "X" o'clock set piece according to its most easily discernible, if not exact, clock position. Finer designations, such as the "9:35 cotton bale," just don't seem to work.)

By now you can see that this simple looking scene change needs thorough evaluation if it is to be done efficiently. These are the kinds of details that you will work out with diagrams and paper cut-out set units as you make your shift plot chart.

The movement of cast members is still another problem with which you must cope. If at the end of I-1, the lights faded on two cast members standing next to the cotton bales, and if in I-2, two different cast members are discovered seated on the stool and chair, then there is the additional consideration of four traveling cast members during the blackout.

The general practice is to specify certain aisles or wing exits for cast exits whenever possible. For entrances, cast members usually follow crew members down the other aisles. During rehearsals you may remind the director to channel cast via aisles reserved for cast exits. When this is not possible for any special reason, you should note it and accommodate unusual cast exits in planning your scene shifts.

It is practical to select the narrower aisles for cast exits, as they are less convenient for moving large set pieces. Location of tent poles or other major fixtures in aisles would also be a factor to consider.

The importance of remembering exit blocking should be stressed to the cast. Obviously, a cast member who dashes up a darkened aisle in a rush to make a quick change only to find her- or himself blocked, does not need to be told twice.

Audience Caution

Members of the audience are usually cautioned in the program to remain seated during blackouts. In many theaters in the round the caution is repeated on the public address system prior to the performance. This responsibility usually rests with the house manager.

Distribution of Scene Diagrams

As soon as the scene designer has completed her or his design, scene diagrams should be made. Haste in this matter should take precedence over accuracy. In the course of building the set pieces and scenery there may be many changes. When the units are gathered all together on stage for the first time at the take-in and the scene designer sees what the set really looks like, as compared to the original perspective sketches, there are likely to be more changes, both in number and arrangement of units.

Yet if you wait until the take-in to make your diagrams, you might find yourself quite rushed. It is much more expedient to make corrections on diagrams with a bold marking pen than to wait for perfect initial copies.

The fastest way of getting the scene diagrams to those who need them is to have the scene designer draw the initial diagrams on spirit duplicator (Ditto) masters. The diagrams can then be used at staff meetings to help everyone understand the sets for the coming production. The scene designer, technical director, master carpenter, property person, stage manager, and assistant stage manager should all be issued a complete set. The producer's secretary tucks still another set into his or her files for coming seasons when the show might be repeated.

The property person uses her or his copies for preset diagrams of props.

The stage manager and assistant stage manager use their copies to help work out their shift plot chart. They note the cast members discovered in each scene and special effects lighting that is initiated during rehearsals.

The technical director and master carpenter use theirs to augment perspective sketches and line drawings in understanding where units are to play.

The making of the diagrams is normally a responsibility of the scene designer (but they have been developed with the director's and your views in mind). You merely see to it that they are duplicated and distributed.

Upkeep of Sets

After opening night you are responsible for upkeep and minor emergency repair of scenery, set pieces, and lighting equipment. You are not expected to reupholster a couch or overhaul a dimmer, but you are expected to patch, shore up, glue together, and generally keep the set fit for the eyes of the audience and the comfort and safety of the cast.

You must always have the tools on hand to carry out this function. Check to see that you have access to appropriate tools.

In the absence of a staff technical director, you might find yourself responsible for the theater's tools. If so:

1. Provide a secure, locked area for storage. Disappearance and theft can thus be considerably reduced. Temporarily, the trunk of a car can serve for tool storage if there is no lockable space in the theater building.
2. No matter how small your tool collection is, it is desirable to make a tool board on which each tool is mounted and outlined or silhouetted. This allows you to easily determine which tools are not in place. It is also convenient since you can always expect to find your tools in the very same place (see Figure 12-7).
3. Painting all of your tools one color can also help to deter loss as there is no possible confusion as to whose tools they are.

Example:

When transient crews come in to work, they sometimes walk off with tools thinking that the tools are theirs. At an all-girls' school the tools were painted pink on the theory that no self-respecting transient male would steal a pink tool.

In non-professional companies where the actors are called upon to help build and paint scenery, you can save the company money by closely supervising the cleanup after work calls. This insures that tools are returned, brushes properly cleaned, and paint cans tightly closed. Close supervision in the proper use of tools can also prevent damage to the tools, and accidents.

You should keep on hand small quantities of the paints used on the set so that you can do touch-up work without having to buy fresh paint that matches the original. Sometimes this merely means having the wisdom to save nearly empty cans of paint until the close of the production.

Photo courtesy of Mel Wixson and the Morgan Theatre.

· **Figure 12-7** ·

A Convenient Setup for a Tool Board. The toolboard above the workbench in the shop at the Morgan Theatre, a community theater in Santa Monica. Note that the tools are silhouetted so that they may be returned easily to their correct places.

· 13 ·

Running the Technical Rehearsal

The purpose of the technical rehearsal is to make a final confirmation and integration of all light and sound cues, special effects, scene changes, and curtain pulling. Every mechanical effect that should happen during the performance should happen at the technical rehearsal, and just the way it is to happen in performance.

It is during the "tech" that you will probably move from the director's side to your work area, usually in the wings, but possibly in a booth behind the audience.

Traditionally the tech is the time when actors stand around, holding positions while lights are refocused, or endlessly repeating cue lines until sound cues are tightened and sound levels are set. It is traditionally a rehearsal where overtime runs long and tempers run short. It need not be so.

The actors, who have rehearsed for weeks, meet the crew, who have possibly never rehearsed. The cast is impatient. They want to do their thing. They can't understand why the director, technical director, and stage manager are now giving their complete attention to the minutiae of mechanical matters that are totally insignificant compared to their performance. So think the actors. They can't understand why the crew can't get things right the first time.

You can most effectively shorten and sweeten the tech by holding a separate crew, and crew only, rehearsal of all the cues and scene changes prior to the tech—sometimes called a paper tech. Many of the problems of the tech can then be ironed out in advance. The crew will be able to do the work involved in smoothing out cues without the cast looking on.

Example:

On paper the light cue looks fine, but because of the design and arrangement of the equipment, it takes three hands on three dimmer handles to execute it. Who provides the third hand? It may take only a few minutes to resolve this situation by assigning another crew member to assist the light tech for that cue. But a few minutes at a "crew-only" rehearsal might save an hour for the cast, staff, and crew at the tech.

The real purpose of the technical rehearsal should be coordination and integration of light, sound, special effects, and scene changes, not the initial attempt at each. The tech should *not* be used to finish the design or devise the effects. If this distinction can be kept in mind, and if time, money, and union rules will allow you to hold a separate crew-only rehearsal prior to the tech, you will be doing a great service to the director, producer, and play by supervising that separate crew rehearsal.

If this is not possible, your burden increases with respect to planning the tech, anticipating problems, and briefing crew members.

The perfect tech is one in which the actors can have the benefits of a run-through while all technical aspects are polished as the play is in progress, or during breaks and intermissions.

This calls for good communications. If the director can talk to you, the technical director, lighting designer, costume designer, and other staff members without noisily interrupting the tech, it will go more smoothly.

Sometimes the seating arrangement of the staff can help. If staff members who do not absolutely have to be backstage will sit in the audience in the row in front of the director, she or he can simply lean forward to whisper comments. All staff members should have paper and pencil. You should provide them with adequate light so that they may take notes.

Since you have moved to your work area, be it backstage or booth, the director must be able to talk to you without running or shouting. You should try to set up whatever communications are necessary.

Many theaters do not have adequate communications. Some times you can improvise. Two prop phones in working order, sound wire, and a battery can be hooked up to give you some link. Of course, headsets would be an improvement.

You will usually need to talk to the lighting board technician, the sound technician, follow spot operator, curtain puller, and others during the tech and during performances (see Chapter Eleven). Ideally you should be able to talk to them via headsets. You should also be able to speak to the dressing rooms and the green room without leaving your work area. (A P.A. system that would allow you to reach the entire audience from your work area in the case of an emergency, monitor equipment enabling cast to hear the performance in the dressing rooms and green room, and a phone would round out most of your communications needs.)

In our age of technology, it is surprising that theater communications have been so neglected that these facilities are usually lacking or inadequate.

When planning for and scheduling your tech rehearsal, plan to give the staff, cast, and crew as much time as possible to work together. Any business other than the prime function of the tech should be relegated to other rehearsals. Directors should accept the fact that the tech is not the time to reblock or polish acting performances.

Cast members should be warned well in advance that they must expect to work late and that they must stay through to the end of the rehearsal.

There is a tendency for the crew to be concerned with their personal comforts and accommodations during the tech. Yes, it is important that the technician on the follow spot have a light in order to follow book. Yes, she or he should have a comfortable chair, since she or he has to sit there throughout the performance. Maybe she or he needs a pillow, too. And it would be desirable to run a phone line to her or him so that you can talk to her or him. But the period of the tech is not the time to take care of these things. They should be seen to before or after, but not while a cast of twenty and staff of ten are waiting to rehearse. Communications, lighting, seating, and other crew necessities and comforts should be anticipated and arranged. If these things cannot be worked out at a separate crew rehearsal, give your crew an early call for the tech and take care of these things before the cast and staff arrive. (See Chapters Eleven and Twelve.)

It is a good practice for you to run the tech by yourself, giving all cues to cast and crew as if it were opening night. If the show can be run as a run-through, do so, stopping only when technical problems make it impossible to go on. In the case of a very heavy technical show, you may wish to skip from technical effect to technical effect instead of running through. In either case, it is important that you have all of your cues clearly marked in your prompt script and all supporting paperwork—scene shift diagrams, shift plot charts (see Chapter Twelve), light tech's lighting sheet (see Chapter Eleven), etc.—distributed and reviewed with those concerned prior to the tech.

In some cases, you may start your tech rehearsal as a run-through and then, seeing that you are falling behind, skip through the remainder of the show from tech effect to tech effect.

If time permits, it is desirable to schedule two technical rehearsals as a safety factor.

The technical rehearsal is one of the biggest tests of your ability, for it is the one single rehearsal where you can save the cast and staff the greatest amount of time and energy.

· 14 ·

Running the Show

Now comes the easy part, the production phase.

The director tells you that it's all yours. There's an audience out there. All you have to do is run the show. You have some long-range responsibilities (see Chapter Sixteen), but your basic functions should now be firmly under control.

An interesting difference between new and experienced stage managers is that the new stage manager thinks of running the show as the most difficult and most demanding part of the job, whereas the experienced stage manager thinks of it as the most relaxing part. Perhaps the reason is that the experienced stage manager has built up work habits that make her or him so thoroughly prepared for the production phase that she or he just sits back during performances to watch that preparation pay off.

Checklists

Pre-curtain, intermission, and post-production checklists will help you to remember all of the little things you must do. These checklists should be placed into your prompt script facing the first page of dialogue, and following the last pages of dialogue, of each act.

A good approach is to think of someone replacing you immediately. Write out your list as if you were telling someone else what

Pre-Curtain Check List

7 P.M.	turn on air conditioning
Dusk	turn on marquee
7:30	check crew present, call late ones
	conduct light, sound check (incl. bell, buzzer)
	unlock props, place on prop tables
	unlock stage door, sweep alley, empty butt cans
	unlock dressing rooms, turn on lights, check paper
	supplies
7:55	final check of stage: sweep it, all set pieces
	in place, all discovered props in place, set hands
	of clock (UR) to 3:45 and check wound
	check all set pieces and props in correct positions
	backstage, ready for changes
	turn off work light, masking tape over switch
	bring in curtain warmers, house lights, cue start
	of taped music
	turn house over to house manager
8:00	give half hour call, check sign-in sheet (post
	new one on Wednesdays), chat with cast, close
	curtain to green room
8:05	call late actors
8:15	turn on stage monitor, give 15 minute call,
	check monitor working in dressing rooms
8:25	give 5 minute call, blink marquee lights
8:30	await house manager's signal to call places (or
	give hold to cast) - call places

· **Figure 14-1** ·

Detailed Pre-Curtain Checklist and Schedule

to do. Write the items in the sequence in which you perform them. Don't be afraid to be too detailed (see Figure 14-1).

Leave space between entries so that you can make last minute additions in sequence.

When you arrive at the theater, open your prompt script to your checklist and mentally check off each entry as you accomplish it. That way, when you call places, there won't be that aggravating question in the back of your mind, "What have I forgotten?"

In stock companies where you do a new show every week or two weeks, each day may bring both a rehearsal and a performance. Instead of pre-rehearsal and pre-curtain checklists, you will want to write out daily checklists covering your procedure for each day.

Your checklists, even if geared to a specific production rather than a season of plays, would be good material to pass on to the person who succeeds you.

A few items on your checklists deserve special comment.

Sweeping the stage, including the backstage walkways between the dressing rooms and the stage, is your responsibility. You may assign this task to someone, but you must make sure that it's done. Following the sweeping you should inspect for nails, screws, stage pegs, splinters, loose edges of rugs, or any other hazards. Only when you are willing to walk barefoot across the stage is the stage ready for the cast.

Besides checking to make sure that the worklight is off prior to curtain, you should check that it is on when needed, and that it is on as fast as possible in order to expedite scene changes and to enable the cast to leave the stage safely (see Chapter Twelve). Remember that the bright stage lights will leave the cast temporarily blinded and that they will need the worklight in order not to trip over set pieces on their way out. Even if the worklight is controlled by a separate switch, and not through the dimmer board, place the cue for it in your prompt script as if it were any other lighting effect. Call for it in the same manner that you cue all other effects.

Giving Cues

To run the show, you must signal or cue lights, sound, special effects (Chapter Eleven), and curtain, and thus coordinate these elements with the action of the play, making them happen at precisely the right time.

Your light pencil lines that identify cues (see Chapter Three) allow you to call the cues during rehearsals when you pinpoint them with the guidance of the director (see Chapter Eight). During the technical rehearsal, or just prior to it (Chapter Thirteen), you confirm the final cues in your prompt script with bold marking pen lines and number the cues (see Figure 14-2). Now you are ready to give the cues to lighting technicians, master electrician, sound technicians, curtain puller, and special effects people.

Following your script through performance, just as you did at rehearsals, you give the cues clearly, firmly, and with certainty. If you do not feel clear, firm, and certain, pretend. The new stage manager may be compared to a person just learning to drive a car; she or he is afraid to step on the gas pedal. The experienced stage manager, on the other hand, gives her or his cues with the authority of a marine drill sergeant, but in a whisper.

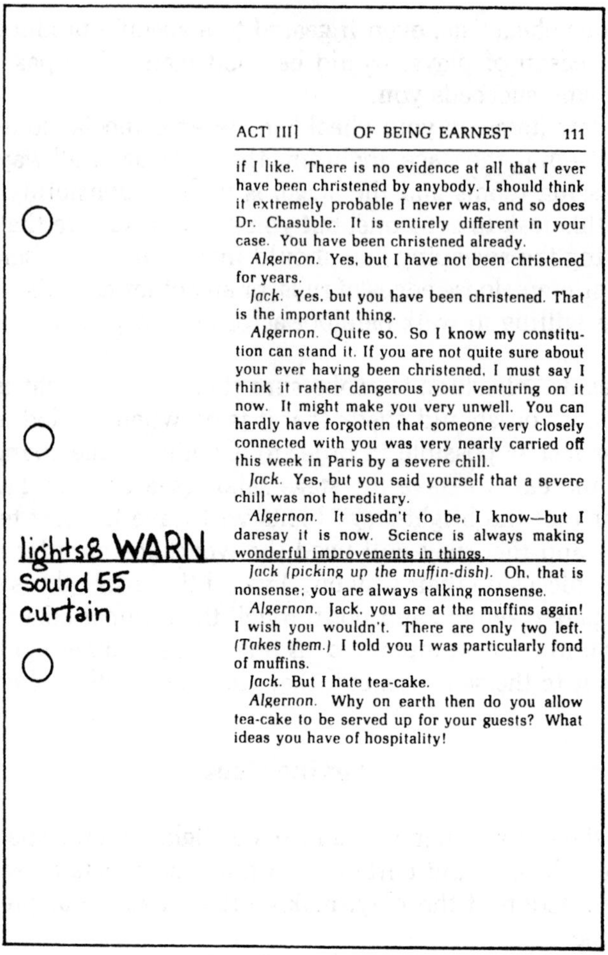

if I like. There is no evidence at all that I ever
have been christened by anybody. I should think
it extremely probable I never was, and so does
Dr. Chasuble. It is entirely different in your
case. You have been christened already.

Algernon. Yes, but I have not been christened
for years.

Jack. Yes, but you have been christened. That
is the important thing.

Algernon. Quite so. So I know my constitu-
tion can stand it. If you are not quite sure about
your ever having been christened, I must say I
think it rather dangerous your venturing on it
now. It might make you very unwell. You can
hardly have forgotten that someone very closely
connected with you was very nearly carried off
this week in Paris by a severe chill.

Jack. Yes, but you said yourself that a severe
chill was not hereditary.

Algernon. It usedn't to be, I know—but I
daresay it is now. Science is always making
wonderful improvements in things.

Jack (picking up the muffin-dish). Oh, that is
nonsense; you are always talking nonsense.

Algernon. Jack, you are at the muffins again!
I wish you wouldn't. There are only two left.
(Takes them.) I told you I was particularly fond
of muffins.

Jack. But I hate tea-cake.

Algernon. Why on earth then do you allow
tea-cake to be served up for your guests? What
ideas you have of hospitality!

Handwritten margin notes: lights 8 **WARN** / Sound 55 / curtain

· **Figure 14-2** ·
Final Cues and Warns Confirmed in Script
with Bold Marking Pen

Generally the cues are, "Warn," "Standby," and "Go." The warn part of the cue is usually accompanied by the cue number so that the technician will know which cue it is that he or she is to execute: "Warn number nine."

If there are sound and light cues in the same general area, you might want to clarify your warn: "Warn lights number nine." If a light cue and a sound cue are to be simultaneous, the warn might be given as, "Warn lights number nine, sound number fifty-three."

The warn is usually given one-and-a-half to two minutes before the cue is to be executed. This is usually a half page to a full page before the cue.

The warn should be given in enough time for the technicians to ready themselves and their equipment for the cue, check the cue on their plot or cue sheet, and give their total attention to executing the cue. If a cue requires extensive preparation—the patching of lines into a dimmer, the changing of reels on a tape recorder—then you might wish to write a separate tech cue into your prompt script to remind the technician to do this page prior to the warn, or immediately following the previous cue.

The standby portion of the cue should precede the go by five or ten seconds, giving the technicians enough time to place their hands in position, flex their muscles, and rivet their eyes and ears on you to await the go. Sometimes the verbal standby is accompanied or replaced by raising the hand.

The go may be given verbally or by lowering the hand.

The exact nature of your cues will depend on the communications equipment backstage, your proximity to your technicians, and their ability to see you and watch their equipment at the same time.

If several cues occur in a fast sequence and there is no time to warn in between them, you will warn and give standby for the series. Then give only your go, or signal for go, once for the whole series. If it is an extremely intricate series of cues, it is probable that you will want to rehearse it carefully, so that the technicians can get a feeling for the timing or rhythm of the series.

Again, all cues—warn, standby, and go—must be given clearly, firmly, and with certainty. Calling cues is another of your sacred duties, a *sine qua non*. You must be able to coordinate lights, sound, special effects, and curtain, and you do it by cuing.

Don't cop out on this responsibility. Don't delegate this responsibility. Even if the light and sound technicians can see and hear the cues and follow book just as well as you can, it is still your job.

Check the result of each cue that you give immediately. If you don't get what you expected, don't panic. Check it out calmly. The tendency is to reach over the technician's shoulder and pull a handle or throw a switch. But keep firmly in mind that the audience is much less aware of gradual changes than abrupt ones. Bringing in the correct effect slowly is usually more desirable than immediate correction of an improper effect.

Mistakes occur in every line of work. Don't allow an error on your part to prevent you from executing all subsequent cues correctly. Don't allow errors to compound. Get a hold on yourself and get the next cue right.

Musical Cues

In musical comedy, opera, and ballet it is often necessary that the stage manager read music and take light cues from a note in the score rather than from a word in the script.

In such cases the stage manager has a copy of the score and marks the cues in the score, spacing "Warn," "Standby," and "Go" as described above with respect to the time needed to alert the technicians. The stage manager might write a cue for her- or himself in the prompt script to go to the score for the next cue, including the page number of the score. Or the stage manager might place the score pages on which there are cues in the prompt script.

If you do not read music, tell your director and don't attempt to fake it. With the director's help you can sometimes get around your deficiency by using a stopwatch. Rather than listening for a note, you would time how far into the music that note occurs and then take the cue from the stopwatch. If there is a fast series of cues from subsequent notes, you would substitute mental counts for listening to notes. Sometimes you can look for concurrent cast movement rather than notes from which to take your cues. These are all cumbersome methods and learning to read music is preferable—and usually a prerequisite for stage management jobs in opera and ballet.

Equipment for Cuing

Should you use verbal and hand signals, or should you use a blinker light, hand held? Or should you wire in sets of red and green lights with buttons at the stage manager's desk so that you can communicate with your technicians? Or should you wear TV-type headsets so that you can talk to, and listen to, your technicians?

There is no best system. It's a question of what will work best for your theater. Expensive headsets won't improve the quality of your performance any more than closed circuit TV in the dressing rooms so that off-stage actors can watch the performance. More important than your cuing equipment is your consistency in using the system of cues described above.

Timing Curtain Calls

You must learn to exercise your best judgment in timing the curtain call. You should insist on ample rehearsal of the curtain call so that it will be as professional as the rest of the play.

Center stage

↓

Shirley-May, Vicky, Dave, JoAnne, Terry, Jonas, Arlene, Rita, Sandy, Norma, Larry,

Enter from off stage right on blackout in this order.	Move center on blackout.	Enter from off stage left on blackout in this order.

↓

Audience

1. Remain silent off stage while waiting for call. Move silently in final blackout. Join hands when in place.

2. Jonas is call leader. He will lead bows and give signal to break formation.

· **Figure 14-3** ·

Curtain Call Order and Instructions

The director usually determines the curtain call order and the effect he or she wants to create in the process of having the actors acknowledge the audience's applause.

In some cases the producer or the management will have a policy on calls for every play performed in that theater. The policy may be, for instance, that the cast form a single line, in order of appearance, left to right. The policy may be that they should take only one bow, regardless of the audience response. This very professional or institutional form of curtain call is hard on the actors' egos, since the stars are not individually acknowledged by the audience, but it usually results in the house lights coming up while the audience clamors for more. This is quite desirable compared to the call where the applause dwindles as the cast takes its last bow.

The design of the call will vary with the taste of directors and producers, ranging from the absolutely simple, as above, to complexly choreographed. I once saw a fancy curtain call add some zest to an overwritten and dull last act of a musical, thus arousing some applause, but this is a highly unusual situation.

Often the planning of the curtain call is left for the very last moment and then done in haste. You can help by making a careful diagram of the call order as set by the director, and by posting this diagram on the callboard (see Figure 14-3).

The timing or running of the call is another of your sacred duties. You must decide how often to bring up the lights and how long to hold them up. Judgment in this matter can come only from experience. You will quickly learn to sense how long and hard the audience will applaud. It is your good judgment that prevents the curtain closing to waning applause.

You should crank the curtain call cues into the lighting plot and rehearse these cues along with all others. It is disturbing to endure a long blackout following the final scene while the crew discovers that they must repatch before they can bring up the stage lights for the call. It is even more disturbing to see the house lights come up for the curtain call rather than the stage lights. We have all seen such incidents mar otherwise technically perfect productions.

When there is no curtain and the call is conducted with lights only, a cast member should be designated the "call leader" and given the responsibility of signaling the cast when to break their call formation and leave the stage. This will prevent a straggling exit that is discernible in the blackout. It also prevents cast members from breaking too early and being caught out of position when the lights come up.

Questions sometimes arise as to whether an actor is to appear in the curtain call and whether he or she must be in costume and makeup. Yes, he or she is just as obligated to appear in the call as he or she was to appear in the play.

"I have such a small part that the audience won't miss me." "I have a date after the show tonight and I don't want to keep her waiting while I get out of makeup." "I die in the first act and I don't want to hang around for two acts." There are many excuses, but no good ones. It is best for you to include a rule on curtain call participation in the company rules (Chapter Four) and carefully explain to the cast what is expected.

Walking the Curtain

Sometime during rehearsals you should have the curtain pulled while you watch from the audience to see how it comes together. If there are no gaps when it is closed, there may be no need to have it walked. But if crew is available, it is always safer to have someone walk the curtain—walk out of sight behind the curtain to insure that it closes smoothly and completely.

Some of the familiar incidents you are guarding against by having the curtain walked are these:

Examples:

The man on the rope hits a snag and thinks the curtain is closed. The actors are hung, waiting for the curtain to close completely.

An actor accidentally jostles a set piece, moving it past the curtain line. The curtain drags the set piece and finally overturns it.

Access to the Control Booth

Only authorized personnel should be allowed in the control booth. Tampering with, or unintentional playing with, sound or lighting equipment by unauthorized personnel could detrimentally affect the running of your show. It is best to post a sign, and enforce it: "No admission," or "Authorized personnel only."

Is the director authorized? It's hard for a stage manager to tell the director to stay out, especially if the stage manager has not discussed this possibility with the director prior to opening night. There is the tendency for the director to want to talk to someone during the performance, someone who will understand his or her anguish, someone who will confirm that all of the actors are not doing what he or she told them to do. Worst of all, the director wants to give last minute notes or make just a little change in some cue or effect.

If you and the director have done your work properly there is absolutely no reason for the director to be in the booth before, during, or after the performance. Make this clear in advance—that his or her presence would be a distraction. The same goes for cast members. Put this item in your company rules—you don't want anyone in the booth unless she or he is there to report a fire!

(Parenthetically, I don't feel that directors should give notes to cast members during intermissions. It's sometimes hard to convince a director that the urgent things she or he wants to say to the cast are not going to make that much difference in the second act. It's very hard to limit my comments about the director's behavior. I have to remind myself that this book is about stage management and not directing. From the stage manager's point of view, there is very little you can do to keep the director out of the backstage area during intermissions. You should discuss this behavior with the director in advance. "I hope you're not the kind of director who comes backstage at intermissions. I've found in the past that this seems to upset cast members more than anything else.")

· **15** ·

Working with
the House Manager

The function of the house manager is to insure the audience's safety and comfort prior to a performance, during intermissions, and after the performance. You must understand the house manager's function and coordinate with her or him in the total effort of assisting the audience to see the production.

Normally, the most important item in your coordination is deciding how the house manager may notify you that the audience is ready to see the production. Will the house manager call you on a backstage phone or intercom and say, "It's all yours"? Or will you run the show at a prearranged time unless the house manager tells you otherwise? How might she or he tell you otherwise? Should you synchronize your watches?

There must be a very definite understanding between you and the house manager. It seems so obvious and yet it is frequently overlooked. How often does the audience return to their seats to find a scene in progress? How often does an audience return to their seats to wait several minutes before the curtain goes up? The audience resents being rushed or having to wait and the actors resent playing to a moving audience. But it does happen and will continue to happen if you fail to coordinate with the house manager.

In large commercial theaters, house managers belong to their own union, the Association of Theatrical Press Agents and Managers

(ATPAM), 268 West 47th Street, New York City, phone 212-582-3750. In a small company, the house manager may be one of the actors, and may have several other duties in addition to house managing and acting.

In some theaters the house manager is in charge of the whole theater plant, box office staff, ushers, custodial staff, etc. He or she turns the house over to the stage manager for the period of the play only, and resumes total responsibility during intermissions and after the final curtain.

In a small theater, the house manager may double as usher, custodian, and assistant director. Halfway through the first act, he or she may turn all of his or her responsibilities over to the stage manager and depart the premises.

In a showcase theater there might be a different house manager every night of the run, and it might be your responsibility to brief each new house manager.

The following discussion of a house manager's duties was written for a showcase theater.

Duties of the House Manager

The house manager acts as the producer's or sponsoring management's representative in greeting and seating the audience. He or she should be well dressed. He or she should wear a badge or ribbon to indicate his or her position. He or she should display his or her best manners. The house manager:

1. Obtains the reservations lists from the reservations clerk and brings them to the theater. This enables him or her to handle future reservations at the theater as well as the reservations for the evening's performance.
2. Arrives at the theater forty-five minutes prior to the curtain. He or she insures that both the sidewalk in front of the theater and the lobby are clean.
3. Checks the condition of the seats and the audience area. Insures that all fire exits may be opened easily, and that alleys beyond them are not blocked. Answers the phones.
4. Greets and seats arriving audience, especially VIP's, and places reserved signs on front row seats for Otto Preminger, Mike Nichols, Rod Steiger, et al.
5. Prevents the audience from bringing food and lighted cigarettes into the theater.

6. Handles reservations problems: people arriving on the wrong night, overbooked audiences, etc. Holds people without reservations until all those with reservations have been seated. Helps people in wheelchairs to find the most convenient aisle space from which to watch the performance. Is alert to other handicaps among audience members and tries to assist if possible.

7. Watches for causes of audience delay—rain, freeway tie-ups, severe parking problems, etc.—and if he or she senses that the audience will be late, he or she asks the stage manager to give the cast a five minute hold.

8. When the audience is seated, he or she closes the back doors, walks to the stage door, and tells the stage manager that he or she may, "Take the show."

9. After the curtain rises, he or she returns to the lobby and seats people who arrive late, cautioning them that the curtain is up and asking them to be as silent as possible. (He or she tries to fill the house tightly from the front so that empty seats will be at the back for late arrivals.)

10. During the acts he or she again checks the sidewalks and lobby so that the audience will find these areas clean when they emerge from the theater during intermissions and after the show.

11. Finds time during acts to sit for a few minutes in the audience to check the temperature in the theater and to observe any audience distractions.

12. At intermissions he or she opens the back doors and outside doors to ventilate the theater. (Body heat and the lighting equipment may make the theater quite grim by the end of each act.)

13. Directs the audience to the rest rooms and the telephone. Insures that the rest rooms are clean and serviceable.

14. Makes any necessary announcements to the audience:
    A. "No smoking." (He speaks to those individuals who haven't read the posted signs and those who don't wish to comply.)
    B. Announces any unusually long delays in the curtain.
    C. "Lights on in car parked outside, license number EMR 223."
    D. "Is there a doctor in the house?"
    E. "Fire!" (The house manager knows exactly what to do to evacuate the theater. He or she knows the numbers to call for fire, police, and ambulance, and always car-

(Varsity. the Stage Daily. August. 1969)

**PROP BURSTS INTO
FLAMES AS PLAY
REACHES HIGHLIGHT**

(Varsity. the Stage Daily.
February, 1969)

**FIRE DEPT
HALTS SHOW**

Murfreesboro. Tenn., Aug. 15—Just
as Mark Antony was about to deliver
his "Friends. Romans, countrymen"
speech in praise of Julius C   - he
was left speechless when a f   *After a thirty minute delay. during*
out on the stage of the And   *which debris was removed and fur-*
Theater during a Rebel The   *ther precautions were taken against*
pany performance of the S   *the outbreak of any other fire, patrons*
ean play last night.   *were permitted to re-enter the the-*
                          ater, still smoke-filled, and the play
The blaze ignited a 1   *continued with Chuck Kitting as An-*
foam and fiberglass bu   *tony resuming his eulogy of Caesar.*
which dominated the Ja   *Most of the audience waited out the*
stage throughout the pl   *firefighting efforts and returned to*
veloped the stage prop   *watch the end of the play. The big-*
the rest of the sevente   *gest ovation of the evening went to*
ater before the eyes c   *five members of the Murfreesboro Fire*
tators.   *Department as they marched out with*
                         full equipment shortly before the play
Stage Manager   *was ready to resume.*
nounced what spectai..
knew. that there was a fire. and ask..
patrons to leave as quietly as possible.
More than a thousand spectators occupying three-fourths of the theater
building managed to file out without
panic. Shortly afterward four fire rigs
arrived to quench the blaze, although
stagehands and actors had already
acted to douse the flames.

**FLAMES CALL OFF
LIVING THEATER**
(Los Angeles Messenger.
February, 1969)

Performances of Liv
ing Theater at USC
cancelled after fire this
ola..

· **Figure 15-1** ·
Onstage Fire Can Threaten
Your Production Any Time, Anywhere

ries an emergency dime with which to use the pay
phone in the lobby. Also see Figure 15-1.)

F. Announces any cast changes and omissions in the program.

15. Times the intermissions and blinks the outside lights
and/or strikes chimes in the lobby and/or announces, "Curtain going up," to bring the audience back in. Closes the
back doors and the street doors at the end of the intermissions. Does not wait ten minutes to bring the audience back
in, but starts them coming back after eight minutes so that
they are seated and ready to go when ten minutes have
elapsed.

16. If there are doctors on call in the audience he or she takes their name and seat location and summons them if they should get a call during the performance.
17. Answers questions of departing audience, notes their complaints and suggestions, and passes them on to the producer.
18. Coordinates with the stage manager in securing the theater when everyone has left. Pushes up the seats and searches for lost items. Before leaving the theater he or she must conduct a sniff test (fire inspection) of every row in the audience and every room and cranny of the theater and dressing rooms to insure that no burning cigarettes have been left anywhere.
19. Returns the reservation lists to the reservations clerk.

Problems frequently occur when you come to your job from one theater and the house manager comes from another. You have different expectations of one another based on different past experiences.

Talk it out. Give it a dry run. Anticipate problems together. What will you each do if it rains torrents, buckets, and cats and dogs on opening night? Who will roll out the heavy duty mats in the lobby? Who will put down the planks in the gulley at the actors' entrance? How will the house manager tell you from out front that the rain has delayed the audience and that she or he wants you to hold the curtain an additional five minutes? Since there's no cloak room, where can the audience store raincoats and umbrellas? Does the house manager lock up the theater? Do you? Or do you both share or alternate shut-down procedures? If you share or alternate, do you both know exactly what is to be done?

Anticipate emergencies together. Review what you each will do in the event of fire, civil disorder, air raid, flood, heart attacks among the audience, animals in the audience, incredibly loud noises emanating from places unknown (see Figure 15-2), and hysterical patrons begging to be let out.

Rotating Duty Rosters

When there is no staff house manager and the cast must carry out the custodial duties, you may find it desirable to prepare a rotating duty roster (see Figure 15-3).

(Los Angeles *Bugle*. 1970)
LETTERS

Nuisance Noises

We recently attended the visiting St. Louis Opera Company's performance of "Aida" at the Municipal Opera Pavilion on December 5. In the middle of the opera we were severely distracted by pulsating drumbeats and musical sounds which seemed to come from the ceiling of the auditorium, as if they emanated from the restaurant upstairs. It was impossible for us to get a clear hearing of the last part of the opera. In order to be sure that the vibrations from above were not somehow imaginary, we turned to a neighbor for confirmation. "Good grief!" he said, "I've been fighting it since the second act." We wrote a strong complaint after the performance, but never received any acknowledgmer very poor taste on the part ment to permit conflicting this to be audible to patrons formances.

Morris and Art Faye
Northeast Cucamonga

Danny Bongo, public relations director for the Pavilion, admits there was no theater employee directly responsible for checking on such intrusive sounds beyond the first few minutes after the performance is under way. "Until somebody gives us the word," he said, "we have no way to be aware there's a problem." However, on December 5, a verbal complaint was made to a guard and, according to Bongo, the sound of the dance band was "totally sealed off" as a result by the end of the opera. Bongo denies that anybody involved received any written protest. But a similar complaint appeared in the Bugle's review of "La Gioconda" as performed by the St. Louis company during the same month here.

—The Editor

· **Figure 15-2** ·
Plan Ahead to Handle Emergencies and Surprise Interruptions

Example:

In a showcase theater situation where there was no budget for cleanup and maintenance of the theater, the cast was called to a discussion by the artistic director (one of the actors). They were asked how to solve the cleanup problem. All agreed that they were the only ones who could solve the problem, that they did not want to levy a tax to pay a custodian, and that their chief concern was an equitable distribution of the work. The artistic director then asked the stage manager (also an actor in the group) to set up a rotating duty roster.

ROSTER

	Thursday	Friday	Saturday	Sunday	Thursday	Friday	Saturday	Sunday
Albert Alvarez	A	B	C	D	E	F	G	H
Ben Blahzay	B	C	D	E	F	G	H	I
Charles Corn	C	D	E	F	G	H	I	J
Dave Dumpling	D	E	F	G	H	I	J	K
Earl Eastman	E	F	G	H	I	J	K	L
Frank Farley	F	G	H	I	J	K	L	A
Gina Glass	G	H	I	J	K	L	A	B
Helen Harvey	H	I	J	K	L	A	B	C
Ida Isely	I	J	K	L	A	B	C	D
Judy Jennings	J	K	L	A	B	C	D	E
Karen Kirsten	K	L	A	B	C	D	E	F
Louise Lehrer	L	A	B	C	D	E	F	G

A Sweep front sidewalk

B Strain sand in all four cans in lobby; move 2 outside

C Sweep/mop lobby

D Put all seats up; sweep/mop audience area

E Clean men's room

F Clean ladies' room

G Clean dressing room tables

H Sweep dressing rooms

I Clean Green Room

J Empty all waste baskets: rest rooms, dressing rooms, Green Room (trash can behind theater)

K Resupply all paper to dressing rooms, rest rooms from supply cupboard

L Dust lobby furniture, straighten

· **Figure 15-3** ·
A Rotating Duty Roster

The rosters were not posted in the dressing rooms or on the callboard, since cast members did not want their friends who visited after performances to see that they were expected to do chores. Instead, each cast member was given a copy of the roster. The stage manager supervised and also carried out his chores.

Cast members were given the option of carrying out their assignments fifteen minutes prior to the call, or after the performance. By doing two chores in an evening, one before and one after the performance, they could work on chores every two nights.

By inviting the cast to participate in solving the problem, the artistic director gained their cooperation. If he had simply ordered the roster posted, it might not have worked as well as it did. A few

ONE FLEW OVER THE CUCKOO'S NEST

VIP LIST

Dale Wasserman	author
Charles Faber	critic - Citizen News
John Houser	critic - Herald Examiner
Phillip Scheuer	critic - L.A. Times
Jimmy Powers	critic - Hollywood Reporter
Dale Olsen	critic - Variety
Robert Lewine	agent V.P. C.M.A.
Milton Lewis	manager
Lurene Tuttle	actress
Jim Lister	cast. dir. Stalmaster-Lister Rawhide Gunsmoke
Boris Kaplan	producer
Gene Banks	casting ABC
Betty Garret	actress
King Donovan	actor-director
Meyer Mishkin	agent Mishkin Agency
Hy Sieger	agent Park-Citron Agency
Norman Pincas	producer
David Graham	agent
Bob Raison	agent Raison-Branden Agency
Harold Swoverland	agent Swoverland Agency
Eddie Foy, Jr.	casting Columbia Screen Gems (I Dream of Jeannie)
Jack Donaldson	agent Donaldson Agency
Bob Bowser	casting Universal
Bob Shapiro	agent William Morris
Naomi Hirshhorn	producer legit
George Pal	producer MGM
Dick Lyons	producer MGM
Al Tresoony	casting MGM
Meryl Abeles	Desilu 20th
Dick Berg	producer Chrysler
Bert Kennedy	director MGM writer
Dale Garrick	agent Garrick Agency
Arthur Kennard	agent Kennard Agency
David Victor	producer Dr. Kildare
Russell Lewis	producer Sacremento legit
Sid Gordon	William Schuller Agency
Walter Grauman	director
Jere Henshaw	casting Revue
Bill Brademan	casting Revue
Walter Doneger	director Peyton Place
June Murray	casting Dr. Kildare
Olga Lee	agent Raison-Branden Agency
Paul Brandon	agent Raison-Brandon
Doug Benton	associate producer Dr. Kildare
Joe Swerling	producer Revue
Marc Miller	producer
Monte Hellman	director
E.J. Newman	director writer Mr. Novak

Lawrence Stern
Stage Manager
AN 8 4855

· **Figure 15-4** ·

A VIP List for the Callboard of a Showcase Theater

minutes of group consultation in advance can prevent a great deal of individual dissent later.

The stage manager also might take pains to explain where the cleanup materials are kept, how a mop wringer is used, and the importance of putting things back where they were found and reporting shortages of materials. (It was discovered, in the example above, that a thirty-year-old actor did not know how to use a mop! He had never used one. The stage manager demonstrated and the actor caught on. Unfortunately he became much more skilled at mopping than acting.)

Not all duty rosters need be of the rotating type if the cast is willing to distribute chores in another way.

Again, a group talk session in advance will help in the voluntary tapping of labor.

VIP Lists

A showcase theater's purpose is to attract to its audience producers, directors, agents, and other very important people (VIP's) who can hire the cast members for roles in movies, television, industrial shows, live theater, and other paying jobs.

Community, educational, and commercial theaters may function as showcases, even though it is not their primary purpose.

If the cast members know which VIP's have seen their performance, they can follow up the impression they've made by sending a résumé and phoning for an interview. They can ask agents who have attended to represent them on the basis of their performance.

So it is desirable that the cast know which VIP's have been in the audience. Posting a VIP list on the callboard is the easiest way to let the cast know (see Figure 15-4).

Posting such a list is not a mandatory function of the stage manager. Anyone who takes the time to check with the box office, house manager, producer, and director might make such a list. But it is one of the extra items that would demonstrate your interest in the welfare of the cast and the reputation of the theater.

· 16 ·

Keeping the Show in Hand

The most difficult problem in a long running production is keeping the quality of each performance as good as it was on opening night. If the director remains with the show, in attendance regularly and in communication with the cast, it is his or her burden. But if he or she says to you on opening night, "It's all yours," and means it, then you have your work cut out for you. It is your basic responsibility to strive toward retaining the director's artistic intent (see Chapter Eight).

In a short run there isn't much of a problem. But as the actors feel more at ease in their roles, especially if the show runs for two weeks or more without the director's presence, "improvements" set in.

Here are some examples of the things that happen in extended runs:

A. *New Business:* An actor sometimes feels "hung up" during the lines of fellow actors. During rehearsals and the first few performances, he was busy thinking of coming lines and business, but with his new-found ease and self-assurance, he begins to feel that he is not doing enough. So he invents new business that he feels is appropriate to his character. He removes his shoe and darns a hole in his red sock with green yarn that he removes from his eyeglass case.

Or it just happens by accident. He trips on the set and hits his head on the door frame, severely shaking the flat, and the audience laughs, so at the next performance. . . .

B. *New Lines:* A late entrance prompts two actors to ad lib some lines while awaiting the late-comer. Next performance the ad lib lines are repeated on the entrance, and at the next performance the entering actor waits for the ad lib lines.

Or, an actor throws in an ad lib line on impulse and gets a laugh, so at the next performance. . . .

C. *Pauses:* The actor now senses that his big moment is being missed by the audience because he doesn't have focus. So he decides he needs a dramatic pause, big enough to drive a truck through. It just seems that long. Actually, his new dramatic pauses and those of his fellow actors only add up to one and a half minutes on your time sheet for the scene—of yawning and coughing in the audience.

D. *Handles:* Suddenly every other line in the script has as preface a new expletive ("Well"), an exclamation ("Wow"), or direct address ("You"). The actors start to make themselves "comfortable" with the playwright's lines. The crispness is gone, the pace is down, but each actor knows in her or his heart that the single word she or he has added is right, just the way the character would say it.

So you observe and listen carefully, and each time you hear new lines, handles or pauses, or observe new business, you make a caret in your prompt script at the place where it occurred and note the new addition carefully. After the performance you bring the changes and improvements to the attention of the actors, privately! (Important: in matters of acting performances, directors give notes to the whole cast but stage managers counsel individual actors privately.)

And that's when you hear wondrous things from the actors in justification and rationalization:

"I've grown in the part."

"It got a laugh."

"It just happened by accident but the audience bought it so why not keep it?"

"I'm experimenting. Don't want to get into a rut."

"Got to keep that magic, spontaneous, first-time quality so I decided to do it for the first time without warning him so he'd give me a response I could play off of, but the dumdum just gave me the same tired line reading he's always been giving me."

Et cetera ad nauseum.

What do you do in the face of such static? You bring as much friendly persuasion as you can to the situation. You remind the actor of the traditional discipline of the theater—that changes in lines, pace, the interpretation of lines, and the inclusion of business are all strictly the prerogative of the director, and that in the absence of the director, they are now the stage manager's prerogative, and you do not approve the changes and improvements the actor wishes to make.

You may or may not go on to explain your reasons for the undesirability of the change or improvement.

You may point out that an actor's reputation for self-discipline is more important in the long run than the change or improvement she or he feels is so important.

You may also point out that historically the worst performances of the best actors have occurred when they undertook to direct themselves.

You might also console the actor that the decision not to accept her or his changes and improvements does not in any way diminish your respect for the actor's excellent taste, inventive genius, great experience despite her or his youth, sagacious artistic judgment, and her or his manifestly sincere desire to improve the production. But cut it!

Finally, you simply do not argue about it. Your authority extends only as far as your persuasive influence in this matter. Never make the actor feel that she or he must apologize, or even agree with you. If she or he gives you static after you have counseled her or him, simply leave her or him with a pleasant, "Why don't you give it some thought?"

You cannot control absolutely an actor's performance. You cannot run out on the stage and twist the actor's arm. Ultimately the actor must realize what you already know—that in live theater, the stage belongs to the actors, not the director or the stage manager. On the other hand, a production is a delicate balance of many performers' efforts, and any actor's reputation can suffer if she or he persists in upsetting this. For the really recalcitrant, the ultimate threat would be replacement with an understudy or a new actor, but this would be an administrative decision.

Cast Morale

Sometimes the gloom in the air at half hour call following a bad review is enough to make any stage manager feel that a comedy could not possibly be performed that evening, or that the tragedy about to be enacted on stage is nothing compared to the one backstage.

Here's how you handle the situation:

1. Don't over-react.
2. Get it out in the open.
3. Don't act elated when others are depressed.
4. Keep your own personal morale high.

It's never quite as bad as you imagine it will be before you get to the theater. Actors and actresses have a way of buoying up their own morale when they get together. Never feel that you must become court jester, or psychiatrist, backstage. This is not the time for a good show biz anecdote. Don't over-react.

Get it out in the open. A casual, "Rough break, Sam," to an actor who has been devastated by bad reviews might get it out from the sulking level to the verbal level and allow the actor to vent his choicest invective about the reviewers. But keep it casual. Show the actor that you don't attach too great importance to it.

Don't be elated when others are depressed. You should be sympathetic enough with the plight of a demoralized cast not to want to appear to be celebrating their disaster.

Keep your own personal morale high. Your morale is dependent on the fact that you are doing a difficult job very well. Continue to do your job very well. Let the cast know, by your deportment, that it is business as usual tonight, that you expect everyone to be on time and to acknowledge their calls cheerfully, regardless of the reviews.

Second-performance slump and "down" performances are other situations that you should be aware of.

The second performance of a run has a tendency to be a poor one. The cast, emotionally up for the opening night, experiences a letdown. The sense of urgency that attended opening night is gone. The second performance seems to be less important. Part of the challenge is missing. They know they can do it because they did it last night. And now they know how good they are. Didn't all of their friends tell them? So the cast relaxes, and the performance quality slips.

Sometimes you are simply not aware of the causes of a down performance. You observe the results. The first scene drags, the audience is unresponsive, and during the intermission it's very quiet in the dressing rooms. The cast is listless.

There is no one way to respond to second performance slump or other down performances. You must judge from your past experience how to best handle the situation. Do you give a pep talk to the cast during the intermission? Do you ask them for the old pzazz? Do you individually enlist the help of the old hands in the cast and ask them to pick up the pace? Have you developed the kind of rapport with the cast during rehearsals or on the tour thus far that enables you to give them the football coach's "You guys are letting me down" routine?

If you feel that you can be effective in fighting down performances, then you should try to do so. But you must not feel that it is an obligation. Simply make sure that you do not contribute to poor cast morale.

Finally, there is one other tradition in the theater with regard to morale that pertains to the stage manager. When a black-edged telegram arrives at the theater for a member of the cast, you hold it until after the performance.

Blocking Replacements
and Rehearsing Understudies

Traditionally, as the closest assistant to the director, you are presumed to have the duty of blocking in replacements and rehearsing understudies. In reality, you rarely get to perform these duties. Sometimes the director wants to do it her- or himself. Sometimes other staff members step in. Sometimes there is simply no need to block replacements or rehearse understudies.

Of course, you should be ready and able to do it since you have the blocking notations in your prompt script.

Rehearsing understudies or replacements is unlike original direction in that you should attempt to prepare the understudy or replacement to fit into the already mounted play. In most cases replacements and understudies have the opportunity to observe the cast and take their own blocking notation during a rehearsal or performance.

If working with an Equity company, you should review the rules concerning understudies with the producer. Some contracts require that understudies be present at the theater while other contracts require that the understudies simply be on call.

You should append the names and phone numbers of potential replacements and understudies to your cast list so that you are able to reach them when the need arises. Since you never can tell when you will need a replacement, it is a good idea to keep the résumés submitted during auditions with your notes of evaluation.

Upkeep of Sets and Costumes

On the very mundane level, the stage manager of a long run becomes responsible for the upkeep of the sets and costumes.

Every member of the cast should be encouraged to report to the stage manager any part of a set piece or set that is becoming worn or unserviceable. This might range from a door that is sticking, to a hole in a flat, to a loose cable backstage.

The stage manager should try to stay ahead of the cast by inspecting sets, set pieces, and costumes periodically and carrying out minor repairs before the cast members notice the need.

The stage manager is also responsible for seeing to it that costumes are laundered when necessary and repaired if necessary (see Figure 16-1).

Costume Problem

☐ clean ☐ repair

Show _____

Name _____ Date _____

Description of problem: _____

· **Figure 16-1** ·

Costume Tag. Tags with eyelets, and preferably wire ties, are available in stationery stores. When you have a large cast, it is important that you get the right costume back to the right actor. Tags should be left in the dressing rooms and actors should be informed via company rules when and where they are to turn in costumes for cleaning or repair.

· 17 ·

Closing and Moving

When the show has completed its run, it is time to strike—tear down the sets and return or store the props and costumes. It is usually desirable to clean the stage area as soon as possible after the last performance.

In union companies the close of the show is announced two weeks in advance by a closing notice signed by the producer and posted on the callboard.

Strike Plan

To accomplish the strike efficiently, you might wish to write out and distribute a strike plan. This plan lets everyone involved know what is expected of them (see Figure 17-1). You should coordinate the plan with all concerned department heads.

Will the actors be involved in the strike, or only the crew? In a union theater situation, cast members do not participate in the strike. In educational, community, and showcase theater, they usually do.

If you are working in the union situation, your strike plan will be very brief. It will advise the union crew of their call. Along with the producer, business manager, or production manager, you will want to evaluate the amount of time required and review the applicable union rules and pay scales to determine whether the strike can most economically be carried out during a night call following the final curtain, or delayed for a future date, even possibly the day that the next set is to be brought in. You will want to evaluate availability of storage space, storage cost, and trucking costs.

It is wise to review the strike plan with the union crew before finalizing it.

In a non-union situation, it is usually best to accomplish the strike as soon after the final curtain as possible. Tools and transportation should be well planned so that your cast, staff, and crew will have everything on hand that they need to accomplish the strike. Be sure that you have enough bags and boxes to get all of the props and costumes properly packed and out of the theater, and enough back seats, trucks, and trunk space to accommodate all of the set pieces, scenery, props, and costumes. Cleaning implements should be in plentiful supply, too, so that the theater may be left clean for the next production.

Most cast members actually enjoy the strike if they know what is expected of them. There is usually a let-down that follows the closing performance, which is buffered when the cast members continue working together for the brief period of the strike. There is a sense of urgency, team play, and accomplishment present at the strike which makes it quite enjoyable.

During the strike, don't tie yourself down with repetitive manual tasks. You should be free to observe and supervise. You should also delegate supervising authority to others, particularly when there is more than one area. Can an actor be put in charge of the shop area while you are on stage? Can one supervise an even smaller area, like a loading dock? Actors who suddenly remember long-lost hernias and war wounds at the mention of the strike have been known to do vast amounts of work when named supervisor.

You must be especially aware of safety problems during the strike, and take time to caution everyone about the most basic of potential dangers: watch where you step; don't step on nails and tools; don't fall into the pit; don't use power tools that you have not operated before until you have been instructed in their use; look above for falling scenery and tools.

Start the strike with a safety lecture and caution workers when you see dangerous practices.

The strike may well be the last chore that cast members see you do. Try to make a good final impression by carrying out the strike

THE TORCH-BEARERS

STRIKE NIGHT PARTY*
Sunday, June 14, 1964
11 pm - 1 am

General
1. Strike can be completed in less than 2 hrs. with the cooperation of all.
2. Please bring hammer and/or crowbar plus at least one lge. corrugated paper box suitable for packing.
3. Please change out of costume and make-up and into work clothes as soon as possible.
4. Urging final night guests to leave as soon as possible will expedite.
5. Remove your own personal costumes, make-up, and prop. to your cars as soon as possible to facilitate cleaning of dressing rooms.
6. Stay off the stage unless specifically assigned there because of falling flats and flying hardware, tools, & crew members. (Use side doors to go between dressing rooms and aud.)
7. Upon completion of assigned tasks, see stage manager.

Assignments
Crew: Dick, John, Fred Barry (others):
   A. Strike front rows of chairs in aud.
   B. Bring in stairs, garbage cans, place in aud. near DSL.
   C. Remove sconces, place in one box;all furn. in aud. near DSR.
   D. Remove all portable lighting equip. to storage room, rear aud.
   E. Remove all flats, stage pos., braces, rigging to aud. near DSL.
   F. When stage strike complete, replace curtains, move furniture to patio.
   G. Dick will be in charge of further refining crew assignments

Doug:
   A. Oversee removal of all items from stage.
   B. Supervise replacement of curtains front and rear.

Len & Hoke, Brett & Ben:
   A. Form 2 teams to work in aud. near DSL area to accept flats, rigging, stage pieces from crew.
   B. Remove hardware & break down to smallest desirable parts.
   C. Store all hardware in box.
   D. Remove all parts to patio & store as directed.
   E. Bring screw driver and/or pliers;work gloves desirable to avoid splinters.

Karl:
   A. Turn on patio lights.
   B. Organize patio area for quick future removal of all materials.
   C. Show Len, Hoke, Brett, Ben where & how to store flats & materials.
   D. When all materials stored, instruct crew to bring out furniture and supervise placement.

Jeanne, Barbara, Margaret, Evelyn, Marlene, Beatriz:
   A. Clean Dressing rooms. B. Store costumes to be ret.

Harvey and Randy: *see me for prop forms*.
   A. Pack all props in boxes.
   B. List contents of box on outside.
   C. Insure with completed forms that we will know what goes where & to whom on Tuesday, June 16th when furniture & props will be returned.

If you anticipate any strike night problems please see me.
Thank you all in advance for the swift, pleasant strike.

· **Figure 17-1** ·
Strike Plan Handout

with the same calm and meticulous organization with which you managed the rest of the production.

Changeover Schedule

In cases where the theater will not have a dark night between two consecutive productions, it is necessary to prepare a changeover schedule. This schedule is actually a combination of strike plan, set-up plan, and rehearsal schedule which aids in smoothing out the transition from one production to another. It tells who has use of the stage space during the critical hours of transition. It coordinates the personnel of the outgoing production, the incoming production, and the house staff (see Figure 17-2).

Before posting it, you should coordinate the schedule with the producer, business manager, production manager, and staffs of the incoming and outgoing productions.

During the changeover you must be on hand to supervise the on-the-spot adjustments that become necessary.

Examples:

When construction takes longer than anticipated, and it frequently does, you must keep the master carpenter from coming to blows with the choreographer of the incoming show who expected those all important ramps to be in place at the beginning of the rehearsal period and not left for last.

You must be forearmed with the authority to make decisions as to whether or not ten members of a union will be paid for an additional four hour call because their services are required for fifteen additional minutes (when the union requires a four hour minimum pay period). Discuss contingencies with the producer. Find out what authority you have to commit her or his money.

Send all personnel concerned a copy of the changeover schedule and post copies on the callboard, in the shop, and in the crew lounge area.

Moving the Show

All moves are alike and all moves are different. They require coordination of staff, crew, and cast in moving the cast, crew, and equipment.

JOHNNY MATHIS/TIJUANA BRASS Changeover

Friday	July 15	8 am to noon	electrics
		1-5 pm	carpentry props electrics
Saturday	July 16	open	
Sunday	July 17	1-6 pm	sound
		8 pm	half hour
		8:30	curtain Mathis show
		end performance	begin strike
Monday	July 18	12:00-3 am	strike/set
		3-6 am	full orchestra dress rehearsal
		6 am to 12 noon	as needed
		1-6 pm	technical cleanup (no performers)
		8 pm	half hour
		8:30	curtain TIJUANA BRASS

· **Figure 17-2** ·

Changeover Schedule between Two Productions

A. You are moving your production from one theater to another. Your lease ran out but your advance sales are great so you have to find another house.
B. You tried out in Azusa and now you're opening in West Covina.
C. You are on a national tour, either via train and/or plane to major cities, or by truck and bus to the hinterlands.
D. Your children's play is traveling to all of the elementary school auditoriums in town.
E. Your industrial show will tour thirty-eight cities in two and a half months.

In any of these situations, here are some of the steps you will want to take:

A. Prepare and distribute an itinerary.
B. Caution the cast/crew on travel deportment.

LOST SHEEP PRODUCTIONS, INC.
12308 BRACKLAND AVE.
LOS ANGELES, CALIFORNIA 90033

ITENERARY - SPRING TOUR

AIR TRANSPORTATION	HOTELS
March 16 leave Los Angeles East. 72/4 PM arrive Miami 9 PM	Everglades Hotel 304 Biscayne St. Miami, Fla. 33101 FR 9 5461
March 19 leave Miami United 395/2:55 PM arrive Jacksonville 3:57 PM	Robert Meyer Hotel 514 Main St. Jacksonville, Fla. 33705 EL 5 4411
March 21 Leave Jacksonville TransFl. 151/1 PM; arrive Tampa 2:17 PM	Manger Motor Inn 200 Ashley Drive Tampa, Fla. 33164 813 223 2456
March 24 Leave Tampa National 462/12 PM arrive Pensacola 1:15 PM	Town House 16 West Cervantes St. Pensacola, Fla. 33225 904 438 4511
March 26 leave Pensacola Eastern 865/ 3:15 PM; arrive Birmingham 4:33 PM	Parliament House 420 18th Street Birmingham, Ala. 35445 205 323 7211
March 28 Leave Birmingham So. Air 285/ 8 AM; arrive Memphis 9:30 AM	Holiday Inn 200 W. Georgia Ave. Memphis, Tenn. 38103 901 525 0102
March 30 leave Memphis United 589/ 10:45 AM; arrive Chattanooga 12:28 PM	Towne House 831 George Ave. Chattanooga, Tenn. 37401 615 266 1255
April 1 leave Chattanooga Delta 736/ 8:30 AM; arrive Charlotte 10:45 AM	Manger Motor Inn 1187 Tenth St. Charlotte, N.C. 28202 704 332 3121
April 3 leave Charlotte Delta 710/2:40 PM; arrive Atlanta 3:33 PM	Marriott Hotel 47 Cain Street Atlantic, Ga. 30303 404 688 6500
April 6 leave Atlanta United 431/2:55 PM; arrive Cleveland 4:30 PM	Pick Carter Hotel 407 E. 9th Street Cleveland, Ohio 44107 216 771 7200
April 9 leave Cleveland American 257/ 11:25 AM; arrive Los Angeles 3:20 PM	

· **Figure 17-3** ·
Itinerary for a Touring Company

C. "Mother-hen" the cast on the road.
D. Supervise the load-in, set-up, strike, and load-out.
E. Pave the way with letters to business agents, host theater owners, etc.

BURT BACHARACH				NOVEMBER 1970		ITINERARY		
DATE	LEAVE	ARRIVE	HOTEL	PLACE OF ENGAGE- MENT OR REHEARSAL	TIME CONCERT	TIME RHRSL.	CALL NEXT DAY	NOTES
THUR. NOV 19 1970	NO GROUP TRAVEL		NONE	ATM RECORDS 1416 N. LABREA LOS ANGLEOS STAGE # 1-555-2711	NONE	7 P.M.	NONE	PARK IN BACK LOT
FRI. NOV 20 1970	NO GROUP TRAVEL		NONE SOUND PSL HOLIDAY IN HYLAND ST. 555-3714	LONGBEACH ARENA 270 E. LAKESIDE LONG BEACH CALIF.	8:30 PM	4 PM	NONE	BE AT AIRPORT ½ HR. BEFORE DEPARTURE
SAT. NOV 21 1970	PERSONNEL AUTO TO TERMINAL #116 (LA)	ARRIVE 1:30 PM SALT LAKE BUS & LIMO	HILTON 200 W. SIXTH SALT LK.	SPECIAL EVENTS CTR. UNIV. OF UTAH 619-555-3719 SALT LAKE CITY	8:00 PM	5 PM	11/22 9 AM	NOON CKOUT. TRVL. W/SAL MONTE TO HOUSTON 11/22
SUN. NOV 22 1970	SLT. LAKE Wal 5 11:00 LAS VAGAS NAT 2 2:30	L. VAGAS 11:00 HOUSTON 6:50	Check RIVIERA HOTEL THEN TO HOUSTON & SAME HOTEL		NONE	NONE	NONE	MERCER MCCUNE
SUN NOV 22 1970	SLT. LAKE WEST. A.L. 410 @ 1:31	DENVER 2:58	SHERATON 777 PARK 555-7010	Note: Wait in Coffee SHOP FOR MERCER & McCUNE & CAR	NONE	NONE	NONE	PUNCH BURNS

· **Figure 17-4** ·

Itinerary for a Touring Musical Show

Itineraries

The first thing you need is an itinerary, whether you are moving across the street or across the nation (see Figures 17-3 and 17-4). What day are you making the move? What time? What is your destination? What's the new address (with zip code)? What's the new phone number (with area code)? What is the rehearsal and perform- ance schedule during the period?

Planning the itinerary is not necessarily your responsibility, but you should contribute. Think through the moves in advance. Has enough time been allotted for set-ups? Try to anticipate prob- lems. Have all of the union rules been considered (i.e., union casts may not travel on their day off)?

It is your responsibility to make sure that every member of the cast and crew has a copy of the itinerary—perhaps two or three for family and friends who will wish to write or phone while the show is on the road.

Touring Agreement

You will want to caution the cast and crew about deportment ex- pected on the road (see Figure 17-5). You are expected to be a model

TO: LOST SHEEP PRODUCTIONS, INC.
12308 Brackland Ave.
Los Angeles, California 90033

Gentlemen

It is my understanding that all personnel employed by,
and who will travel with, the Lost Sheep road company
must agree to the following:

That while we are in the employ of Lost Sheep Productions, Inc., we will conduct ourselves in a manner that
will not bring any adverse criticism to Lost Sheep
Productions or its clients.

That our manner of dress will be businesslike, neat and
in good taste, particularly when traveling.

That we will travel with the group as assigned and ask
for no changes or deviations from travel schedules and
itineraries. All travel departures are final and no
changes can be made except by Lost Sheep Productions or
representatives who have been instructed that the only
change that can be made is a change for the entire group.
The reason for this is that changes affect price and
budget and will not be allowed.

It is our understanding that we are on a job and a
business trip and not on a paid vacation. The show and
any rehearsals are to take first consideration in any
planning of extracurricular activities.

That when technical rehearsals are called, all personnel
involved are expected to put the same effort into them
as into the performances.

That all personnel will be prompt at any and all calls
for fittings, rehearsals or performances as called by
the stage manager.

AGREED TO:_____
(name)

DATE:_____

· **Figure 17-5** ·
Touring Agreement for Cast and Staff

for the rest of the company. You must advise the company members
if things get out of hand. In the absence of a regular company manager
on the road you may be expected to do some "mother-henning."
You should tactfully remind cast members that their health, as it
affects their performances, is the first concern of the management,
and it is for that reason that you are cautioning them to watch their
health.

The most common occurrence for touring companies is simply
making too much whoopee once out of town, resulting in reduced
energy levels that bring down the quality of performances. You can't
always prevent such things, but you can caution. If tactful influence
fails and an actor's performance suffers as a result of his or her offstage activities, you must inform the producer or the management.

The packing, padding, and care of sets, props, costumes, and
technical equipment concern every department head. You coordi-

LOST SHEEP PRODUCTIONS, INC.
12308 BRACKLAND AVE.
LOS ANGELES, CALIFORNIA 90033

Mr. Victor M. Otorino
General Manager
The Chechonovitz Civic Light Opera
2020 Himmelfarb Drive
Chechonovitz, California

Dear Mr. Otorino,

On November 18, 1970, we will be setting up the Lost Sheep
production of THE MAGNIFICENT EIGHT. Our truck should
arrive on Thursday at 11 AM.

We would appreciate it if you would take the necessary
measures to clear any alley or passageway to allow our
truck access to your loading dock at that time. Because of
a very tight schedule, it is essential that our truck be
allowed to unload immediately upon arrival and if elevators
are involved, that a man be placed on duty on a freight
elevator for our use at the time above until we have
finished carrying in our equipment.

Our stage manager will be Mr. Lawrence Stern. Anything
he asks of you will be in the name of Lost Sheep Productions and your cooperation will be appreciated.

We would like your house electrician, when we unload, to
answer any questions of our technical crew. Mr. Chris
Papadapoulos will be our carpenter. We will be carrying
all of our own stage draperies, lights, PA system and
projection equipment.

We will be coming in on a yellow card and we will be
employing union stagehands. Our carpenter will be in
touch with your local business agent concerning calls
for local men to assist us.

We will need a grand piano, tuned to 440 pitch, piano
bench and a 12' X 12' rug for the musicians at stage right.

Thank you for your cooperation. We look forward to
working with you in your facility.

Sincerely

Sid Rosenwald

SID ROSENWALD
Executive Producer

· **Figure 17-6** ·
Advance Letter to Host Theater Manager

nate with them in planning every move. You are the overseer of the
move.

It is particularly important that set diagrams be accurate
and that all flats be marked with accurate butting guides so that
crews who have never seen the assembled set can put it together
with ease.

On arrival at a new location, you first go to the theater. You
inspect the premises to insure that your set-up plans are workable
(see Chapter Five, "Information Packets"). You assign dressing
rooms and make sure that they are in serviceable condition. You
supervise the set-up and check your personal equipment. You greet
the new crew members who will run the show and review the run-

ning order, lighting sheet, sound plot, and shift plot chart with them (see Chapter Twelve).

Before leaving the theater, you post your local address and phone number on the callboard so that it is available in an emergency for the management of the theater and the local crew members.

You should then check with the cast to insure that their hotel accommodations are satisfactory.

Advance Letters

In very large companies there are sometimes advance people who go to a new location ahead of the company to prepare for their arrival. Sometimes an assistant stage manager may be dispatched in advance. But in many cases the problems of a traveling company can be anticipated and smoothed out via letter (see Figure 17-6 and Chapter Five, "Information Packets," and also Figure 5-6). Letters requesting specific support (to hotels for accommodations, to business agents of unions for local personnel, to host theater owners, etc.) are usually sent out over the signature of the producer or company management. You can contribute to these letters by letting management know what problems you anticipate or encounter, e.g., difficulty of hotels cashing checks for cast members on paydays, unavailability of an elevator during a load-in, etc.

Calling a special staff meeting to brainstorm a move or series of moves can save time and money on the road.

· **18** ·

Organizing Information

We are in the midst of an information explosion. The availability of books, magazines, newspapers, radio and TV broadcasts, microfilm, Xerox copies, and computer printouts is almost overwhelming. As the amount of information available to every stage manager increases, she or he must decide on how to organize it so that she or he can make use of it.

Local Theater

You might want to start your personal acquisition of theater information by sending a postcard to every live theater in town asking to be placed on their mailing lists. Write to commercial, educational, showcase, community, and children's theaters. You will soon receive information in the mail about who's doing what, and you will receive more complete and accurate information than you can find in your newspaper.

Go to the theater as often as you can. Make notes in your programs as to outstanding acting and technical credits. Save your programs.

Newspapers and Magazines

Read local newspapers and national magazines regularly. Making a scrapbook of theater information is the easiest way of keeping abreast of live theater (see Figure 18-1).

Clip local reviews of plays. Note the technical credits. You may soon discover, for instance, that just a handful of people are getting all of the good lighting reviews. Even if you have never worked with these people, you will start to know who they are.

You will also be able to determine trends. What type of plays are being done by the many community theaters in your area? What

(Varsity, the *Stage Daily*,
May, 1969)

**LEGIT TECH MEN
CONVENE IN L.A.**

The United Institute for Theat
Technology will hold its ninth
conference at the Los Ang
today through Thursd
287 professionals
nected with
tending.
T
Tota
will b
and le
week.
Between
and the Le
panel chaire
fessor from N
tomorrow morn.
The next sess
noon, is "New Tec
computers in theatr
be discussed. Wedne
tour the Music Cent
"Building Codes and S
sion at Ahmanson Theati
noon session will be "Pro,
ery," conducted at L.A. Ci
"Electronics in the The
"Techniques of the Thrust Sta
be subjects of the final m
Thursday at the Hilton.

(Varsity, the *Stage Daily*,
December, 1969)

BROADWAY OPENINGS

Last of the Red Hot Lovers

New York, December 29—Neil
Simon does it again in this new
comedy, which opened last
night at the O'Neill Theater to a

(The Los Angeles *Bugle*,
January, 1970)

STAGE NEWS

**Top Billing for Computer in
"Tommy"**

If you want information about
the production of the rock op-
ra "Tommy," now playing at
Roxy Theater as directed by
Rosen and starring Teddy
in the title role, then go
the stage manager.
to 's that? The stage man-
'ell, why not? Stage
are in a pretty good
know what's going
say, directors are
etter one—except
here some very
's recording the
'rector would
's stage man-

*(Los Angeles Messenger,
February, 1969)*

**NEW THEATER GROUP
IN EAST CUCAMONGA**

Northeast Cucamonga—A new community theatrical group is forming
here to bring back the flavor of the
straw hat summer theater circuit to
this bustling area, long destitute of
its former theatrical ornament. The
Greater Cucamonga and Operatic Pavilion.

The Cucamonga Caperers, a group form-
composed of theatrical people
active in Anaheim and Azusa,
under the leadership of Fred Freedley,
stage director, George Geomble, sce
nic designer, Louis Lumber, music di
rector, and Archie Arkwright, legal
and business adviser. The non-profit
organization will provide talented lo
cals with an outlet for their creative
energies, and visiting stage favorites
with a chance to show their stuff to
a summer audience.

Four plays are yet to be selected
as kickoff items to get the group moving, the first due to open in late May
or early June of this year.
you don't upstage your
ors. And we have just the
man to do the delicate handling:
our audio-visual programmer-
director, Jim McKie.

· **Figure 18-1** ·
Likely Items for a Manager's Scrapbook

types of plays are the educational theaters doing? The showcase theaters? The commercial theaters? The experimental theaters? By reading naticnally published reviews of Broadway and off-Broadway openings, you can learn to anticipate which of these plays will later be done by certain local theaters.

Which local producers do consistently good work? By judging the type of plays they do and the quality of their work, which producers would you prefer to work for or learn more from? The largest, most plush plant in town may not be doing the kind of work with which you would want to associate yourself. By going to the theater and reading reviews, you can discover the theaters you would most like to be your own.

Also, clip articles on all aspects of production, and reviews of new books about theater.

A subscription to one or more of the trade papers might provide you with good current information.

Variety
154 West 46th Street
New York City 10036

Daily Variety
1400 N. Cahuenga Blvd.
Hollywood 90028

Hollywood Reporter
6715 West Sunset Blvd.
Hollywood 90028

The Hollywood Drama-Logue
P.O. Box 38771
Los Angeles 90038

There are many excellent magazines devoted exclusively to live theater:

The Drama Review
51 W. 4th Street, Room 300
New York City 10012

Dramatics
3368 Central Parkway
Cincinnati, Ohio 45224

Educational Theatre Journal
1029 Vermont Ave. N.W.
Washington, D.C. 20005

Plays
8 Arlington Street
Boston, Massachusetts 02116

Plays and Players
Box 294
2–4 Old Pye Street
London, SW1 2LR England

Theater
Box 2046 Yale Station
New Haven, Connecticut 06520

Theatre Crafts
33 East Minor Street
Emmaus, Pennsylvania 18049

In addition to those listed above, *The Standard Periodical Directory* (Oxbridge Publishers, Inc.; 420 Lexington Avenue, NYC 10017) lists 111 separate entries of publications devoted to theater, each having a distinct point of view. Review the entire list at your library and see if some of the titles appeal to you.

Guides to Goods and Services

A fast reference that you will want to index into your prompt script is the theatrical supply listings from the yellow pages of your local phone directory. You might enclose the listings in a mylar sheet protector for convenience.

Where can you get lighting supplies in a hurry? Where can you send someone to repair a damaged wig? Who has Max Factor pancake makeup in 7A on hand? Get the answers fast. Use your yellow pages.

How many times have you driven to a supply house only to find on arrival that they don't have what you need in stock? Call ahead.

Simon's Directory of Theatrical Materials Services & Information is a national directory of theater information and should be in every stage manager's library. If it is not available through your bookstore, you may write to the publisher: Package Publicity Service, Inc., 1564 Broadway, New York City 10036.

Collect catalogues from theatrical supply manufacturers throughout the country. You can learn a lot by studying catalogues. Here is a very small starter selection of manufacturers and suppliers.

Altman Stage Lighting
57 Alexander
Yonkers, N.Y. 10701

Kliegl Bros. Inc.
32–32 48th Ave.
Long Island City, N.Y. 11101

Olesen Company
1535 Ivar Avenue
Hollywood, California 90028

Package Publicity Service, Inc.
1564 Broadway
New York City 10036

Rosco
36 Bush Ave.
Port Chester, N.Y. 10573

Strong Electric
1 City Park Ave.
Toledo, Ohio 43697

Theatre Production Service
45 West 46th Street
New York City 10036

See Simon's Directory for additional selection.

Studying a few catalogues will help to make you aware of the industry that is ready to back up the theater. It will help you keep abreast of new products. What do you know about quartz lights? Black light? Foam scenery? Solid state communications equipment?

You will want to send for samples, swatches, and gel books. Services and demonstrations are sometimes available from manufacturers who wish to promote their products. Can you get lighting equipment sales representatives to come out to your theater to help you analyze the problem of augmenting your lighting equipment for a particularly heavy show? Can he help you with the know-how to create special effects?

Before you buy, compare products carefully. Not all of the factors are always stated in brochures about the product. You will want to evaluate cost, durability, repair costs, availability of spare parts, capability of the product, ease of cleaning, ease of repairing or replacing worn parts, proximity to a repair facility, ease in use, unique advantages, and peculiar disadvantages.

Contact File

Use 3 × 5 " or 4 × 6" note cards to assemble information: names, addresses, and phone numbers of people who may be helpful to you in your theater work (see Figure 18-2). You will want to keep cards for actors, producers, directors, designers, technicians, costume designers, suppliers of equipment, sources of props, unions, and others. You will want to alphabetize your cards and you might even want to use some sort of code—various color cards or flags—to help you pull information quickly.

A durable metal or wooden box to keep the cards in is a must.

You may be able to help in casting by keeping tabs on the various fine actors that you discover in plays that you see. Write a card for each actor whose work impresses you. Get his or her address and phone number. Get his or her agent's name and number, too, if he or she has one. Go out of your way to see him or her in the next play that he or she does.

Books

You should have available a few books on theater that can recharge your intellectual batteries, the type of book that you can read more than once and still find interesting and helpful. These might be considered your "clothesline" books, giving you the basic information that will allow you to assimilate other information, pinning it up on the "clothesline" in your mind.

What seven books would you take with you to another planet if you expected to establish a live theater there (see Figure 18-3)?

Perhaps these seven "other planet" books would be a good start for your own personal library. It is better to know seven books well than to own a huge collection of books with uncut pages.

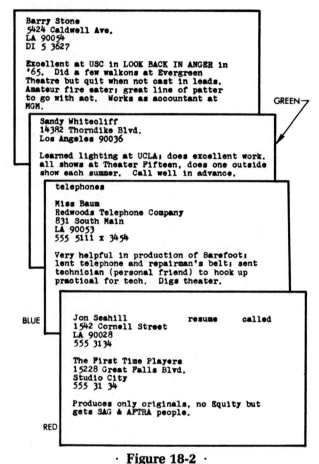

Barry Stone
5424 Caldwell Ave.
LA 90054
DI 5 3627

Excellent at USC in LOOK BACK IN ANGER in
'65. Did a few walkons at Evergreen
Theatre but quit when not cast in leads.
Amateur fire eater; great line of patter
to go with act. Works as accountant at
MGM.

GREEN

Sandy Whitecliff
14382 Thorndike Blvd.
Los Angeles 90036

Learned lighting at UCLA; does excellent work.
all shows at Theater Fifteen, does one outside
show each summer. Call well in advance.

telephones

Miss Baum
Redwoods Telephone Company
831 South Main
LA 90053
555 5111 x 3454

Very helpful in production of Barefoot;
lent telephone and repairman's belt; sent
technician (personal friend) to hook up
practical for tech. Digs theater.

BLUE

Jon Seahill   resume   called
1542 Cornell Street
LA 90028
555 3134

The First Time Players
15228 Great Falls Blvd.
Studio City
555 31 34

Produces only originals, no Equity but
gets SAG & AFTRA people.

RED

· **Figure 18-2** ·
Contact Cards:
White, Actors; Green, Technicians;
Blue, Suppliers, Red, Producers

Extensive bibliographies for every theater arts subject may be found in your local library.

In addition, if you are interested in a program of directed reading, many graduate schools of theater arts publish graduate reading lists. Contact the university nearest you.

Or you may wish to add your name to the mailing lists of the several publishers who specialize in books on theater arts.

Allyn and Bacon, Inc.   Burt Franklin, Publisher
Longwood Division   235 East 44th Street
470 Atlantic Avenue   New York City 10017
Boston, Massachusetts 02210

"What Seven Books Would I Take to Another Planet if I Expected to Establish a Live Theater There?"
(a small, prejudiced, but useful selection)

ACTING

Actors on Acting
Cole, Toby and Helen Krich Chinoy
Crown, New York 1970

DIRECTING

Directors on Directing
Cole, Toby and Helen Krich Chinoy
Bobbs-Merrill, Indianapolis 1963

MAKEUP/COSTUMING

Stage Makeup
Corson, Richard
Appleton-Century-Crofts, New York 1967

Costume in the Theatre
Laver, James
Hill and Wang, New York 1964

SCENE DESIGN/SET CONSTRUCTION/LIGHTING

Scene Design and Stage Lighting
Parker, W. Oren and Harvey K. Smith
Holt, New York 1968

HISTORY

History of the Theater, Third Edition
Brockett, Oscar G.
Allyn and Bacon, Boston 1977

PLAYWRIGHTING

Playwrighting
Bernard Grebanier
Thomas Y. Crowell Company, New York 1961

· **Figure 18-3** ·
Seven Titles to Start a Theater Library

AMS Press, Inc.
56 East 13th Street
New York City 10003

Cornell University Press
124 Roberts Place
Ithaca, New York 14850

Crown Publishers, Inc.
50-10 34th Street
Long Island City, New York 11101

The Fireside Theater
Garden City, New York 11530

Indiana University Press
10th and Morton Streets
Bloomington, Indiana 47401

University of Miami Press
Drawer 9088
Coral Gables, Florida 33124

University of Washington Press
Seattle, Washington 98105

Annotated Bibliography of New
Publications in the Performing Arts
The Drama Book Shop
150 West 52nd Street
New York City 10019

Postcards sent to the publishers above will bring you the latest information about new books on theater as well as lists and mail order prices of hard cover and paperback editions of interest to you.

Police, Fire, and Municipal Regulations

You should be aware that there are police regulations, fire laws, and municipal codes which may control the operations of all theaters, if and when applied (see Figure 18-4).

These regulations vary with each city, and within cities depending on the size of the theater. They are generally written in the form of ordinances and sections of the city code. The ordinances and codes are available in the offices of city administrators concerned, and in public libraries. Unfortunately, not all regulations pertaining to live theater are neatly grouped together. They may be found under such diverse headings as "Rules Governing Café Entertainment and Shows," "Assemblage Occupancies," "Safety to Life Requirements," and others.

Experts are usually available to assist theater owners and producers who may call to request inspections of their facilities, or submit plans for approval. The stage manager does not normally do this.

Occasionally, whether requested or not, fire marshals inspect theaters just prior to the opening of new productions to check fireproofing, exits, smoking signs, and other public safety features. Theaters have been closed and performances postponed as a result of such inspections (see Figure 18-5).

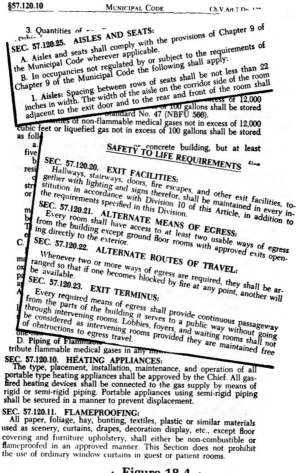

§57.120.10   MUNICIPAL CODE   Ch.V.Art.7 Div. 12°

3. Quantities of ——

SEC. 57.120.25. **AISLES AND SEATS:**
A. Aisles and seats shall comply with the provisions of Chapter 9 of the Municipal Code wherever applicable.
B. In occupancies not regulated by or subject to the requirements of Chapter 9 of the Municipal Code the following shall apply:
1. Aisles: Spacing between rows of seats shall be not less than 22 inches in width. The width of the aisle on the corridor side of the room adjacent to the exit door and to the rear and front of the room shall
...ess of 12,000
...r 100 gallons shall be stored
...ndard No. 47 (NBFU 566).
...ies of non-flammable medical gases not in excess of 12,000
cubic feet or liquefied gas not in excess of 100 gallons shall be stored
as foll
a.
five
b
resi
str
or
SAFETY TO LIFE REQUIREMENTS
... concrete building, but at least
fire

SEC. 57.120.20. **EXIT FACILITIES:**
Hallways, stairways, doors, fire escapes, and other exit facilities, together with lighting and signs therefor, shall be maintained in every institution in accordance with Division 10 of this Article, in addition to the requirements specified in this Division.

SEC. 57.120.21. **ALTERNATE MEANS OF EGRESS:**
Every room shall have access to at least two usable ways of egress from the building except ground floor rooms with approved exits opening directly to the exterior.

SEC. 57.120.22. **ALTERNATE ROUTES OF TRAVEL:**
Whenever two or more ways of egress are required, they shall be arranged so that if one becomes blocked by fire at any point, another will be available.

SEC. 57.120.23. **EXIT TERMINUS:**
Every required means of egress shall provide continuous passageway from the parts of the building it serves to a public way without going through intervening rooms. Lobbies, foyers, and waiting rooms shall not be considered as intervening rooms provided they are maintained free of obstructions to egress travel.

D. Piping of Flammable...
...one...
tribute flammable medical gases in any ins...

SEC. 57.120.10. **HEATING APPLIANCES:**
The type, placement, installation, maintenance, and operation of all portable type heating appliances shall be approved by the Chief. All gas-fired heating devices shall be connected to the gas supply by means of rigid or semi-rigid piping. Portable appliances using semi-rigid piping shall be secured in a manner to prevent displacement.

SEC. 57.120.11. **FLAMEPROOFING:**
All paper, foliage, hay, bunting, textiles, plastic or similar materials used as scenery, curtains, drapes, decoration display, etc., except floor covering and furniture upholstery, shall either be non-combustible or flameproofed in an approved manner. This Section does not prohibit the use of ordinary window curtains in guest or patient rooms.

· **Figure 18-4** ·
Typical Theater Safety Regulations

You should review public safety requirements with the staff of your theater. The entire staff should take the time to review plans for emergencies.

Frequently in small theaters, scene designers and technical directors build into the audience, covering exit lights and no smoking signs, and blocking exit aisles with scenery. You should prevent this by calling their attention to the rules.

If you are involved in opening a show in a building that has been newly converted into a theater, you should ask the producer or management if local regulations have been checked. The number

(Los Angeles *Bugle*, July, 1969)

STAGE NEWS TODAY

*

The Awareness Theater, recently closed by the fire marshall, has relocated temporarily at the Psychiatry Center Auditorium at the UCLA Medical Center where Bella Harpman is directing two one-acts by Harry Rose on Friday and Sunday nights. The plays are "Big Sol" about an aging convict who fantasizes about the blonde he murdered so effec- tively that he has his cellmate seeing things, and also "Time Charlie" which deals with an opium addict who dreams peddling dope on horseback.

Mrs. Harpman say the university will reinstate the Awareness Theater, starting when other members of the Drama Students' Guild can be found, while the theater does the production on of the Medical Center present its ovation to the Awareness theater apparently

(Los Angeles *Messenger*, February, 1969)

USC LIVING THEATER CALLED OFF

Performances of the Living Theater Saturday night and tonight were canceled at USC following apparent violations of fire safety regulations.

Police called a tactical alert on the campus Friday evening after learning that fire safety laws had been violated and that too many persons were occupying the sized stage at once in regulations.

executive di- university rela- that the per- had been can- cause the theater staff were "inade- to assure that the ssary compliance with safety codes and audi- nce safety would be car- ried out in accordance with municipal regulations."

Refund information is available by telephone at the following numbers: 555-7834, 555-6093, 555-8427.

(Varsity, February, the Stage Daily, 1969)

FIRE DEPT HALTS SHOW OF LIVING THEATER

Performances of the Living Theater at USC were cancelled this weekend after fire safety code violations were alleged by fire marshalls.

A tactical alert was called by police Friday after notification that fire safety codes were ap- parently being ignored and that too many peo- ple were being allowed on stage. Refunds were made available.

· **Figure 18-5** ·
A Theater in Violation of Safety Laws
Can Be Closed Down

of people allowed in the building, the number of off-street parking spaces necessary, and even the amount of lavatory space, are all the subjects of city regulations.

If you are working in an Equity company and feel that the producer is failing to comply with regulations, thus endangering public safety, and you have discussed it with him, then take the issue to your union and let the union take up the issue with the producer.

If you are in a non-union theater situation and can't convince your management or producer to make the theater safe, quit first. Then call for fire, police, and building code inspections as a con- cerned citizen.

People die in theaters as the result of negligence—failure to know and obey the law. As a stage manager, the lives of your cast, crew, and audience may depend on your knowledge and application of the law.

Getting to Know the Unions

"You can't join Equity until you have a job in an Equity company, and you can't get a job in an Equity company until you are a member of Equity." This seeming paradox is often quoted but quite misleading. As soon as you can convince an Equity producer or director that you should be his or her stage manager, the doors of the union will open to you. Equity is not one of the closed unions where nepotism reigns or where "blood is thicker than talent."

If it is your intent to become an Equity stage manager, don't wait for an Equity job to get acquainted with the union. Try to understand the benefits and disadvantages of union membership. Go out of your way to meet a union stage manager. Engage her or him in conversation about her or his work and union. If you live in a city with an Equity office (N.Y.C., L.A., S.F., Toronto), visit it and get to know the people in the office. The union office is not a placement service, but the union staff is in a good position to know what producers are anticipating productions or casting. Bulletin boards in the union offices frequently display information useful to stage managers. Sometimes the union has available handouts, such as lists of union-approved theaters where you might apply for work.

If you accept a job as a stage manager with an Equity company, you must join the union. Thereafter you may never legally work in a non-Equity company without first getting a waiver from Equity.

Once in a union position, you may quickly find it necessary to deal with members of other unions, depending on the size of your theater staff:

Screen Actors Guild (SAG)
American Federation of Television and Radio Artists (AFTRA)
American Guild of Variety Artists (AGVA)
International Alliance of Theatrical Stage Employees (IATSE)
Association of Theatrical Press Agents and Managers (ATPAM)
Theatrical Wardrobe Attendants
Treasurers and Ticket Sellers Union
Musicians Union
Teamsters

As closely related unions for performers, SAG, AFTRA, and AGVA have reciprocal agreements as to when and how their members may perform in jurisdictions of the other unions. The producer normally handles arrangements with the unions and insures that all members of his cast are members of Equity, or have been cleared by Equity to work in the production.

Union composition of a staff varies from theater to theater, depending on size and on the arrangements that producers have made with union locals. In a small union house, all of the cast may be Equity and there may be only one non-Equity union member, an IATSE master electrician.

In another larger house, there may be three IATSE members (carpenter, lights, props); two Theatrical Wardrobe Attendants members; five Treasurers and Ticket Sellers members in the box office; two members of ATPAM (publicist and house manager); and five musicians from the AFM (who are paid to play bridge in the wings during a play in which there is no music).

In a huge outdoor theater, Teamster truckers may refuse to leave their trucks and enter the stage area to pick up scenery, insisting that the scenery be loaded out by IATSE stagehands and handed to them on their truck, while IATSE stagehands will refuse to get on a truck, insisting that Teamsters must be present to stack the scenery.

In still another tent theater, four well-paid IATSE crew members may work right alongside six non-union "apprentices" who are not paid at all; both union and non-union crew members do the same work, but at the end of the union work call period, the union men go home while the non-paid "apprentices" continue to work to the end of the rehearsal period.

The stage manager need never feel that he or she must contest the inequities of union regulations. This is a responsibility of management or the producer.

The stage manager should do his or her best to understand the rules that apply to other union members with whom he or she must work: hours, minimum calls, overtime rules, and working restrictions and jurisdictions.

Examples:

A union property master may be prohibited from moving any lighting equipment, so he looks on while the master electrician, his friend and a member of the same union, toils.

A union carpenter may be paid to be on hand for a show in which he has no duties other than pulling the curtain, but his union rules will not allow him to use that paid time to work on the sets of the next show which follows in the same house for the same company.

Start by asking the producer or administrative manager for the information you will need to know about union calls to enable you to plan work calls most efficiently.

If she or he cannot give you sufficient information, request permission to call the business agents of the unions to get this information. Usually the producer or business manager will want to handle this for you.

Discuss work rules with the individual union members concerned. In informal chats, find out what union members feel are their obligations to their employer, as well as what they consider the benefits of their union membership.

In the long run, the more you know about the work rules of the other unions, the more money you will be able to save the producer in scheduling calls.

Union rules cannot be summarized here, ₃ince they vary from local to local, and since they are also dependent on agreements that each producer makes with each local business agent. It is a mistake to infer that wage scales, hours, and work restrictions are not locally negotiable, regardless of nationally distributed union literature. Stage managers do not negotiate, but producers and business managers do.

Inexperienced stage managers are frequently apprehensive about working with IATSE personnel for the first time. Perhaps this is because the veteran IATSE members are often much older than the new stage managers. There is nothing to fear. Treat members of all other unions with professional courtesy. Give them the same respect for the job they are doing as you expect for yours. Assume that they are trained specialists who know exactly how to carry out their work once you have scheduled it.

It is wrong for a stage manager to harbor contempt or resentment for a member of another union simply because his or her union prevents his or her exploitation by the producer.

· 19 ·

Correspondence

The stage manager has little need to write extensive correspondence, but you will want to consider writing a letter to the next stage manager, critiques, letters of recommendation, and thank-you notes.

A Letter to the Next Stage Manager

Turnover of stage managers is very frequent. Sometimes they are there for a season only, and next season a new person is holding the clipboard, starting anew, running into the same problems that you ran into last season. Sometimes stage managers are replaced in the middle of a season, and sometimes a theater has a different stage manager for every single production.

No matter what your length of service, you have found out some things that your replacement can only learn by time-consuming research, trial, and error.

Where did you take the tape recorder to be serviced last time it broke down? When was the last time it was serviced? How frequently should preventive maintenance be done?

Where is the key to the metal bulb protectors for the dressing room lights?

Who services the air conditioning units?

What ceiling outlets are on what lines into the booth?

What mistakes did you make that the next stage manager should avoid?

What working diagrams and templates, applicable to this theater only, can you turn over to your replacement?

There are many little things that only you know. When you leave, the staff cannot be expected to pass this information on to the new stage manager. Some of it may be trivia. Some is important. But all of it would help the new stage manager to adjust to the job more easily.

If you are not going to be around to break in the new stage manager, why not leave a letter to make the adjustment easier? Simply write the same kind of letter that you would like to find if you were coming to the job instead of leaving.

Critiques

The purpose of a written critique is to help you to improve your work on future productions. It is intended to remind you of mistakes you made, problems you solved, and methods you devised. It need not be formal and it need not go anywhere. Don't feel that you have to turn it over to a producer or director because you wrote it. It is for you.

Experience is a great teacher. If the critique reminds you of your experience it will be a great self-improvement aid. As history students know, mistakes of the past are too soon forgotten and too often repeated.

In your theater career what seems unforgettable to you today will be just a hazy, useless memory tomorrow unless you write it out, review it, and apply it.

As you start into your next production, review your old critiques and try to see how you can contribute more effectively to better theater.

It is the exceptional theater that holds critiquing sessions following productions or seasons. If you should be asked to contribute to such a critique, select one significant item from your written critique to present. Using your most tactful manner, present that one item from the point of view of how best to improve the next production or season. Make sure your suggestions are concrete. Don't offer vague censure or praise. Remember the effective critique should be concerned with locating the "curse" rather than the "culprit." Be hesitant of giving adverse criticism on techniques or devices that have produced desired effects.

Letters of Recommendation

You can help capable people with whom you work by writing a letter of recommendation for them (see Figure 19-1). It will help their morale to know that their work was appreciated, and it may help them to secure better jobs in the future.

Use the theater's letterhead stationery when available.

In your letters of recommendation, (1) cite the exact work that the individual performed, (2) give your evaluation of his or her work, (3) state whether or not you would wish to work with him or her again in the same capacity, (4) evaluate the individual's potential

THE CHECHONOVITZ CIVIC LIGHT OPERA

CHECHONOVITZ, CALIFORNIA

August 29, 1969

To Whom It May Concern
c/o Mr. George Spelvin
335 Ostrova Drive
Bialistok, California

During the 1969 season I had the pleasure of working with George Spelvin. He was the company "gopher", a title given in summer stock to the first person called upon when there is work to be done.

As a member of the stage crew George set and struck scenery up and down the aisles of our theater in the round, seven nights every week. During the day his duties varied. He assisted me as shipping clerk, errand runner, truck driver and typist. He helped the property master in collecting and returning props. On loan to the technical director, he helped build sets. He painted scenery, properties and the stage.

It was always a pleasure to assign George to a job, because you knew it would be done right -- the first time. He always accepted assignments cheerfully and was alert in seeing if there was a better way to do a job. Despite his long hours George was always willing to do a little more, and often recognized and did work before I could assign it.

George earned the respect of the production staff and cast members for his dependability and quiet, courteous, unassuming ways.

I would be very pleased to work with George again. I feel that he is ready for an assignment of greater responsibility. He would make an excellent assistant stage manager.

Sincerely

Lawrence Stern

LAWRENCE STERN
Production Stage Manager

LS:lh

· Figure 19-1 ·
Letter of Recommendation from a Manager

for doing other related work, and for advancement, and (5) be sure to give your title and relationship to the individual.

If she or he was property master this season, do you think she or ne might make a good assistant stage manager next season? If she or ne was assistant stage manager, do you think sne or ne is ready for stage manager, business manager, or technical director?

If you feel that you have performed well in your position, don't be reluctant to ask for a letter of recommendation from your immediate supervisor.

Copies of letters of recommendation may sometimes be enclosed with résumés when applying for a job.

Thank-You Notes

Don't forget to write thank-you notes, letters of thanks, or letters of appreciation. Let the capable people with whom you worked know that you cared.

· 20 ·

Getting a Job

Your First Job as Stage Manager

There is no minimum number of college credits that qualifies an individual to become a professional stage manager. Outside of educational theater situations, no producer (or anyone else who hires stage managers) will ask to see your college diploma, your high school diploma, or any other kind of certificate. Producers might ask to see your résumé and will probably ask you about your past experience.

The two factors that count most heavily are your feeling of competence and your ability to sell yourself. If you have read this manual this far, understand it, and feel that you can apply everything in it, you are ready to stage manage. Now, can you convince someone else that you are ready?

In seeking your first job, my recommendation is that you apply immediately as stage manager at the theater closest to your home. If you are not accepted, ask if you may work as assistant stage manager, property person, assistant property person, or on the crew. Once working in any subordinate position, demonstrate your competence and tell the producer that you want to work your way up.

The frequent pattern is that if hired as props, no matter how competent you prove yourself, you will always be seen by that producer as props. So, with the experience you have, start applying to other theaters for positions of greater responsibility. Later, when you

243

have worked at another theater as stage manager, the producer for whom you propped will welcome you back as stage manager.

The best time to get a paid stage management position is when you already have a job in community, educational, or showcase theater. This might mean taking a bread and butter daytime job while you work in community theater at night until you can get the experience and credits you need.

If you are considering going to college specifically with a career in theater in mind, I suggest that you visit possible campuses and talk to the students who are in the theater program. It is too easy to be misled by advertisements and catalogues. From the students seek the answers to the following questions:

1. How many main stage and little theater productions are put on every year? Some colleges provide the opportunity to make theater happen. Others have very limited production opportunities even though they may have fine academic programs. Your concern is whether or not you will have a chance to work. In some schools where there are many productions every year, there may also be very large numbers of students. Will you be a small fish in a large pond? Perhaps it would be better to go to a smaller school where everyone works without waiting to be in the junior class. Ask the students about this; they know.

2. Does any one faculty member teach with passion? Well, if not passion, a point of view? Well, lacking a point of view, how about a sense of joy? You can't write to a prospective teacher and ask, "Will you light my fire?" But you can ask the students if they have found any faculty members they can endorse as enthusiastic. Again, the students generally know.

By the time you have discussed these two questions with prospective fellow students you will have a good idea if you will fit into their theater community just from the vibes you get.

There are many different atmospheres in which to study theater. Check around at junior colleges, private and state supported colleges and universities, and independent theater programs before making up your mind. Don't feel trapped if you don't find what you want the first semester; you can usually transfer credits to other institutions.

Résumés

A résumé is a letter of introduction that you write on behalf of yourself to a prospective employer.

Put yourself in her or his shoes. What does she or he want to know about you? Your past experience is most important. What have you done? Put your most recent credit at the top of the page. Whom did you work with? At what theaters? The faster that the prospective employer can find the information she or he wants, the better (see Figure 20-1).

```
                        C R E D I T S

        PLAY                    THEATER              DIRECTOR(PROD)
*MIDDLE OF THE NIGHT      JCA Center Playhouse    (Bill Miller)
 (J. Rimson, Arlene
  Schwimmer)
*THE TUNNEL OF LOVE       Theatre Rapport         (Bob Cole)
 (R. Doyle, L. Priest)
●THE ANTHEM SPRINTERS     Actors Studio West      Ch. Rome Smith
 (P. Burke, G. Walberg)
*A MY NAME IS ALICE       JCA Center Playhouse    (Bill Miller)
 (D. Babbitt, Wadsworth
  Taylor)
+THE GLASS MENAGERIE      Huntington Hartford     G. Keathley
 (P. Laurie, A. Sothern)
-THE FANTASTICKS          Immaculate Heart        P. Madsen
 (J. Hague, Michael
  McGiveney)
-THE VOYAGE                   "      "            R. Montgomery
 (R. Stevens, W. Taylor)
*CRAWLING ARNOLD          JCA Center Playhouse    (Bill Miller)
 (Hal.Adelson,
  Shirley-May Pilnick)
●AFFAIRS OF STATE         Orange County Theatre   Reid Lowden
 (J. Caulfield, J. Himes)
●FUNNY THING HAPPENED ON  Fresno Music Circus     J. Lucas
 WAY TO FORUM
 (St. Holloway, G. Lamb)
+FUNNY THING HAPPENED ON  Sacramento Mus. Circ.   "     "
 WAY TO FORUM
 (D. Dee, Sh. Spilane)
●SHOW BOAT                    "      "      "     Milton Lyon
 (A. Gilbert, M. Miller)
●GUYS AND DOLLS               "      "      "     J. Lucas
 (E. Ames, J. Jameson)
●TAKE ME ALONG                "      "      "      "    "
 (J. Conte, D. Lockin)
+110 IN THE SHADE            "      "      "      "    "
 (G. Byrne, J. Davidson)
+MUSIC MAN                   "      "      "      "    "
 (K. Freeman, N. Smith)
+PAJAMA GAME                 "      "      "      "    "
 (W. Griffin, P. Karr)
+BYE BYE BIRDIE
 (Peter Marshall, Jess
  Pearson)                   "      "      "      "    "
+CAMELOT
 (K. Nelson, L. Talbot)
●NOBODY LOVES AN ALBATROSS Las Palmas            Alan DeWitt
 (Fr. Aletter, K. Freeman)
●ONE FLEW OVER THE CUCKOO'S Player's Ring        John Erman
 NEST                      Gallery
 (W. Oates, Wm. Smith)        "      "      "    H. Korman
●ENTER LAUGHING
 (L. Adams, A. Peterson)
●THE TORCH BEARERS         Equity Library Theat.  "    "
 (J. Arnold, L. Lesser)
●THE EMPEROR               Cahuenga Playhouse     B. Wintersole
 (H. Darrow, B. Heyman)

*director                  resume January '69
-technical director        Lawrence Stern
●stage manager             Main P.O. Box 1901
+assistant stage manager   Los Angeles 90053
                           (213) 555 2424
```

· **Figure 20-1** ·

Short Form Résumé

Showing Varieties of Theatrical Management Experience

It's a good idea to list the names of a few prominent cast members along with your credits. It is name dropping in its most obvious and honest application.

A more formal résumé, including schooling, unrelated work experience, and biographical data might be desirable if you want the producer to know more about you (see Figure 20-2). The problem with the long form is getting the producer or administrator to read it. You should assume that a producer is a very busy person who doesn't have time to read. Put the most important, earth-shaking words at the top: HIS OR HER NAME, i.e., "Mr. or Ms. Wheeler-dealer, I want to work for you." This sentence, written legibly at the top of your résumé, besides informalizing and possibly getting his or her attention, also states your immediate goal.

The Harvard Business School recommends that an accurate statement of your goals be the first item in your résumé. However, in the case of the stage manager, a concise statement of goals might severely limit the application of your résumé. If you are a stage manager this week, you may want to work as a road manager for a music group, advance person for a circus, light designer for an ice show, or guest director for a resident theater next week.

Instead of printing your goal as part of your résumé, tailor each résumé to the specific prospective employer with a cover letter or a hand-written note. Tell him or her concisely how you think you can serve him or her best.

Your address and phone number(s) are essential.

Note that race, religion, national origin, and age are not included in the résumé.

Send your résumé out regularly to every theater in town, and if you're willing to travel, to selected theaters out of town. Every three months is not too often. It is absolutely impossible for you to know exactly when a theater will be in need of new personnel.

A résumé is usually worthless unless it is followed up with personal contact. Start with a phone call. Ask if your résumé arrived. Then ask if there are any openings now or if any are expected. Ask if you might drop by for a chat in the hopes of getting acquainted and being kept in mind for some future opening. At the very least, get the name of the person who actually hires the stage manager at that theater.

In your contact file keep a record of the theaters to which you've sent your résumé, and the names of the people to whom you've spoken in your follow-up phone conversations. Note their comments carefully. Who is the stage manager now? Could you work without salary on the crew until a paying slot opens up? During pre-opening rush, could you work with the crew just to get acquainted with their staff?

Hiring is usually done face to face, and personality may be a much more significant factor than experience. For the novice it is

RESUME

LAWRENCE STERN

Main Post Office Box 1901   213/555-2424
Los Angeles, California, 90053

Single   6 feet   155 lbs.   Good health

CURRENTLY   **Assistant Production Manager, Greek Theatre Assoc.**

Year round operation of Huntington Hartford
Theatre (1,000 seats, legitimate local productions
and touring companies) in Hollywood and summer
operation of Greek Theatre (4,400 seats, outdoor
amphitheater; popular attractions, musicals, opera,
ballet, dance) in Los Angeles, as well as packa-
ger of touring attractions for San Francisco,
San Diego, Sacramento, Santa Barbara, and Hono-
lulu. Responsible for research of Broadway productions and touring attractions, cost analysis,
and coordination with producers of incoming productions.

RECENT   Technical director, Immaculate Heart College
THEATER   for productions of THE VOYAGE and THE FANTASTICS,
EXPERIENCE   1966. Responsible for construction of sets and
1963 - 1966   coordination with art department, as well as
instruction of student crew. Worked with di-
rectors Ray Montgomery and Patricia Madsen.

Production Stage Manager, Sacramento Music Circus
(1,700 seat tent theater in the round) for
CAMELOT, BYE BYE BIRDIE, PAJAMA GAME, 110 IN THE
SHADE, TAKE ME ALONG, MUSIC MAN, GUYS AND DOLLS,
SHOW BOAT, and A FUNNY THING HAPPENED ON THE
WAY TO THE FORUM, 1965. Worked with directors
Jonathan Lucas and Milton Lyon. Responsible for
the coordination of department heads in production phase, management of the company in rehearsals, and light, sound and music cues during
performance.

Since February 1963, stage managed Center
Playhouse's THE CRUCIBLE directed by Frank
Bessell, and PALACE OF A THOUSAND DREAMS
(children's play) directed by George Werler.
At Cahuenga Playhouse stage managed THE EMPEROR
produced by Lou Rifkin, directed by William
Wintersole. Stage managed THE TORCH-BEARERS
for director Harvey Korman at Equity Library
Theater West and ENTER LAUGHING (also directed
by Mr. Korman) and ONE FLEW OVER THE CUCKOO'S
NEST (directed by John Erman) at Paul Levitt's
Players' Ring Gallery. Last Hollywood assignment was stage managing Dorothy Roth's production of NOBODY LOVES AN ALBATROSS at the Las
Palmas Theatre. Have written, produced and
directed parodies of plays I've worked on since
high school days.

· **Figure 20-2** ·

Long Form Résumé for a Theatrical Manager

MILITARY
EXPERIENCE
1959 - 1963

Commissioned second lieutenant through ROTC, June 1957, as Station Manager, Armed Forces Radio and Television Service, Island of Crete, was responsible for producing 130 hours per week of radio and 70 hours per week of television. Produced, directed, wrote, supervised a staff of 20 military announcers and Greek national technicians, scheduled, surveyed, punched, floor managed, worked camera, reorganized film and record libraries, supervised a radio station in Athens, hosted frequent visitors to the only TV facility in Greece. Won three network awards for outstanding programs.

Served as Wing Information Officer for 3rd Weather Wing, Offutt Air Force Base, headquarters Strategic Air Command (SAC). Responsible for nation-wide news releases and public information. Edited monthly newsletter to 100 subordinate units. Organized and directed base little theater group producing VISIT TO A SMALL PLANET, NIGHT MUST FALL, THE CURIOUS SAVAGE and THE SEVEN YEAR ITCH. Drama critic for base newspaper.

Final Air Force assignment, Assistant Director, Candidate Advisory Service, United States Air Force Academy, Colorado. Traveled from state to state in public relations capacity bringing Academy to attention of educators. Arranged for displays at state and national educational conferences and presented slide briefings. Won first place in Academy's annual short story contest, 1962. Honorable discharge as first lieutenant, February 1963. No Reserve obligation.

EDUCATION
1953 - 1958

WESTERN RESERVE UNIVERSITY, Cleveland, Ohio. Master of Arts in theater (direction, scene design, lighting, television production, playwriting). BA in English, 1957, minored in theater arts. Reported for school paper, debated, served as class and student council officer, wrote book and lyrics "Letter Girl" (annual college musical) in junior year. Cum laude graduate, elected to Omicron Delta Kappa, national honorary leadership fraternity. Worked way through college as nightshift lathe operator at Thompson Ramo Wooldridge, bakery hand for Fisher Brothers, page at Cleveland Public and Western Reserve University libraries, playground supervisor, counter boy at Lake Shore Country Club.

EARLY
BACKGROUND

Grew up in Cleveland, Ohio. Father was a watchmaker. Attended public schools: Hazeldell Elementary, Patrick Henry Junior High, Glenville High School. Graduated January 1953 in upper 10 percent of class. Active in high school dramatics under Eugine C. Davis. Class officer. Held part-time jobs as machinist and library page.

REFERENCES

Personal references will be forward upon request.

· **Figure 20-2** ·

(Continued)

important to realize that although you may be the best stage manager in the world, there are directors, production managers, and producers who will not care to work with you because they feel that your personality will not mesh with theirs in what they consider to be the best interest of production. Over the years they have become able to make this evaluation instantaneously. It is something that does not lend itself to open expression in the interview process. If you are rejected and feel there is no reason other than the interviewer's feeling against you, try to trust his or her judgment and try someplace else.

When you have several credits you may wish to have your name and capsule résumé published in the *Players' Guide*, an annual pictorial directory for stage, screen, radio and television, published by Paul L. Ross, 165 West 46th Street, New York City 10036, phone: (212) 869-3570. The section devoted exclusively to stage managers might bring your name to the attention of a prospective employer.

When your level of experience warrants it, you might also wish to submit your résumé to the Theatre Communications Group (TCG), 355 Lexington Ave., New York City 10017, phone: (212) 697-5230. TCG assists in the exchange of information among theater people nationwide. They have their own résumé format and will send you their form on request.

The trade papers rarely contain advertisements for stage managers. It is definitely a producers' market with supply exceeding demand in situations where the stage manager is paid. And yet, in community and little theaters where the stage manager is not paid, or is dreadfully underpaid, it is almost impossible to get competent people to serve as stage manager.

This means that the novice can easily gain the valuable experience she or he needs if she or he wants to work up to the level of the professional stage manager.

Do not underestimate yourself. Send your résumés to theaters which you feel require greater experience than you possess. You might make a valuable contact that will pay off later. Or you may be hired for a slot far above what you're seeking by a producer who recognizes your potential.

When you are "at liberty," you will have plenty of time to send out résumés and to update your contact file so that you can get off your next round with far less effort. From your file you will be able to pull the addresses of the theaters, and you can send them out marked to the attention of the specific individual who does the hiring.

It is a Hollywood aphorism that "the best time to get a job is when you have one." Even if you are happily employed in what seems like a long range situation, get out your résumé regularly and keep up your contacts.

Personal Mailing List

In addition to mailing out résumés to prospective employers, you may wish to keep up your contacts with people in the business by regularly sending them notes on your progress, invitations to shows you're doing, and programs of shows you've done (not to mention Christmas and New Year's greetings).

It takes very little effort and does not cost much in postage and stationery to let your theater acquaintances know what you're doing—and it can pay off in many pleasant ways.

Three months after your present show closes, ten members of your cast, staff, and crew may be working in ten different theater situations. Each represents a possible introduction for you to another set of directors and producers. But three months after you close you may run into an actor with whom you worked nightly, and he or she may not remember your name.

The theater scene is both fluid and forgetful. To exploit the former quality, you have to overcome the latter.

Your personal mailing list might consist of all of your cast lists with crew and staff members added.

Long-Range Goals

Where are you going, Stage Manager? Do you want to stagemanage for the rest of your life? Do you want to find some big, cushy theater with stable management and move in to stay—to sixty-five or senility, whichever comes first?

There seem to be too few career stage managers in the business. There are a lot of aspiring actors, aspiring directors, aspiring producers, and aspiring writers who call themselves stage managers. There are a lot of stage managers who are on their way out of theater— on their way to law school, teaching English, programming a computer, or selling shoes. Stage management seems frequently to be a phase rather than a career.

If you make a career of it, you can hope for a salary of $300 per week. If you get to Broadway, your salary might go as high as $825 per week as production manager for a musical. (These figures reflect the equity contracts of 1982. For more current information, call your local equity office.)

But that's the optimistic viewpoint. You must expect feast and famine, periods of high pay and periods of unemployment.

Unlike many careers, stage management does not offer regular promotions, hours, vacations, and retirement. A few benefits are provided by union membership, but it is up to the individual to plan her or his own career progress. Promotions are yours for the getting, the hustling, and the self-promoting. If you plan to be a career stage manager, you must evaluate your own aggressiveness as a very significant factor in your potential career. If you are not aggressive, you will drift from one union minimum situation to the next.

If stage management is just a phase for you, here is my best advice: get out just as soon as you can and do your thing. Stage management demands too much of your organizational ability, energy, time, and emotional juices for you to think of it as a bread-and-butter job to support your real interest in life. When you have stage managed three or four shows in two or more theaters, you will have a fair understanding of the job, and certainly adequate background for any related theater work. It won't take you more than six months of steady work to know if you want to make it a career. Then if you want to be an actor, director, producer, writer, or shoe salesperson get out and act, direct, produce, write, or sell shoes.

But if you want to be a stage manager (give it all you've got); be a great stage manager!

· Appendix ·
A Few Theater Stories

Knowing jokes is not a substitute for having a sense of humor. There are occasions, however, when a good theater anecdote can be helpful.

1. Fresh from grad school and the Actor's Studio, the young director's first assignment was with an old, established Yiddish theater company. On his first day with the group, he assembled the entire company on stage and delivered to them The Method.

He spoke eloquently for *five hours*(!): inner stress, remembered emotion, Stanislavsky, Vahktangov, Strasberg, everything. And when he was through, dripping with perspiration, he knew in his heart that he had just delivered the definitive lecture on The Method. He strode away triumphantly to let them think it over.

One old time Yiddish actor turned to another. "So how does he want, louder or softer?"

2. A hastily assembled and rehearsed cast of *Stalag 17* was in the hushed conspiracy sequence when the stage manager noticed that the dialogue on stage had decreased to an inaudible whisper. He prompted with a line that would lead the cast out of this sequence. There was only silence on stage. So the stage manager prompted again. Another silence. Finally an actor broke the silence with a harsh whisper: "We all know *what* the line is, but *who* says it?"

3. The wedding of the daughter of a very famous Hollywood character actor brought out many producers, directors, and agents. As the proud father

253

escorted the bride down the aisle, this whisper was overheard: "Will you look who they got to play the father!"

4. The old circus worker came home drenched from a storm. For years and years his job had been to follow the elephants in the parades and clean up after them.

His wife pleaded with him. "Why do you do it? You're past retirement age. It's bad for your health—out in all kinds of weather. Please, I beg you, retire."

"What," he answered, "and give up show biz!"

5. The novice actor was elated by a call from his agent. It was just a one-line walk-on in an historical play, but it was work. The actor who was to do the part had been taken ill. They opened that night. The agent explained that he would get his costume and full particulars at the theater.

"By the way," said the agent, "your line is, 'Hark, I hear a cannon.' "

On the way to the theater the novice rehearsed his line: "**Hark,** I hear a cannon." "Hark **I** hear a cannon." "Hark, I hear a **cannon.**" He was absolutely determined to deliver his one line well.

He got into his costume and the stage manage briefed him. His cue would be the firing of the cannon.

He went on stage. He waited. His moment was coming. He became more and more excited. Finally the cannon exploded.

And the novice delivered his line as follows: "What the hell was that?!!"

6. The old stripper had been out of work for years. Her agent called to ask her if she would do a Seal Lodge in Draidel, North Dakota. She was desperate; she agreed.

Sure enough, it was popping-out-of-the-cake time, as the band played, on a table surrounded by aging Seals in their purple fezzes. But something happened. As she danced the men started to clap. Then they started pounding on the table. They rose out of their seats, banged harder and faster on the table, stamped on the floor, became excited and then frenzied. Some started jumping up onto the table. Then they started grabbing for her. She pushed them away. They grabbed some more. She pushed, fought, clawed, shoved, kicked and, fighting off their hands, somehow managed to escape to her dressing room. She slammed and bolted the door and turned to her agent, who was reading the trades with his feet sprawled over her make-up table. In an angry voice she asked, "Did you hear that band?"

7. Following his debut at Carnegie Hall, the soloist was overwhelmed by the audience which rose as one man yelled, "Again, Again, Again."

The singer repeated his last number, and when he finished, his bow to the audience was again met with screams of "Again, Again, Again."

He repeated each number in his program until the audience had called him back for a total of twelve encores, and in total exhaustion tried to thank his audience for their enthusiastic reception: "I thank you, but I am simply too fatigued to continue."

Above the audience's chant of "Again, Again, Again," rose a single voice shouting, "You gonna keep on singing until you get it right."

8. Cecil B. De Mille was about to shoot his greatest, most costly epic scene. He had stationed his three best cameramen strategically. In the scene a herd of elephants stampeded through a native village, an earthquake swallowed up half the village, a tidal wave covered everything else and, as the waters receded, a volcano erupted spewing hot lava and burning the remaining huts. Then the Yugoslavian army on horseback, dressed as the hordes of Ghengis Khan, swept through the remains, raping and pillaging, only to be in turn swept off by a tornado.

Eighty-seven assistant directors and the headquarters staff of the Yugoslavian army held the thousands of extras in place. Three hundred and seventeen special effects men readied the wind machines, dynamite, and chicken feathers.

Then C.B. gave the command, "Lights, cameras, action."

And it all happened beautifully—the elephants, earthquake, tidal wave, lava, burning, the Yugoslavian army, raping, pillaging, and the tornado. And when the last chicken feather had settled to the ground, Cecil B. De Mille knew that he had produced the most incredible sequence ever captured on film.

"Did you get that, Dick?" he asked his ace cameraman.

"Gosh, C.B., I forget to take the lens cover off the camera."

"Never mind," said C.B. "Did you get that Roger?" he asked his second cameraman.

"Oh, boy, C.B. I forgot to load the film."

"Never mind," De Mille said and shouted up to the third cameraman on the dolly, "Did you get that, Arthur?"

Arthur shouted back, "I'm ready when you are, C.B."

9. The community theater in Frigidoria, Maine, was about to open when the prompter came down with pimples. Fortunately, the ingenue had a maiden aunt who lived only a few blocks from the theater. Hastily she was summoned and installed behind the scenery with a script and flashlight, and instructed to watch the lines. She was told to let the actors know if they gave the wrong ones.

All went smoothly until the third act. The leading man went up. There was silence on stage. Then he repeated his last line, "Behold, the moon rises by yonder peak."

Nothing.

So he moved upstage to the flat which hid the ingenue's aunt, kicked the flat, and delivered his last line once again. "Behold, the moon rises by yonder peak."

And then he heard the ingenue's aunt whispering, "Wrong."

10. The Boy Scout saw a nun trying to cross a busy intersection near Broadway. He offered to help her.

"Oh, thank you, young man, but I can make it."

"Please, sister, let me help," said the scout. "We're supposed to do good deeds."

When they had crossed he said, "May I ask what order you're with so I can tell my scoutmaster?"

"Oh, for Pete's sake," she said, "I'm with *The Sound of Music.*"

11. The last act of the college's production of *Hedda Gabler* was building to its melodramatic conclusion in which Hedda takes the pistols which the playwright has so conspicuously planted, and exits into the library to shoot herself. After a shot is heard, Tesman crosses to the library door, peers offstage, and announces to the audience, "Shot herself. Shot herself in the temple. Fancy that."

The student actor playing Tesman waited for the shot. Finally he heard—click, click. He crossed to the library door, peered offstage, and said, "Oh my God, she stabbed herself to death."

12. We were rehearsing a play called *Golden Boy*. Charlie Lynch was playing the part of Tom, a prize-fighter, and Dorothy Kilheffer was playing the part of Lorna. These two are in love. In the process of finding out that they are in love they have a violent quarrel. During this quarrel he says to her, "I wouldn't look at you wice if they hung you naked from a Christmas tree."

At this moment I heard a quite audible gasp from John Schaeffer (President of the College). I thought to myself, "Uh-uh, we may be going to get the blue pencil." But we went on without interruption.

At the end of the scene, Dr. Schaeffer called Dotty to him and said something to her in a rather agitated whisper.

After rehearsal I asked Dotty what had happened. He had said to her, "Dotty, that's a terrible thing for a man to say to a woman. That's the worst thing he can possibly say. Don't worry, Dotty, if they hung you naked from a Christmas tree, I'd look at you twice."—(Darrell D. Larsen, retiring after 35 years as director of theater for Franklin and Marshall College, *Alumnus Magazine*, July, 1962).

13. Sammy Ginsburg had been in show biz for eighty years as a stunt man in a circus. His specialty was diving one hundred feet into a barrel of water. As he began his act, he addressed the crowd.

"Ladies and gentlemen, good evening. Tonight for the forty-seven thousandth, four hundred and fifty-third consecutive time you will see me climb up on this one hundred foot ladder and dive into this barrel of water."

A hush fell over the audience. The drums started to roll.

"Of course," Sammy continued, "it's not like in the old days. I've been doing this same stunt for sixty-five years, and I'm a little slower now—my arthritis."

He reached for the ladder and moaned. "Also a little bursitis I have it in my right arm. But I have to go on with the show because I'm the sole support of a family of fourteen."

He slowly pulled himself up on the second rung and groaned low again.

The crowd became apprehensive at the sight of this old man groaning up the ladder. "Don't jump," shouted a member of the audience. Soon several others joined in and it became a chant, "Don't jump, Sammy, don't jump." Finally the whole audience was standing up, chanting, shouting, imploring Sammy not to go through with it.

"Okay, okay already." said Sammy, stopping his climb and addressing the audience. "The next performance is at 10:30."

14. Edward G. Robinson once said that you could always tell if he was a good guy or a bad guy in a movie by the angle of the brim of his hat. If it was up, he was usually a detective, and if it was down, he was the heavy. While filming a flick in which he was a terrible villain, his hat brim suddenly popped up.

"What did you do?" asked a friend.

"What could I do?" replied Robinson. "Why I arrested myself, of course."

15. A local high school interviewer asked John Barrymore if he thought Romeo and Juliet had been sexually intimate. "Well," replied Barrymore, "in the Chicago company they were."

16. When Cecil B. De Mille arrived at the Pearly Gates, St. Peter asked him to produce a film.

C.B. said no.

"But you can use all the greatest talent we have here," St. Peter persisted. "Directors: Stanislavsky, Eisenstein, Griffith...."

"No," said C.B.

"Actors: Barrymore, Gable, Cooper, Bogart...."

"No," said C.B.

"Composers: Beethoven, Tschaikovsky, Mozart, Gershwin, Hammerstein...."

"Well," said C.B.

"Writers: Shakespeare, Shaw, O'Neil, anyone you want."

"Okay," said C.B., "with talent like that, how can I refuse. I can start this afternoon."

"Great," said St. Peter, "but first I'd like you to read this girl I know. She hasn't had much experience, but she's really cute."

· Glossary ·

The terms compiled in this glossary are the special vocabulary of the stage manager.

Abstract Set Nonrepresentational set that suggests rather than simulates appropriate surroundings.

Accent Emphasis placed on an action or phase of a play by lighting or staging technique.

Achromatic Lens A lens that transmits light without separating it into its spectral colors. Lenses should be achromatic.

Acoustics The qualities of sound transmission within a theater.

Act Curtain See Curtain.

Acting Area That part of the stage used by actors during the performance; may be extended to aisles or elsewhere if the action of the play takes place there.

Ad Lib (1) Anything said by actors on stage other than the lines of the script, (2) to extemporize in a performance or interpolate impromptu remarks possibly because of a lapse of memory, as a reaction to an unplanned incident, or to cover a late entrance.

Adaptor Short length of cable with a different type of plug on each end (i.e., twistlock to pin, or pin to stage plug); also, a plug inserted into a socket so that it will accept a different type of lamp base.

AEA Actors Equity Association. Union for stage actors and stage managers.

AFTRA American Federation of Television and Radio Artists. Radio and TV entertainers' union.

AGVA American Guild of Variety Artists. Nightclub entertainers' union.

Amateur Anyone whose work in or for the theater is without financial reward.

Amber   A popular yellowish-orange color.

Ampere   Unit of electric current; one ampere is the amount of current sent by one volt through a resistance of one ohm.

Amphitheater   An oval or circular building with rising tiers of seats about an open space.

Anchor   To fasten to the floor.

Angel   One who invests money in a production.

Antagonist   Adversary of the hero or protagonist.

Anti-pros   Lighting instruments hung in front of the proscenium.

Anticipate   React to a cue that has not yet occurred (i.e., actor falls before shot is fired; actor turns to door before knock, etc.)

Antique   To make props or set pieces appear old.

Appliqué   Ornamentation cut from one material and applied to another

Apprentice   Individual who works in the theater for the learning experience, usually not paid.

Apron   The part of the stage in front of the proscenium.

Arbor   Metal frame supporting counterweights in system for flying scenery.

Arc Spotlight   Spotlight in which the source of light is an arc of electric current jumping a small gap between two carbon sticks; the carbon sticks are either hand adjusted or driven electrically to remain a constant distance apart; an iris shutter is used to control the size of the beam or to shut it off completely.

Arena Theater   A theater having the acting area in the center of the auditorium with the audience seated on all sides.

Arm   A batten supporting a curtain; usually a short batten used for wings.

Asbestos Curtain   Fireproof curtain located immediately in front of the front curtain. In some areas it is required by law that this curtain be raised and lowered in sight of the audience during a performance. Also called Fire Curtain and Fireproof Curtain.

Aside   Dramatic device in which the character speaks directly to the audience while other characters on stage supposedly do not hear him or her.

At Liberty   Euphemism for unemployed.

ATPAM   Association of Theatrical Press Agents and Managers. Union for theater publicists and house managers.

Audition   Tryout performance before producers, directors, casting directors, or others for the purpose of obtaining a part in a production; may be acting, singing or dancing.

Auditorium Lights   See House Lights.

Baby Spot   Small spotlight, usually 100, 250, or 400 watts; lens is ordinarily 5", 4½", or smaller in diameter.

Back Light   To focus lighting instruments on the backs (shoulders) of actors to produce emphasis or separation from background.

Backdrop   A large area of painted canvas fastened to a batten and used for a background which hangs straight, i.e., sky drop, woodland drop, lake drop, etc. Contrast to Cyclorama which is not painted but lighted.

Backing Light   Illumination behind a set used to give a lighting effect on a backdrop.

Backing Unit Any piece or pieces of scenery placed behind an opening (door, window, etc.) to limit the view from the audience of the off-stage areas.

Backstage (1) The entire area behind the curtain line: stage, dressing rooms, green room, etc., (2) any part of the stage outside of the acting area during a performance.

Baffle Metal or wood screen used to prevent light spill.

Balcony Front Spotlights Spotlights that are mounted on the front of the balcony or related locations to light the acting area.

Barndoor A metal shutter with doors to control light spill.

Batten (1) A length of rigid material, usually wood, fastened to the top and bottom of a drop or leg, (2) the 1″ × 3″ lumber used to construct scenery, (3) the wood or pipe on a set of lines to which scenery or lights are fastened.

Beam, Ceiling Beam in ceiling of an auditorium in which spotlights are concealed.

Beam Front Spots Spotlights mounted high in the beams (or prepared slots) of the auditorium ceiling for the purpose of lighting the acting area from above.

Belaying Pin A hardwood pin or pipe used in pin rails to tie ropes from gridiron.

Bit Part Small role in a production, rarely with more than two or three lines. *See* Walk On.

Black Light Light that causes certain colors and materials to glow in the dark.

Blackout Closing of a scene, act, or the play itself, usually on a particularly effective line, by a sudden extinguishing of the lights. Used frequently in musical revues.

Blacks Black draperies or curtains.

Bleed When a prior color is seen through a subsequent coat, it is said to bleed.

Block A pulley or pulleys in a frame, part of counterweight flying system.

Blocking Movement of actors in the acting area.

Blocking Notation Written description of actors' movement.

Boards The stage. "To walk the boards" means to appear on stage.

Bobbinet Transparent curtain of silken texture. *See* Scrim.

Book Play manuscript. In musical productions, the libretto without the music.

Boomerang Color wheel. A box attached to a lighting instrument to hold color frames. Makes color changes convenient. *See* Color Box.

Border *Scenery:* An abbreviated drop at the top of the set, which masks the flies from the audience. May represent sky, foliage, etc. *Lighting:* row of overhead lights on stage. First row behind the proscenium arch is called the concert border, X-Ray border, or first border. Others are numbered from down- to upstage: second border, third border, etc.

Border Lights Strips of lights mounted in a metal trough divided into compartments with individual color frame holders. Instruments are normally wired into three or four different circuits and are used for general lighting in the stage area.

Bottle   Slang for bulb or lamp that is used in a stage lighting instrument.

Box Set   Traditional set of three walls.

Brace, Stage   An adjustable device made of two lengths of 1″ × 1″ wood held between clamps, used to support scenery from behind. A forked iron hook fastened to one end of the brace is twist-hooked into a brace cleat attached to the unit requiring support, and an iron foot at the other end of the brace is secured to the floor by means of a stage screw.

Brace Cleat   A small metal plate attached to the frame of a flat. A stage brace is hooked into it to brace a flat.

"Break a Leg"   Traditional wish of good luck exchanged between theatrical people prior to opening night curtain instead of "good luck."

Breakaway   Scenery or props that disappear, break, or change form in full view of the audience.

Break Character   To say or do anything, as an actor, during a rehearsal or performance, which is not consistent with what the character portrayed would say or do.

Bridge   A long, narrow platform hung from the grid immediately adjacent to a light pipe or attached to it, for the purpose of allowing a technician access to lighting instruments.

Bridge Lights   Those lights that are mounted on the bridge.

Bridge, Paint   A long narrow platform hung from the grid at the back wall, upstage from which a scenic artist may paint scenery or drops attached to a frame on the wall.

Bring Up   To increase the intensity of the lights. *See* Dim In.

Build   Accumulation and gradual acceleration of tempo, emotional intensity, and action by dramatist, actors, or director at any point in a play, but particularly in the approach to the climax.

Bump It   To hit the floor forcefully with flown scenery in order to trim the scenery.

Bump Up   To bring up as fast as possible.

Burn In   The first red glow emitted by the filament of a lighting instrument before full intensity light is emitted.

Bury the Show   To strike sets, costumes, and props after the final performance.

Cable   Flexible wire for conducting current from dimmers to lighting units or effects equipment.

Cage   Wire enclosure used to separate lighting equipment or sound equipment from the stage.

Call   (1) Notice to actors backstage announcing the amount of time before the curtain, normally half hour call, fifteen minute call, and five minute call, (2) notice of rehearsal or performance placed on the call board and reiterated by the stage manager.

Call Board   Bulletin board for actors.

Call Boy   Individual who gives calls to the actors. It is advised that the stage manager do this her- or himself.

Candlepower   Illuminating capacity of an instrument.

Carpenter Stagehand responsible for handling scenery, building and repairing the set.

Cast (1) Players in a play, (2) to select actors to play roles.

Caster A small wheel used to make moveable scenery.

Ceiling A large horizontal canvas-covered frame hung on two or more sets of lines, used to close in the top of an interior set. *Book ceiling:* built in two pieces which fold together at the middle (book-like) parallel to the footlights, to permit flying. *Roll ceiling:* canvas is attached to front and back battens and rolled around them for storing and transportation

Ceiling Plate A plate for bolting together and hanging a ceiling piece.

Center Stage The area in the center of the acting area.

Central Staging Placing the audience area on all four sides of the acting area.

Chalk Line A long length of string rubbed with chalk which is snapped to transfer straight chalk line to floor or flat.

Characterization Delineation by dramatist of a role in a play or portrayal by an actor of a role on stage.

Cheesecloth An open weave cotton cloth sometimes used as scrim.

Chew the Scenery To rant and rave on stage.

Cinemoid A colored plastic sheet used for producing color in light.

Clamp Most lighting instruments come with a C-type clamp to fasten them to a pipe. There is a similar cable clamp used to hold heavy quantities of cable to a light batten, but this is most frequently done with tape.

Claque Paid members of an audience hired to applaud.

Clavilux An instrument invented by Thomas Wilfred for throwing upon a screen varying patterns of light and color which permit combinations analogous to the successive phrases and themes of music.

Clear Please (1) Order to strike props or get out of the way, (2) warning that the curtain is going up.

Cleat Metal hardware used for securing flat.

Clew A metal plate that holds several lines so that they can be handled by a single line.

Climax That part of the central action, usually near the close, in which tensions are greatest and in which the theme is finally and fully revealed.

Clincheplate A metal plate used to back clout nails.

Clip Board A board with a metal clamp on the top for holding plots, cue sheets, etc.

Clout Nails A type of nail used in scenery construction, which bends to hold materials together when it strikes the clincheplate.

Color Box A metal container of six color frames that may be attached to the front of a spotlight for color changes. Some of these are controlled remotely from a switchboard or from the spotlight. See Boomerang.

Color Frame A metal, wood, or cardboard holder for the color medium in the front of a lighting instrument. More frequently called a Gel Frame.

Color Medium A transparent material such as glass, gelatine, or cinemoid, which is placed in front of lighting instruments to produce color.

Color Wheel A device to make color changes. A large cumbersome, wheel.

mounted on the front of a spotlight, that has four to six openings for different colored gelatines. It may be manually operated by the spotlight operator or it may be motor driven.

Come Down   To move toward the downstage area, or toward the audience. See Downstage.

Comedy   (1) Style of drama characterized by the humorous and amiable, (2) a play in which the protagonist fights a winning battle.

Composite   (1) Several pictures showing an actor in various costumes and poses, (2) part of an actor's résumé.

Concert Border   Lights mounted on the first pipe upstage of the proscenium.

Connector   A device for connecting two cables together or a cable to a switchboard or unit. Each connector consists of two parts, a female or receiving part and a male which has studs or prongs which fit into the female. Multiple connectors are female connectors to which more than one male connector may be fastened. A number of units may be attached to one cable easily by use of branch-offs or multiple connectors.

Contour Curtain   A curtain that is gathered up in scallops.

Conversation Piece   A comedy in which there is much talk and little action.

Corner Iron   Right angle iron strap or L-shaped plate used for support or reinforcement.

Corner Plate   A triangle of 3/16" or 1/4" plywood used to reinforce corners of flats in scenery construction.

Counterweight System   Mechanical use of weights to help balance heavy flow scenery, curtains, etc.

Crash Box   A box filled with broken glass or small metal parts used for sound effects.

Crisis   Turning point in a play.

Crosspiece   Horizontal batten in a flat.

Cue   A signal in dialogue, action or music for an actor's action or speech or a technician's duty backstage.

Cue Sheet   A list of the exact cues for the execution of specific duties by the crew.

Clip Cues   To speak one's lines before the preceding actor has had time to finish the cue phrase. This usually destroys the meaning or effectiveness of the final words.

Curtain   A hanging drapery that conceals the stage or scene from the audience. It may rise, part, fold, drape, or sink. Also called Front Curtain, Main Curtain, Act Curtain, House Curtain, Flag, and Rag.

Curtain Line   (1) An imaginary line across the stage which marks the position of the front curtain when it is closed, (2) the last line of a scene or act which is the cue for the curtain to close.

Cut   (1) To remove a line or lines from a script, (2) order to stop rehearsal.

Cut Drop   A drop which has pieces cut out or is edged to represent leaves, foliage, or other decoration.

Cut Line   A trip line that is cut to release the asbestos curtain in case of fire.

Cutout *See* Groundrow.

Cutting List A list of the pieces of wood with their dimensions needed for scenery and set pieces.

Cyclorama (CYC) A huge, seamless backing sheet of material, usually white, which may be lit to indicate sky. Sometimes it is hung in a semi-circle with the sides coming well downstage to enclose the acting area.

Cyclorama Lights High-powered individual reflector type border lights mounted on a castered frame (or hung from a light batten) to light the cyclorama.

Dark Night(s) Period when theater is not open to the public.

Dead Spot Area in acting area that is insufficiently lit.

Diffused Light Nearly shadowless light.

Dim To decrease the intensity of the light on the stage by means of rheostats or dimmers. Also called Take Down.

Dim In To increase the intensity of the light. Also called Dim Up or Bring Up.

Dimmer An electrical device used in a switchboard to regulate current. Types: Resistance, Slide, Plate, Transformer Vacuum, Remote Control, Silicon Rectifier.

Dip in Intensity Unplanned lowering in intensity of stage lighting.

Direct Beam Lenseless projection equipment used to cast shadow or project translucency on a screen, cyc, or flat.

Discovered at Rise On stage when the curtain goes up.

Distemper Paint made by mixing dry pigment with size. Scene paint.

Dolly A low truck with casters used for moving scenery, set pieces, or theatrical equipment.

Dome A permanent plaster cyclorama.

Dope Glue used for attaching canvas flats.

Douser Cutoff device in arc light or follow spot.

Downstage Toward the footlights (or if no footlights, toward the pit, apron, or audience).

Draw Curtain A type of curtain suspended from an overhead track that opens from center to each side. Also called a Traveler Curtain.

Dress Parade On stage, under the lights (preferably before appropriate flats) check of costumes to be worn by each character.

Dress Rehearsal Final rehearsal before opening.

Dressing a Set Adding minor decorations to the set, usually the ornamental touches as opposed to functional props that must be on the set for use of actors.

Drop *See* Backdrop.

Drop Curtain A curtain that rolls up from the bottom.

Duck Strong cotton material.

Dutchman A strip of material, usually muslin, about three inches wide, which is used to cover cracks where flats meet. Masking tape is sometimes called Instant Dutchman.

Duvetyn Velvety cotton fabric.

Effect   The impression given to an audience of a particular thing by a technical achievement: a rainbow produced by lights, wind produced by a wind machine, etc.

Electrician   The operator of the control board and lighting instruments. Not necessarily an electrician in the non-theater meaning of the word. Also called Boardman, Lighting Technician, or Tech.

Elevations   (1) Working drawings of the flats of a setting, (2) risers, platforms, etc., which give variety to the stage level.

Elevator Stage   A section or sections of the stage floor which may be lowered and raised by hydraulic process.

Entr'acte   (1) Intermission, (2) short scenes performed before the curtain

Entrance   Actor's appearance on stage.

Epilogue   A scene that follows the end of the play.

Equity   See AEA.

Expressionism   From a school of thought that developed in Germany in the late 19th Century. Really an extension of impressionism and opposed to realism and naturalism. Expressionists are concerned with producing an inner emotional, sensuous, or intellectual reaction. It is this inner emotion that they try to express, and they maintain that it does not necessarily bear a relation to the outer aspect of life.

Exteriors   Settings painted to represent outdoor scenes.

Facing   Decorative trim, painted or applied around doors, windows, flats, etc.

Fade In   Gradual dim up of light or sound.

Fade Out   Gradual dim out of light or sound.

Fall   Rope used with block and tackle.

False Blackout   A blackout that occurs within a scene but does not call for a scenery or prop change. Usually denotes passage of time. See Blackout.

False Proscenium   An inner frame especially built for a production to close down a large proscenium, to mask lighting equipment or to give special design to the production. See Proscenium.

Fantasy   Play unrestricted by literal and realistic conventions of the theater and usually distinguished by imaginative uses of the supernatural and the mythological.

Farce   Play designed only for entertainment and laughter; there is no serious or sincere attempt to depict character nor is there genuine concern with probabilities or realities.

Farce-Comedy   A form halfway between farce and comedy which contains elements of both.

Feedback   Undesirable noise in sound system; sometimes caused by mike being too close to speaker.

Filament Image   Projection of filament from spot, to be corrected by adjustment of spot or diffusion.

Fill Light   Addition of light to blend areas or reduce shadows.

Fire Curtain   See Asbestos Curtain.

Fireplace Unit   A fireplace frame made to fit a flat opening.

Fireproof Curtain   See Asbestos Curtain.

First Border *See* Border.

Flag *See* Curtain.

Flaking Paint coming off of flat that need‹ to be refinished.

Flameproofing Solution sprayed or brushed on flats or fabric‹ t‹ retard flames.

Flash Pot A box device in which a smoke oι flash effect is created, also called flash box.

Flat A wooden frame covered with canvas used as a scenic unit. It may be from 10 to 20 feet in height and vary in widths. The widest flat is usually 5'9″ so that it will go through the six foot openings in freight cars. This one is called a "six" or full flat. Other flats are named by their conventional widths.

Flat Paint Paint that absorbs light, opposed to glossy, which you would not want to use generally for scene paint.

Flies The space above the stage occupied by sets of lines and hanging scenery.

Flipper A small piece of scenery hinged to a larger flat.

Float To lower a covered flat by placing the foot against the bottom rail and allowing it to float down so it is lying flat on the floor. The flat will fall slowly because of air resistance.

Floodlights Light units which give a general diffused light. Also called Olivette.

Floor Cloth Canvas or duck covering for the stage floor. Also called Ground Cloth.

Floor Plan A scale drawing of a stage setting showing the position on the floor of the walls, windows, openings, etc.

Floor Plate Metal plate with ring used for tying lines to the floor.

Floor Pocket An opening in the stage floor which contains a receptacle for large stage electrical plugs and is metal covered.

Flown Term applied to condition of scenery which has been raised into the flies.

Fly To lift scenery above the level of the stage floor, out of view of the audience by means of lines from the gridiron.

Fly Curtain A curtain that is raised and lowered.

Fly Gallery A narrow bridge or gallery running along the side of the stage, well above the floor, from which are operated ropes secured to the pin rail.

Fly Man Name applied to any stagehand who is to fly scenery.

Fly Rope *See* Lines, Fly Rope.

Follow Spot A spotlight on a movable joint, operated so as to follow a player on the stage with a beam of light.

Foot To apply the foot to the bottom rail of a flat or the base of a ladder so that another stagehand may raise it.

Foot-Candle A unit for measuring the illumination given by an instrument: it is equal to the amount of direct light thrown by one international candle on a square foot of surface, every part of which is one foot away.

Foot Iron A steel brace bolted to the bottom of a piece of scenery or set piece so that it may be fastened to the stage floor by means of a stage screw.

Footlights   Strip lights, a source of illumination for the acting area, which may be portable, permanent, open trough type or disappearing. Being used less and less in modern theaters.

Fortuny System   Indirect lighting, using spotlights focused on colored silk fabrics. The silk redirects the light to the stage. It is shadowless, diffuse and allows for subtle color changes but is impractical because of expense and space required.

Foul   To cause scenery or lights hung in the flies to become entangled with each other.

Fourfold   Four flats hinged together.

Fourth Wall   Name given to the hypothetical wall of separation between the stage and the audience in a proscenium theater.

Foyer   Entrance hall into a theater.

French Scene   The division of an act in which the number of characters is constant. Entrance or exit of character(s) marks the beginning of the next French scene.

Fresnel   Type of spotlight using a Fresnel lens or step lens. Lens is named for French physicist Fresnel who developed it for lighthouse beacons. The Fresnel produces an even field with soft edges.

Front Curtain   See Curtain.

Frost   Translucent gel used to diffuse light.

Full   Maximum intensity of lighting or sound.

Full Stage   The entire area of the stage that can be used as the acting area.

Funnel   A cylinder of cardboard or thin sheet metal fastened perpendicularly to a square of the same material. Also called Snoot, and Highhat.

Fuse   A strip of metal with a low melting point, usually in an insulated fireproof container, which breaks when the current becomes too strong.

Gaffer   Stage crew head.

Gagging   Slang for unauthorized improvisation or revision of lines by an actor.

Gain   Volume control on an amplifier.

Gallery   Highest balcony in a theater.

Gang   (1) To hook together, (2) to move two dimmers together.

Gelatin (Gel)   Thin, transparent sheet of material for producing colored light.

Gel Frame   A metal, wood, or cardboard holder for the color medium which is placed in front of a lighting instrument. Also called Color Frame.

Ghost   A streak of light which leaks from some light source and falls where it is not wanted. See Spill.

Ghost Load   An offstage lighting instrument used to load a resistance dimmer so that it will dim out an onstage instrument properly.

Gimp Tacks   Small roundheaded tacks used for furniture upholstery.

Gimp Tape   A decorative upholstry tape used as a finish strip on the edges of furniture.

Give Stage To move on stage so that the center of interest will be thrown to another actor.

Glare Light reflection too uncomfortable for the audience.

Glass Crash *See* Crash Box.

Glue Burn Stain on flats caused by glue.

Glue Gun Small, hand-held electrical device for heating and applying glue.

Go Order to take a cue, execute an effect.

Go On To enter on the stage.

Go Up To forget one's lines and to be unable to resume without assistance.

Gobo (1) Metal plate with pattern used in lighting instrument to project pattern on cyc or lighting effect on flat, (2) a louvre, usually of metal, used to prevent spill from lighting instrument.

Good Theater Any piece of business which clicks with the audience, or which communicates surely and easily with the audience.

Gopher (Gofer) A production assistant who gets his or her title from the fact that he or she is frequently sent to "go fer" something.

Grand Drape Curtain extending width of the stage opening, which is hung just back of the proscenium and in front of the front curtain. It can be lowered to cut the height of the stage opening.

Grand Valence The first drapery border in front of the main act curtain, usually of the same material.

Green Room Waiting or reception room, behind, near, or under the stage, used by authors, directors, actors, to meet their public. So called because the first "retiring" room in Covent Garden Theatre in London was all in green. Most professional theaters do not have Green Rooms today, but many little community and university theaters provide such meeting places.

Gridiron (Grid) The framework of steel or wooden beams above the stage, which supports the rigging used in flying scenery.

Grip A stagehand who assists the master carpenter in moving settings.

Grommet Metal eye hole, usually found at the top of drapes and through which ties are run.

Ground Cloth *See* Floor Cloth.

Ground Plans Layout of the stage showing location of set, properties and lights for a production. *See* Floor Plan.

Ground Row (1) A row of lights on the floor to light lower area of a cyc or drop, (2) a low profile of scenery designed to represent rocks, earth, skyline, etc., that stands self-supported on the ground, usually in front of the cyc, and is used to conceal the base of the cyc, the lighting equipment and cables, as well as to help give the illusion of depth and/or horizon.

Grouping Placing the cast about the stage.

Guy Line Rope or wire from high scenery to floor used to steady or strengthen.

Half Hour Warning by the stage manager a half hour before the curtain goes up.

Ham An actor who is bad or pretentious, or both.

Handle A word that an actor adds to the beginning of a line, that was not originally written in the script: Oh, gee, gosh, well, but, etc.

Hand Prop Any property which is handled by the actor during the course of the play, but particularly those props which the actor carries onto the stage as opposed to those which are discovered. See Properties.

Hanger Iron Hardware for hanging scenery. It has a ring attached to one end of a steel plate which is bolted to the scenery.

Hanging the Show Putting up the sets of a play: flats, doorways, lights, etc. So called because originally the show was set with wings and backdrops which had to be hung from the grid. Also called Mounting.

Head Block Three or more pulley blocks framed together and placed on the gridiron above the outer edge of the fly floor. The ropes from three or more loft blocks come together at the head block and pass down to the pin rail. Also called Lead Block.

Heads Up Order to watch for moving scenery.

Highhat See Funnel.

Hold (1) To sustain an effect for audience response, (2) to pause in delivering a line so that audience may react.

Hood See Funnel.

Horseshoe Stage A stage that is surrounded on three sides by the audience.

House The auditorium and front of the theater, as contrasted with the stage and backstage areas. Also used to refer to the size of the audience as in, "How's the house?"

House Lights Electrical fixtures that provide light for the audience. Sometimes called Auditorium Lights.

Hung Up Condition of being unable to continue one's lines or business because another actor is ad libbing or because another actor has already taken the position you were to take.

IATSE International Alliance of Theatrical and Stage Employees. Union for stagehands.

Impressionism Theory that productions should be concerned with artistic interpretation rather than with reality. Strives for psychological reaction by use of color and line.

Ingenue Young girl in a play, usually providing the love interest.

Inner Proscenium See False Proscenium.

In One, Two, Three "In one" is the area on stage just upstage of the curtain line five or six feet. "In two" is the first area plus the next five or six feet upstage. "In three" adds the next five or six feet upstage or full stage.

Inset A small scene set inside a large one.

Interiors Sets representing indoor scenes.

Iris Shutter A manually operated shutter for varying the size of a light beam emitted from a lighting instrument.

Jack A triangular device made of wood, which is hinged to the back of a ground row or other set piece for the purpose of bracing it from behind.

Jackknife Stage Two portable stages with narrow ends parallel to foots, and on pivots. When one stage has been used, it is swung offstage into the wings. From the wings on the other side of the stage the second stage is swung into position on the acting area. The jackknife stage permits quick changes of scenery, as do elevator and revolving stages.

Jog   A narrow flat.

Juicer   Electrician.

Juvenile   Player of youthful male roles.

Keep Alive   To store scenery or properties so that they will be readily available.

Keyboard   A switchboard, usually with slide controls.

Key Light   The main source of light.

Keystone   A small piece of 3/16" or 1/4" plywood cut in the wedge shape of a keystone and used to reinforce joints in scenery.

Kill   (1) To take an article off of a set, (2) to extinguish lights or stop sound effects or other effects.

Klieglight   Trade name for spotlights.

Lamp   Source of light. See Bottle.

Lamp Dip   Lamp coloring lacquer which gives a durable transparent color tint.

Lash   To bind two flats together with a lash line.

Lash Cleat   A small metal hook on the frame of a flat, behind which a lash line is thrown to bind the flat to the edge of another flat.

Lash Line   Length of #8 sash cord fastened to the back of a flat and used to lash flats together.

Lash Line Eye   The metal eye to which the lash line is secured.

Lead   Principal role in a play, or actor or actress playing the role.

Lead Block   See Head Block.

Leg Drop   A drop from which the entire center portion has been omitted.

Left Stage   The area on stage at the actor's left as he or she stands center stage facing the audience. Stage left.

Legit   Popular abbreviation for the legitimate stage, live theatre as opposed to movies.

Leko   Once a brand name, now a generic term for any ellipsoidal reflector spotlight. (Compare to Fresnel and P.C.)

Lekolite   Trade name for spotlight.

Lens   Glass cut for the purpose of condensing and concentrating the rays of light from lamp source and reflector.

Levels   (1) A platform, set of steps, or ramp that raises the playing space above the level of the stage (also called Risers, Elevators and Platforms), (2) an imaginary line drawn across the stage at any distance from the curtain line but parallel to it.

Lid   Top of platform or ceiling.

Light Batten   A pipe or batten to which lighting instruments are clamped and along which lighting cables are run.

Light Plot   Sequence of light changes from beginning to end of the play, with lines or business that immediately precede each change. Each change is described.

Light Towers   Poles mounted at the sides of the stage or audience area to mount lighting instruments. Also called Light Trees.

Light Tree Tower of pipe or wood used to hang lighting instruments in the wings.

Line, Lines Speech or speeches in a play.

Line (of Business) Type of role or roles in which an actor specializes.

Line Drawings Blueprints from which sets and set pieces may be constructed without reference to any other drawings or specifications.

Fly Rope Lines The ropes from the grid which raise and lower scenery. One end is attached to the batten and the other is secured on the fly gallery. Three ropes are usually used on each batten. The nearest one to the gallery is called the short line. The one in the middle is the center line. The farthest is the long line.

Linnebach Projector A large metal box with concentrated light source for projecting pictures from a gelatin or glass slide.

Lintel Horizontal crosspiece over door, window, or arch.

Live Weight Weight of moving body as opposed to weight of inert body.

Load, Electrical (1) Amount of current used in a circuit, (2) electrical equipment to be connected to a line.

Load In Process of moving all of a company's equipment (scenery, props, costumes, etc.) into a theater.

Load Out Process of moving all of a company's equipment out of a theater.

Lobby That part of the theater between the entrance and the last row of seats, usually separated by a wall and doors.

Lobster-Scope A spotlight effect machine producing a flicker of light.

Loft Block A pulley block in the gridiron through which a line may be run.

Louvers (1) Concentric rings of thin metal strips fitted to the front of a projector to cut off all but the straight beam of light (also called Spill Rings and Baffles), (2) parallel strips of wood or metal used to mask a light source from the audience.

Make Fast To tie off securely or fasten any line.

Manager There are various types other than stage manager. *Producers* are sometimes called managers. *House Manager*: responsible for all details in management of the theater building. *Business Manager*: handles money, payrolls, accounts, contracts, etc. *Company Manager*: responsible for the company, usually on the road. *Personal Manager*: acts as a representative for an author or actor.

Manuscript (ms) Written or typed play, or the book of a musical. Usually used in rehearsal.

Mark It Order to record level of intensity of light or sound cue.

Martingale A two-fer or branchoff connector. Two lines with female plugs spliced into one line with a male plug used to connect two instruments to one cable. (I have heard this term pronounced "Martin-dale" in supply houses on the West Coast. If any reader knows the origin or correct spelling of this term, please let me know. Thanks.)

Mask (1) To hide from sight, or to conceal from the audience, (2) any sort of cardboard or sheet metal slide to be placed in the guides of a spotlight to restrict the light to various shapes. Also called a Mat.

Masking (Piece) A piece of scenery used to conceal backstage from the audience.

Mat See Mask.

M.C. Master of Ceremonies, introducer of acts or participants in a variety program.

Medium See Color Medium.

Melodrama An exaggerated, romantic, exciting, and improbable play. Incident and situation are important, characterization is not.

Mezzanine (1) Sometimes the first balcony of a theater having more than one; (2) the first few rows of the balcony and separated from the balcony proper.

Milk It Dry, To squeeze the maximum laughs out of a line, bit of business or situation.

Mopboard Baseboard.

Motivation Reason behind all stage action and speech. Skill with which the director and actors find the motivation for characters and incidents will determine the quality of the play.

Mounting See Hanging.

Movement Passing of actors from place to place on stage. See Blocking.

Mugging Excessive facial contortions during a performance.

Mule Block A block with pulley used to change the horizontal direction of a line.

Mullion Slender vertical bar between windows.

Multiple Pin Connector A female receptacle that accepts three male pin connectors.

Muslin Material frequently used for covering flats.

Naturalism Same in external form as realism but emphasizes the natural function in life as opposed to realism which is more selective.

Newel Post that supports handrails of steps, also called newel post.

Notices Reviews, dramatic criticism.

Offstage Area backstage, outside of the acting area.

Ohm Unit of electrical resistance.

Olio A mixture, medley, miscellaneous collection. Usually variety acts following an old fashioned melodrama.

Olio Curtain A curtain that rolls up from the bottom. Also called Drop Curtain.

Olivette See Floodlight.

Onstage Inside the acting area.

O.P. Opposite Prompt, usually the left side backstage.

Open Cold To give the first public performance for critics without out-of-town tryouts or invitational previews.

Orchestra Lower floor of the auditorium.

Organic Blocking Process of blocking in which the director allows the actors to move at will and then uses their movement as the basis for his blocking.

Out Front (1) The part of a theater that is beyond the front curtain—lobby, box office, seats, etc., (2) any area occupied by members of the audience.

Outlet Box Heavy metal fireproof box containing two to four female receptacles, porcelain insulated.

Overture and Beginners, Please The British equivalent of Places, Please.

P.A. System Public address system. Microphone and loudspeakers, or any sound amplification equipment.

Pace To the theater what tempo is to music. The timing of lines and business. Not to be confused with speed.

Paper Tech A crew only technical rehearsal to iron out the mechanical bugs.

Parallel A collapsible frame support for a stage platform.

Part (1) Character assigned to an actor in a play, (2) typewritten portion of a play which pertains to an actor's scenes and contains all of his or her lines and cues. See Side.

Patch Panel A plugging panel used to interconnect dimmers and outlets, also called plugging panel.

Pay Out Order to allow rope to pass through hands.

P.C. Plano convex spotlight. Compare to Leko and Fresnel.

Peep Hole Stage Stage with definite division between acting area and audience, such as a proscenium arch. Also called a Picture Frame Stage. Compare to Central Staging and Horseshoe Stage.

Periactus A three-sided revolving apparatus painted with scenery.

Period Plays Costume plays of other eras.

Perspective Drawing Rendering of floorplan and elevations to perspective of audience.

Phantom Load Added resistance to a dimmer so that it will dim out a spot too small to dim ordinarily.

Picture Frame Stage See Peep Hole Stage.

Pigtail See Martingale.

Pilot Light Dim light used by stage manager to follow prompt script.

Pin Rail A rail with holes in it, into which wooden pins are placed to secure lines. See Fly Gallery.

Pipe Batten See Batten.

Pipe Clamp An adjustable metal jaw for mounting lighting instruments on pipe battens.

Pit Sunken space in front of stage, usually where orchestra performs.

Pivot Stage See Jackknife Stage.

Places, Please Signal given by stage manager to the cast for taking their respective positions preparatory to the rise of the curtain.

Plano-Convex Type of lens or type of spotlight using that type of lens.

Plant (1) Member of the acting company who is placed in the audience for the purpose of fostering the illusion that the audience is taking part in the performance, (2) a prop on stage at curtain rise, particularly one concealed from the audience.

Platform A collapsible and portable unit used to add levels to the stage, or to provide an additional acting area.

Playing Space Stage space, inside or outside the set, visible to the audience and used for acting during the play.

Plot (1) List of what is required of each technical department in order to make a play work (light plot, sound plot, property plot, costume plot, special effects plot, etc.), (2) planned action or intrigue of a play.

Plug (1) A scenic unit placed in or in front of another piece of scenery to change it. For example, an arch for one act may be changed for the next act by placing it in a window plug, a fountain plug, etc., (2) a male connector with insulated handle, with two strips of copper along the side to make contact with similar strips in the outlet box.

Plugging Box Portable outlet box.

Position An actor's place on the stage as set by the director.

Practical Something that is usable. For example, a pair of French doors might be constructed so that only one opens. The one that does open is the practical one.

Preset To place props, costumes, or any materials in position prior to curtain or prior to use.

Pre-set (or Pre-select) Switchboard A switchboard where one or more complete changes can be set up in advance without interfering with the lighting of the scene in progress.

Preview Performance given prior to formal opening.

Principals Actors who carry major roles in a production.

Problem Play Play built around a difficulty of society. Its characters personify the various forces and their conflict is the subject matter of the play.

Producer The individual (amateur or professional) who accepts the responsibility for obtaining the personnel and the materials to make theatei happen.

Profile Board Plywood, 3/16″ or 1/4″, used to edge a flat.

Projector Directional floodlight, using a metal parabolic reflector to project parallel light rays.

Prompt Book Book of the play including all business, action, plans, and plots needed for the production. Also called Prompt Script.

Prompt Script See Prompt Book.

Prompt Side (P.S.) Side of the stage from which the stage manager runs the show, usually the right side.

Prompter One who stands in the wings or out of sight of the audience, and assists actors with their lines and cues. Usually utters only the first few words of a line that an actor forgets, or significant words of the line.

Prop Box Box kept offstage in which props are stored.

Properties (Props) Articles used for a play—hand props, trim props, and set props.

Prop Table Table offstage where props are set prior to the curtain. Actors are conditioned to obtain their hand props from the same place on the table at each performance, and return their props there if they carry them off stage.

Proscenium The wall dividing the auditorium from the stage.

Proscenium Arch The edge of the opening of the proscenium.

Proscenium Opening The opening in the proscenium through which the audience views the play.

Protagonist Hero of a play or the character who carries its principal idea.

Put Together A rehearsal at which all elements of the production are brought together in their appropriate sequence.

Quartz-Iodine A long life lamp used in lighting instruments.

Quick Study Hurried and technical memorization of a part and its business by an actor, usually in an emergency when a part must be learned at a moment's notice. Also refers to an actor whose memorization comes easily to him.

Quiet Please Order for silence.

Rag See Curtain.

Rail The top or bottom board in the frame of a flat.

Raked Stage A stage slanted down toward the audience.

Raking (1) Placing the side walls of a set at an angle to improve the sight lines, (2) slanting stage area, platform, or audience seating area to improve sight lines.

Ramp Inclined platform.

Rant To deliver lines in a shouting, melodramatic and extravagant manner.

Readthrough Rehearsal at which the script is read from beginning to end.

Realism Fidelity to nature or real life. Representation without idealization. Adherance to actual fact.

Reflectors Shiny metal surfaces used in spotlights and projectors in back of the light source to intensify the light and give it direction: spherical, ellipsoidal, and parabolic.

Rehearsal Repetition of scene or practice of a production in private, preliminary to public performance, and for the perfection of that performance.

Rep Company Company playing repertory.

Repertory Collection of plays, operas, or parts which may be readily performed because of familiarity with them on the part of a cast or actor. A repertory company is one in which, instead of performing one play continuously, there are several productions ready and they are varied each night or week. Usually the same actors have parts in several productions.

Reprise Repeat of a musical number.

Resistance Dimmer A type of stage dimmer used to decrease intensity of lighting instruments.

Return Piece A flat set at right angles to the downstage corner of a set. It is parallel with the footlights or curtain and runs offstage to mask the wings.

Reveal See Thickness.

Revolving Stage One or more circular stages (mounted on top of the permanent stage) electrically or manually revolved to effect scene changes or special effects.

Right Stage The area on stage at the actor's right as he stands center stage facing the audience. Stage right.

Ring Down To drop the front curtain on the last scene or act. Based on an old theatrical custom of ringing a bell to denote the closing of the show.

Risers See Levels.

Road Irons Angle irons placed at corners of flats to protect them when they must be moved frequently as on tour.

Road Show A theatrical production which tours several cities and towns.

Rococo Over-elaborate style of decoration.

Roll Curtain A curtain that rolls up from the bottom. Also called Olio Curtain and Drop Curtain.

Rondel See Roundel.

Rosin Box A box, large enough to stand in, containing rosin used by actors or dancers to rosin shoes or slippers.

Roundels Circular heat-resisting glass color media.

Royalty Compensation to authors and composers paid for permission to perform their works.

Run Length of a stage engagement or the total number of performances.

Runway Extension of stage into audience area.

Saddle Iron A narrow strip of iron used to brace the bottom of a door flat. Also called Door Iron and Sill Iron.

Safety Factor Safe percentage by which load on ropes, cables, and dimmers may be exceeded.

SAG Screen Actors Guild. A union for actors working in filmed entertainment.

Sandbags Canvas bags filled with sand used to weight lines or the jacks behind scenery.

Satire A form of comedy in which sharp derision is aimed at an idea or individual.

Scene (1) Setting of an action, (2) division of an act or play.

Scene Dock A storage area for flats and other scenic units, usually located in either wing area of the stage.

Scioptican Device used to create moving effects such as clouds, flames, waves, etc.

Scrim A finely woven material through which light may or may not be seen, depending on how it is lit. Also called Theatrical Gauze and Bobbinet.

Selvage The edge on either side of a woven or flatknitted fabric, so finished as to prevent raveling.

Set To prepare the stage for the scene that is to be performed.

Set Dressing Props arranged to decorate the set. Also called Trim Props.

Set of Lines A unit group of ropes hanging from the gridiron used to fly scenery. There are usually three or four lines in a set.

Set Piece A unit of scenery standing alone.

Set Props Those props which stand on the stage floor, or other props not carried on by the actors. Compare to Hand Props.

Set Up To erect a set and install related equipment.

Shift To change scenery and properties from one setting to another.

Shoe A block of wood enforcing the joint between toggle and stile.

Showcase Theater A theater whose main purpose is to obtain paid work for members of the cast.

Show Curtain A drop or curtain behind the front curtain which is painted to give atmosphere to the particular play being presented.

Shtick Slang: business, usually comedy business.

Shutter An apparatus mounted on the front of a spotlight, or designed into it, which cuts entirely, or in part, the rays of light. There are iris, combination, funnel, and slide shutters. Also called Cut-Off.

Side Page of an actor's part. Usually half the size of a standard typewritten sheet. When bound together called Sides.

Sight Lines Lines, painted or imagined, which divide area the audience can see from area the audience cannot see.

Sitting on Their Hands Phrase used describe an unresponsive audience.

Situation Relationship of characters to one another or to a condition. A play may have a series of situations. The basic situation refers to that one problem that is central to the play.

Size Water A thin solution of glue and water used in mixing scene paint.

Sky Drop A drop painted blue to represent the sky.

Smoke Pocket Steel channels on each side of the proscenium arch which guide the ends of the asbestos curtain.

Snatch To hook or unhook flown scenery during a scene change.

Snatch Lines Adjustable ropes or chains used to fasten scenery to a counter-weighted batten.

Sneak To bring in a light or sound cue imperceptibly.

Snoot See Funnel.

Snow Cradle Device for making snow effect.

Soft Light Diffused light with little or no shadow.

Soubrette A minor female part in comedies whose characterization call for pertness, coyness, coquetry, intrigue, etc., and is frequently a show part.

Sound Effects Sounds performed offstage in relation to stage action.

Space Stage Method of staging plays with lights focused on actors so that no setting is necessary.

Spelvin, George Ficticious name used on a program by an actor whose real name already appears in the program. George Spelvin was first used by a minor actor who doubled in the cast of *Brewster's Millions* in 1907. The play was so successful that its author, Winchell Smith, continued to have George Spelvin listed in the rest of his productions for luck. Harry Selby is another name that is similarly used.

Spike To mark the position of a set piece on the stage floor, usually with tape.

Spike Marks Those marks, colored crayon, luminous paint, or tape used to help stage crew position set pieces. Infrequently used to help actors determine where they should be.

Spill Unwanted light due to a poorly focused or shuttered spotlight. Sometimes spill is unavoidable because it is emitted from a lighting instrument which cannot be shuttered.

Split Stage Two or more scenes placed on stage simultaneously.

Spotlight Lighting instrument designea to produce a concentrated beam of light.

Spot Line A single rope specifically rigged from the gridiron to fly a piece of scenery which cannot be handled by the regular lines.

Glossary

S.R.O.   Standing Room Only.

Stage   Entire floor space behind the proscenium arch.

Stage Brace   See Brace.

Stage Call   Meeting of the cast and director on stage to discuss problems before a performance or rehearsal.

Stage Directions   Instructions in the script concerning movements and arrangements on the stage.

Stagehand   An individual who is always present backstage when an actress has to make a quick change in the wings.

Stage Manager   The individual who accepts responsibility for the smooth running of the production on stage and backstage in pre-rehearsal, rehearsal, performance, and post-performance phases.

Stage Pocket   Outlet box distributed about the stage, usually sunken into floor and equipped with a self-closing slotted cover.

Stage Screw (Peg)   A large, tapered screw with a handle used to secure stage braces to the floor.

Stage Wait   Period of time when there is no dialogue or action on stage, usually an undesirable situation caused by a late entrance or a dropped line.

Stage Whisper   A stage convention in which one actor whispers loud enough for the entire audience to hear, but is assumed to be heard only by those to whom he or she is whispering and not by other actors on stage.

Stand By   An order to be alert for a cue.

Standby   Understudy.

Stands   Metal devices for holding and mounting spotlights, floodlights, and projectors.

Star   Leading actor or actress.

Stile   The vertical piece of wood that forms the slide in the frame of a flat.

Stock   Resident company of players performing one play nightly for a week and rehearsing another play for the following week.

Stock Scenery   Flats and other scene units kept on hand for repeated use.

Straight   Refers to a role or performance that is natural, normal, and uncolored by eccentricities.

Strap Hinge   A hinge with long tapered flaps used for hanging windows and doors.

Strike   To clear the stage of scenery, props, etc.

Strip Light   A long, trough-like reflector with sockets for lamps of small wattage, or a row of individual reflectors housed in a rigid sheet metal structure. Used to produce general illumination.

Stroboscope   An instrument for producing the illusion of motion by a series of pictures viewed in rapid succession.

Subtext   Meaning underlying the lines.

Supernumerary (Super)   An extra or walk-on in a production. A person who merely appears in a mob scene or in the background, and who has no individual lines of her or his own to speak.

Swatch   Sample of material or paint.

Sweep   A method used for setting up and cutting circles or arches.

Switchboard A combination of switches, dimmer plates, and fuses for controlling light. Also called Dimmerboard.

Tab A sheet of canvas or other material, framed or unframed, narrower than a drop but suspended like a drop, used chiefly for masking offstage spaces. Also called a Leg.

Tableau Curtain A curtain that is gathered up in an ornamental arch. See Curtain.

Tag Term for the final speech of a scene, act or play, serving as a cue for the curtain.

Takedown See Dim.

Take-in Process of moving all of the sets and set pieces for the forthcoming production to the acting area for the first time and setting it all up as it is supposed to play.

Take It Out Order to raise scenery.

Take Stage To move into an area of greater prominence on the stage with other actors yielding focus.

Teaser (1) Scenery border suspended from the grid just back of the front curtain used to mask from the audience anything in the flies, edge of a ceiling piece, etc. It can be raised or lowered to change the height of the stage curtain. It is often used in place of a grand drape, (2) any short drop suspended above to mask.

Technical Director Individual responsible for construction of scenery and set pieces.

Technical Rehearsal (Tech) A rehearsal at which the technical aspects of the production are integrated.

Technician (Tech) An individual who runs lights, sound, or special effects equipment.

Template A pattern made of cardboard or plastic—most useful to the stage manager are those for furniture and lighting instruments.

Template Table (1) A special type of work bench used in the construction of flats, (2) a pattern.

Theatrical Guide See Scrim.

Thickness A width of lumber or other material attached to the edge of an opening—doorway, arch, window—to give the edge the effect of depth or thickness. Also called Reveal or Return.

Three Dimensional Scenery Scenery that will be seen from all sides and is therefore finished on all sides.

Three Fold Three flats hinged together.

Throw Distance between lighting instrument and surface to be lit.

Throw It Away To give no particular emphasis or expression to a speech or line in a play.

Thrust Stage Acting area of stage that extends into the audience, or the audience is seated on three sides of the apron.

Tie Off To secure lines to hardware or the pin rail.

Time Sheet Record kept by stage manager of exact times of each act, scene, and scene change.

Title Role   Character whose name appears in the title of the play, usually the most important role.

Toggle (Bar)   The crosspiece in the frame of a flat.

Top It   To build or increase the volume or emotional intensity of a line to a greater level than the previous line.

Tormentor   Long, narrow curtains or flats, upstage on either side of the proscenium arch, used to mask the wings. *See* Leg.

Tormentor Lights   A number of spotlights mounted on a vertical pipe batten on either side of the stage, just behind the tormentors.

Trades   Newspapers and magazines devoted to the theater, or any other special interest.

Tragedy   Drama in which the protagonist fights a losing battle.

Translucency   A sheet of treated, thin material. When back-lighted, may be used to produce silhouette effects.

Traps   Trap doors which open into the basement trap room and permit the use of sunken stairways, scenery, or actors rising from or sinking into the ground.

Traveler   A curtain that opens to the sides.

Treadmill Stage   Machine device consisting of belts running on the stage floor, on which scenery or actors may give the illusion of traveling over a distance.

Trim   To hang and adjust drops or borders so that the lower edge is parallel to the floor.

Trim Props   Those properties that are placed within the set or hung on the walls of the set for ornamentation.

Trip   To elevate the bottom of a drop or other flown scenery, with an auxiliary set of lines, in such a way as to make it occupy a space approximately half its height. Tripping is used on a stage where there is not enough fly space to get a unit out of sight by taking it straight up with one set of lines.

Trip Line   A line or lines to a batten used to adjust its position.

Truck   A dolly.

Tungsten-Halogen   Long life lamps used in lighting equipment.

Turkey   A show that is a failure. The term originated when bad shows were opened on Thanksgiving Day to clear expenses and make a little money in the two or three holiday performances. Any badly cast or badly produced show.

Turntable   Moving stage, revolving stage.

Twist Lock   Electrical connectors which have to be twisted into place and therefore cannot easily be withdrawn. They are especially useful where cords must lie on the stage floor and are in danger of being kicked out of an outlet.

Two Fold   Two flats hinged together. Also called a Wing.

Twofor   Two-fer or martengale or multiple connector. Two female plugs spliced into one male plug in order to plug two lighting instruments into a single cable.

Type Casting Selecting actors for roles because they resemble in real life the characters they will portray.

Ultraviolet Light See Black Light.

Understudy An actor who must be perfect in a given role, know all the lines and businesses, but who appears only when the person playing that role is taken ill or for some other reason cannot appear.

Unit Set Set built of scenic units which can be used together in various combinations for forming different settings.

Upstage (1) Away from the footlights or audience, (2) to move upstage of another cast member and thereby compel that cast member to turn his back to the audience if he wishes to speak to the "upstager."

Valance Teaser or border

Vampire Trap Double faced section of a flat that revolves on a pivot for fast escapes or disappearance of props.

Velours Curtains used to dress a stage, made of velour, usually consisting of a backdrop with wing curtains for side masking.

Velveteen Imitation velvet material used for draperies.

Voltage The measurement of the force needed for the flow of electricity.

Wagon (Stage) A low platform on wheels or casters on which a set may be placed and then moved quickly into place.

Walk On A very small part, with or without lines.

Walk the Curtain To walk behind the curtain as it closes to insure that it closes properly.

Walk Through A rehearsal in which actors get out of their chairs and walk through their movements on stage.

Walk Up To raise a flat from the floor to a vertical position, by hand.

Wardrobe (1) Costumes and all articles of dress of a play or production, (2) room in which costumes are stored or fitted.

Wardrobe Person The person in charge of costumes and their upkeep.

Warn A signal that a cue is due within a short time, usually within a minute.

Watt A unit of electric power equal to a current of one ampere under one volt of pressure.

Wing See Two Fold.

Wings (1) Space outside the acting area, at the right and left of stage, (2) draperies that hang at the sides of the stage to mask the offstage areas.

Working Drawings Blueprints made from the designer's drawings. See Line Drawings

Work Light Light for the stage area used during rehearsals, scene shifts, and construction Work lights are usually controlled by a wall switch instead of from the dimmerboard.

Yoke The metal, U-shaped support which holds a lighting instrument.

Zip Cord Lightweight household electrical wire that should not be used for stage lighting, except for practical lights on the set.

Reader's Comments Form

Does this book meet your needs?

Did you find it easy to read and understand?

Was it organized for convenient use and application?

Was it complete?

Was it well illustrated?

Was it suitable for your theater?

The name of your theater:

    Type (circle one): professional—educational—community—
    showcase—children's—religious

Your name and job title:

Did you use this book (check appropriate lines):
☐ As an introduction to the subject?
☐ For advanced guidance on the subject?
☐ As an instructor?
☐ As a student?

Your comments:

☐ I wish to make reference to Chapter_____:
I feel additional information or examples should be included in
the area of _____:

Please use the reverse side or attach additional pages for yo ir comments if necessary.

Perhaps in your work you have discovered a management procedure,
a method, or a technique that would be of help to future stage managers. Insights into the peculiarities of dance, ballet, opera, ice
shows, theme park, dinner theater, puppetry, magic, and variety
shows would be especially appreciated. Your comments or additions
could help to improve the next edition of this manual.

Send to: THE STAGE MANAGER
         P.O. Box 1901
         Los Angeles, California 90053